Don't Think It Hasn't Been Fun

SARAH JO BURKE

Don't Think It Hasn't Been Fun

THE STORY OF
THE BURKE FAMILY SINGERS

LIMELIGHT EDITIONS • NEW YORK

First Limelight Edition August 2003
Copyright 2003 by Sarah Jo Burke

Published in the United States by
Proscenium Publishers, Inc., New York

Interior design by Rachel Reiss

Manufactured in the United States of America

LIBRARY OF CONGRESS CATALOGING-IN-PUBLICATION DATA

Burke, Sarah Jo, 1952-
Don't think it hasn't been fun : the story of the Burke Family
Singers / Sarah Jo Burke.— 1st Limelight ed.
p. cm.
ISBN 0-87910-987-4 (hardcover)
1. Burke Family Singers. 2. Singers—
United States—Biography. I. Title.
ML421.B86B87 2003
782.5'092'2—dc21
2003007669

For those who have forgotten their stories and for my mother who scribbled notes in between feedings and laundry, knowing that we would want to remember what she would forget.

Acknowledgments

I'D LIKE TO THANK Mel Zerman and Jenna Young at Limelight for making this book a reality. Thanks to Sam (Susan A. McGregor) for all her wonderful support, encouragement and know-how. Thanks to Britt Bell of Moyer Bell for leading me to Mel. My thanks to Scott Edelstein, writer and literary agent, who read the first twelve-chapter draft, looked me in the eye and told me my story began at Chapter Eleven. Wise man. Thank you for all the advice you have given since then. Thanks to Marshall Cook at UW-Madison for his encouragement and to Joan Strausbaugh (Jones Books), the editor who first championed this manuscript. Your support and vision have been consistent and invaluable. I heartily acknowledge Karlé Lester, dear friend and editor who happened to live next door; and Patricia Mazzarella, a New England editor who kindly read it and was one of the first to say, "Use one voice." My thanks to Ernestine Gilbreth-Carey for your encouraging letters and postcards; and to Buck Spurr, kind friend and good story-teller, thanks for the stories about Jimmy Durante.

I am grateful to all my brothers and sisters for their stories and support—especially to Steve for answering so many questions, and to my sister Gemma, who let me read the whole manuscript to her in three days. In her woods. While she cooked. Propped up on pillows. Thank you, Gem, for your laughter and your tears during those days—for totally "getting it"—and for all the advice since. (Don't forget. I always stand just left of you.) Thank you, Marie Jo Bohan, for your enthusiasm and good ideas and continued friendship. Thanks to the guys at Bob's Copy Shop in Madison who were so helpful, and to Susan at another copy shop who read half of it while she copied—I hope you get to finish it. Thank you to Sheila Faulkner, who has fed me with good books to read for many years now. Sheila, they have been a constant flow of inspiration during the writing of this book. And to Karen Ryker, my dear Karen, who has been an incredible support in every way possible, a listening ear as I read each new paragraph; thank you for your gentle diplomacy. We have dreamed this together.

And lastly, though this goes without saying, I thank the young mother who wrote notes, the middle-aged woman who kept a log, and the old lady who found a box in the cellar...

Contents

Don't Think It
Hasn't Been Fun

Ed Sullivan Show, December 1963

Prologue

December 22, 1963—CBS Studios in New York City

Waiting backstage. The smell of old sweat and pancake makeup, sour breath and VO-5 styling gel. Light bulbs line the mirrors in the dressing room. Their harsh light shows every flaw. An hour and a half to wait.

My oldest sister, Marty, works on Dad's hair, then Mum's, and on to Florrie's, Gemma's, Annie's and finally, mine. Steve, John, Jim, Walter and Peter have crew cuts. No loose ends, so she gives them a dab of VO-5 for shine.

The makeup man comes in with his box of colored creams

and sponges, pencils and brushes. Marty, Florrie and Gemma watch him as he leans over my face. He talks as he works. Says he did the makeup for "The Hunchback of Notre Dame" and I wonder if that's how I'm going to look. He reads my mind and grins. "You're gonna look great," he says.

Groomed and ready to go, I'm leaning in the doorway when Tessie O'Shea arrives. She's out of breath, dimpled and dumpled, full of life and theatre rouge. The singers and dancers from her London theatre troupe follow on her heels, and with their entrance the backstage becomes a whirl of buttons, cleavage and fishnet stockings. The men wear derby hats and three-piece suits covered entirely with rows and rows of buttons, and the women are positively squeezed into outfits short on cloth but with enough fishnet to rival Gloucester harbor. Dad tells me to go wait in the dressing room.

Buster Keaton, half-deaf and still wearing that old crumpled hat, waits near the stage curtain and keeps to himself. Throughout his career he was known for his deadpan expression on camera. As far as I can see, he doesn't smile off-camera, either.

Along with Buster, Tessie and her London gang, and us waiting on the left wing, George Kirby, Frank Ifield, comics Paul Dooley and Dick Libertini, the Hermannis jugglers, badminton comedy star Hugh Forgie and that little mouse, Topo Gigio are also waiting in dressing rooms on the right wing. True to form, Ed Sullivan is having another "reelybig shew." But this Sunday night, I am not sitting at home tuned in along with millions of other Americans. Tonight, I am standing backstage waiting to go on.

Ray Block and his orchestra warm up on the other side of the curtain. Horns, woodwinds and strings fill in the sporadic backstage chatter. I can hear the bass player practicing the fast runs of the Bach "Alleluia." Dad wrote that part and it sounded tough. I had no idea that Dad could even orchestrate until yesterday at the rehearsal, when he passed out hand-written sheet music to all the sections.

Soon, another sound begins to compete with the musicians. It is the low hum of an audience gathering and taking their seats, the buzz of excited, hushed voices accented by bubbles of intermittent laughter.

The show finally begins. One act follows another. Topo Gigio, the little mouse who reappears about every three weeks, tells the host again, "I love you, Eddie...Kiss me, Eddie."

Applause for Topo. It's time to go out there. I stand fifth in line, with Jim ahead of me and Gemma behind. A stagehand holds the curtain and he smiles down at me. My legs are shaking, everything itches and I've got to go to the bathroom. Too late now. The pink and blue footlights and hot white television lights are blinding as I walk to the chalk circle that marks my place on stage. I stand there, bowlegged with feet together and hands folded and look out into the black beyond the lights. It is unnerving to hear the loud, faceless applause and I quickly glance to either side for reassurance.

Standing elbow to elbow, we make a long line of family, of sopranos, altos, tenors and basses. The remarkable blend of our twelve voices is the result of shared blood and a shared life. We are the Burke Family Singers and this is our story...

Peace Dale days—1954

CHAPTER 1

"Roma Dixit!"

December 1991

Mother came up from the cellar carrying a dusty cardboard box and looking as if she'd just discovered electricity. "Will you look at these!" she cried, making a space on the table with one hand and grabbing my arm with the other. What she'd found was a bunch of old notepads.

They were of the five-and-dime variety and old enough to have cost just a dime, some thirty, some forty years old. I watched her count. There were twelve of them. On one yellowed page was the tracing of a five-year-old's hand and on another, a few kid scribblings, but all the rest were filled with my mother's neat Palmer-method handwriting.

The Christmas lights (the reason for her trip to the cellar) were forgotten. Eyes glittering like an old rock hound with a fabulous new find, she looked at me and said, "Do you know what these are?"

Inside the older pads were stories and new ideas or just thoughts that she wanted to keep. The later ones were a daily log of all the tours.

The stories were mostly about her children. Mother had ten children who made sure that she was never at a loss for new material. How she had time for anything but changing diapers, washing clothes and the kids who wore them, making meals and packing school lunches is beyond me, but she somehow made the time. She jotted down not only which child said what funny or enlightened thing but other items as well. She wrote down recipes like "French Goulash," "Aunt Ollie's Chocolate Cake" and "Easy Divinity." She wrote lists of Christmas cards sent and received, the names and addresses of different Catholic comic books to send away for, and the words of an author that touched her, like this one:

> "If you forgive people enough, you belong to them, whether either person likes it or not—squatter's rights of the heart."
>
> —James Hilton

There was the Christmas list that reflected the meager salary of a church organist. It must have been written for the first six of us: Steve, Marty, Florrie, Gemma, John and Jim: 1. Wool shirt 2. doll 3. doll 4. doll 5. train/gun 6. cart/gun.

And there were ideas for projects such as how to make a mini-terrarium or angels from styrofoam, strips of sheeting and old lace soaked in wheat paste and sprayed gold. She even made a list of which plants made natural dyes followed by dyeing instructions.

There was no point in trying to read one notebook while she read another. She nudged me. "Listen to this: 'November 1955—The switch on the bathroom light is broken again. It was still dark when I came downstairs to get Peter's bottle this morning. John was in the bathroom, sitting on the throne of his ancestors. There were two lighted candles behind him. When I walked in on him he just glanced up at me and said 'Liberace!'"

"Here's another," she said, just after I'd found my place in the pad I was reading. "1959—Yesterday I told Pete to go to the bathroom to get his sneakers. He came back to say there was nobody in the bathroom but the door was locked. I went to investigate and Jim came out laughing. When Pete had called out, 'Who's in there?' Jim had answered, 'Nobody!' Pete took him at his word!"

While we were laughing over that, a folded yellow sheet of paper slipped out of the notepad in her hand. She opened it up and didn't say a word for a while, then nudged me again.

What she passed to me was the temporary remedy for a situation gone out of control. The situation was ten kids moving in ten different directions with only one Mother to follow them and the remedy, according to Dad, was organization. He had decided to step in and organize the household.

Poor man. Although he loved us all, he never should have had ten children. He just didn't have the psyche for it. He was a nervous type. He came from a line of musicians long enough to thin his blood and cause the neurons in his brain to synapse faster than most.

Mother, on the other hand, was descended from politicians, longshoremen and Boston cops and could have had thirty children. She was into a free-flow sort of existence—even if the flow occasionally backed up on her. Dad's cure for her exhaustion was to reinvent Parris Island. His blueprint was written in pencil on a long yellow sheet from the lawyer's pads he always used.

ROMA DIXIT!
(Rome has spoken!)

SCHEDULE

A.M.

7:00   *John & Gemma rise (John has clock)*

7:10   *John—orange juice & yeast & serve*

7:10   *Gemma—Make cold cereal, eggs &*
bread Mon Wed Fri (No toast!)
Make hot cereal & bread Tues. Thurs.
(No toast!)

7:00   *Steve, Martha, Florrie rise (John wake them)*

7:30   *Breakfast—5 older children—EACH PUT DISHES IN SINK*

7:30   *Anne, Jim, Walter & Sarah rise (John wake them)*
       Jim—Dress Walter   Anne—Dress Sarah

7:40   *John wash dishes*

7:45   *Gemma inspects Anne, Jim, Walter & Sarah*

7:55   *Jim—put breakfast on table.*

7:55   *Walter—empty rubbish*

7:55   *Anne—get Peter up and dress him*

8:00   *Breakfast—EACH ONE PUT DISHES IN SINK!*

8:15   *Jim washes dishes*

P.M.

5:00   *Gemma check bread, spread & milk & cereal.*
       Small children put toys away, etc.

5:10   *Rosary*

5:30   *Supper—5 older children (Anne help Mother)*

6:00   *Supper—5 smaller children (Motts and Flotts do dishes)*

6:30   *Gemma put Sarah & Peter to bed— Walter bed at 7:00.*

8:00   *John, Jim & Anne—BED—Ha! ha!*

9:30   Steve, Martha, Florence, Gemma—
*   BED—Ho! Ho!*

I was amazed at Dad's attention to detail and curious about why we couldn't have toast. Suddenly, it came back to me. This was the pre-Burke Family Singers-and-Toast Era. This was the Peace Dale Period, when every penny counted.

Before we began to sing professionally, we lived in Peace Dale, Rhode Island. My parents' first home was a small, two-storey house on the corner of Sweet Fern Lane and Rodman Street. About the only thing it had to recommend itself was the fact that it was within reach of my father's job and his budget. Mother called it a "glorified root cellar" but Dad said, "Never mind, hon, it's ours," and had indoor plumbing put in and the outhouse removed.

The front door on Rodman Street opened to the living room, where Dad kept his piano. It was an upright model and it got a lot of use. Dad composed and arranged church music on it and every once in a long while he'd surprise us and play some mean boogie-woogie. Later on, Dad used it to teach us about pitch and rhythm and harmony.

When we had more money, the old upright was replaced by a baby grand that, besides my mother, was the love of his life. He'd look at her and say, "You know, Anne? One day that baby grand is going to bury me." It was his insurance policy and he was right—it did bury him. My mother sold it to pay for a large part of his funeral costs, and sometimes, even now, when I go to visit her, I half-expect to hear him there, working out harmonies on the piano, sorting the notes until he got them just right.

Television first appeared at the New York World's Fair of 1939 and by 1949 American families were buying 100,000 television sets a week—but we weren't one of them. We had just moved to Rodman Street, and though there were now two adults and eight kids roaming around the property, my sister Gemma still couldn't prove it to one neighborhood boy:

"What are you doing here?"

"I live here."

"No, you don't. It's Mr. Burke's house."

"I'm his little child."

"No, you're not. Anyway you couldn't be moved in. There's no TV antenna."

"We don't have TV."

"Why not?"

"We can't afford it."

"Yes, you can."

"No, we can't. We have eight children."

"We have a piggy bank half-full. We can buy anything."

This stops Gemma.

Six years later we finally got a TV set. Hopalong Cassidy became the rage in the under-thirteen set, Dad got to watch the fights on Friday nights, and we all watched Arthur Godfrey. Mother, horrified by the fights, wrote, "I can't stand seeing one temple of the Holy Spirit pummeling the hell out of another temple of the Holy Spirit." Soon there was a lace cloth and a statue of Our Lady on top of the TV set, and we said the evening rosary in the living room.

Beyond the living room with the upright piano and the TV set with Mary on top, there was a small middle room that we used as a catchall. It trapped the ever-present ironing pile and was the place where sewing skills passed from Mum to Florrie and Gemma, and eventually to Annie.

In one corner of the room was a pot-bellied kerosene stove, known as a "pot-burner," which served as the only means of heat for the house.

Off the middle room was the only bathroom and it was by far the busiest room in the house. With ten kids, there was often a line formed outside the door. The only way to jump to the head of the line was to pound on the door and dance around while presenting a face of exquisite agony. Yelling "I gotta go!" over and over again was good too. Then the judges, who were also waiting, voted on the evidence.

You had to demonstrate not only an emergency but the most dire emergency and competition was stiff, especially among the boys, who were particularly uninhibited. However, if you grinned at any point during your performance, your first place in line was immediately forfeited. Grinning just before you closed and locked the bathroom door on those waiting was considered suicidal behavior—but it was done, and paid for dearly.

Mother spent more time in that bathroom than anyone else. She was especially familiar with the contours of the bathtub because that was where she washed all the laundry. She used a broom handle stick to move the heavy towels, sheets, diapers and clothes around before she scrubbed them on a washboard. Then she wrung them through a roller attached to the edge of the bathtub and hung them out to dry. This was usually on a Saturday morning. By Saturday night all ten kids had been in that same tub for baths and a hair wash. One of Mum's notations sums up her Saturday nights. It was written when she had only 8 children:

> Saturday—8 baths—80 toenails—80 fingernails—16 ears—8 noses—8 headwashes—banana curls—confessions

The kitchen was relatively large, with a big cast-iron stove and a kitchen table where we ate in two shifts. The fridge moaned quietly in one corner, and the glass on the window over the sink was shiny due to almost constant pane replacements. From outside, the windowpanes winked defiantly in the sunlight, daring Jim to try for another homer.

There was a beat-up wood floor in the kitchen that Dad covered with linoleum, but the threshold under the back door was so worn down that the wet weather seeped in and the floor was often muddy. All the other floors in the house were of old wood, dried out and splintered from the heat of the kerosene stove. We had some throw rugs that were moved periodically to cover the worst spots and though Dad was always telling us to keep our shoes on in the house, we often ran around bare-foot in the summer. Before long, we'd be looking for the tweezers and my older sister Marty to remove a splinter.

Upstairs was just for sleeping. The heat from the kerosene stove came up through a ceiling grate to the hallway upstairs and eventually to the three bedrooms on the second floor.

My parents slept in what they jokingly called the "Master Bedroom." It had the only closet in the house. In the second bedroom, four of the boys slept on two sets of bunk beds and the fifth slept on a cot in a wider part of the hallway. The five girls shared the third bedroom—with two double beds, a twin bed, a desk, two bureaus and a hang-up rack on wheels.

Living in close quarters can create anything from intimacy and tolerance to the urge to strangle someone, and we ran the gamut from tenderness to everything short of murder.

"Friends may come and go, but your family will always be there," so my mother said, and it was true: they *were* always there—whether I liked it or not. They were there whether *she* liked it or not, for that matter. She was obviously losing the battle the day she wrote: "Some days you feel like you're climbing a greased pole." Dad's consoling words as he left the child-filled house on a rainy day were: "Remember Anne, they can't get any younger."

On rainy days we must've torn that place apart, and on sunny days Mother was so busy with cooking, laundry, projects and us that housecleaning was low on the list of priorities.

Priorities, however, seem to swing like a pendulum with the next generation and this particular swing produced five daughters who are killer house cleaners. Believe me. Our floors are always clean. But back then, even after our best efforts, the small house on Rodman Street never looked clean. It had seen too much living before we got there and our arrival hadn't helped matters. We lived hard, especially the five boys.

In 1957, Mother wrote: "What a day! Father Joe Murphy arrives with 3 bushels of tomatoes. Everything stops while the tomatoes get canned. Jim and John take apart a comforter—enter kitchen with feathers in their hair, eyebrows and clothes. John grins 'It looks like fur, doesn't it?'"

And then there was Walter. He had a solo act and that was good because more than one of him would have been overkill. He was the reason Mother said she should have entered the convent.

As he got older, we realized that Walter didn't labor under the fear of death that keeps most of the rest of us in check. He attempted everything from reshaping the iron monkey bars at St. Francis playground with his face to breaking his arm while jumping imaginary barrels at Meehan ice-skating rink to getting hit by a Short Line bus, bouncing head-first into the curb, and then back into the bus and spending six weeks on the Danger List at South County Hospital. To this day he says he wasn't accident prone, but for many years Dad kept a list of doctors that he owed money to on his long yellow lawyer's tablet. There were usually about 14 names on that list and many of them were on a first-name basis with my brother Walter.

While Dad sweated out the five or ten dollars a month to pay off each of those doctors, Mother was usually around when the accident happened and was just grateful that we survived. She blamed it on heavenly protectors:

"When the little dears are asleep at night I can visualize the relief of their guardian angels. They shake hands, kick off their shoes, sprawl across the foot of the boys' cots with a 'Whew! Thank God that day is over!'"

My father paid $2,200 for the house on the corner of Rodman Street and Sweet Fern Lane and a thousand of it was given to us by the pastor of St. Francis, Father Greenan. That was in 1949. My parents' next negotiation with the bank was in January, 1954. "Preventive medicine" was the term Dad used with the bank president when he asked why Dad wanted the vacation loan.

They were exhausted. Dad had been working three jobs and getting very little sleep. He sold cars over at Wiebel Ford in Wakefield and had made the "500 Club" selling over 500 cars in one year, he was organist and choirmaster at St. Francis Church and did the Minstrel Shows there, and he had a job repairing and selling TVs at Bob Warner's shop. And we know that Mother, the lazy thing, was just sitting around eating chocolates, polishing her nails and reading fashion magazines.

The bank manager looked at Dad, heard his story and then personally typed out a loan agreement for $253.50. Under Collateral, he typed "Character."

So they shipped us off, two by two, to friends and neighbors and went up to Canada for a week. It was their first vacation in twelve years and we weren't sure if they were going to come back, but they did, with smiles and a thick red record album that was to change the way we woke up in the morning.

It was a recording of a French boys' choir singing the Gelineau Psalms and Mother played it on the turntable every morning. What a wonderful way to wake up! The choirboys sounded like angels and sweetened our dispositions, which was good because some of the older ones, who no longer woke at the crack of dawn, were not disposed to be sweet in the morning.

Dad, who discouraged any form of laziness, including sleeping in, sometimes added to their foul humor. He'd come back from playing Masses on a Saturday morning, find us still in bed, and yell up the stairs Marine-style, "All Right! Haul Ass! Feet On The Floor!"

He continued to do that after their vacation and the combination got a little bizarre: Mother patiently wooing us awake with "You who dwell in the shelter of the Most High..." and Dad suddenly shouting up to us like a drill sergeant!

Alice, Maerose, Bill, Francis, Walter—The Dancing Burkes, 1924

Anne and Walter, 1935

...and the first three of us

CHAPTER 2

"A pretty girl—BLAT!— is like a melody!"

THEY WERE QUITE A pair, those two: so different in temperament and style and yet equally strong willed. When they disagreed, it was usually about some aspect of child rearing; my father intent on sparing us from the unhappy consequences of an undisciplined youth, knowledge for which he had paid dearly, and my mother determined that our spirits not get squelched in the process. In a contest of wills each was a power to be reckoned with, but when they agreed on something, they were unshakable. They were not boring people. They had presence. You knew it when either one of them walked into a room for each was equally capable of making an entrance.

Actually, that's how they met. It was 1935. Dad was hired for a gig at the Notre Dame Academy Fashion Show and mother was making an entrance. Modeling a very form-fitting white satin evening gown with a white ermine jacket, Anne Devine (that's right, Devine) walked out onto the stage. She was a tall Irish beauty with intelligent blue eyes, a patrician nose, full lips and a dimple in her chin. She had a light complexion that turned to a high color when she blushed, and she blushed easily. She wore her long dark hair combed back from her face and up in a French roll at the nape of her neck.

Mother knew how to carry herself. As a graduate of the Notre Dame Academy on the Charles River, she had been trained in etiquette and elegance as well as the standard school subjects. She successfully ignored the whistles of the Harvard and Boston University sculling teams on her way to school, and she was not daunted by the local Dorchester boys who would look up as she passed and say, "How's the weather up there?" She was now learning to hold her head even higher at the Miss Mary Francis Rooney School, where she was preparing to teach Elocution, Posture and Drama.

Though I never had the opportunity to meet Miss Rooney, her admonishments have dogged me right up to this day. One of Miss Rooney's more famous axioms cautioned against evil nocturnal habits. I write it as it has been so often quoted to me: "Only barbarians go to sleep without first reading." When Mother was trying to get me to dress properly and not slouch, which was and is a lost cause, she'd use the other popular Miss

Rooney maxim: "Before you speak a word, people have all ready made a judgment by what they have seen." Unlike myself, mother had learned both lessons.

She was first-generation Boston Irish and the oldest daughter of a Dorchester police sargeant named Jack Devine, who had come over from Ireland with a sixth-grade education and a determination that his kids would be college-educated. Her mother, Margaret Roche, known affectionately as "Maggie Jiggs," was a milkman's daughter with a fifth-grade education who felt the same way. They had worked hard and wanted their children to have the advantages that an education in those days could afford. Her brothers went to Boston Latin and would later play on the Harvard football team with the Kennedys. Anne Devine was raised to succeed in the Boston of 1935 and it showed.

She walked gracefully down the ramp to the music of a young piano-player and faltered only slightly when she saw him—which was just about a second before he saw her and stumbled on the fingering of the song he was playing: "A pretty girl—blat!—is like a melody...." To hear her tell it, there was such a charge in the air that lighting a cigarette anywhere in the vicinity at that moment would've been a really bad idea.

He looked like he worked at night. His skin was white, his hands were soft, and he was definitely not what Jack Devine had in mind for his oldest daughter. He had green eyes and a shock of white running through his wavy black hair. The white streak was the result of a head-on collision with a fast-moving hockey puck in high school. It may have hurt at the time, but it sure didn't harm his looks. He was striking. Along with his physical appearance, he had a naturally strong musical talent which was trained just enough to harness and finally, the man had charisma.

Walter Vincent Burke enjoyed the position of eldest child and first-born son in an Irish Catholic family. His parents met at the New England Conservatory of Music. T. Francis Burke was on scholarship for piano and Mae T. Gormley studied on a scholarship in voice. They got married and passed a double dose of musical talent, nervous energy and quick wit on to their six children who were natural performers; singers, dancers and instrumentalists.

T. Francis taught them piano, and their mother, Mae T., encouraged their talents in singing and dance. As soon as they were old enough, she enrolled them at the Molly Hurley Dance School, where they appeared in Minstrel Shows as "The Dancing Burkes." Years later, two of the girls would run their own dance school in Boston.

T. Francis Burke, the father of this mad brood, was a church organist, a published composer and Director of Music at Boston College. I knew him as a gentle, quiet old man who sometimes left a gathering in his own living room to go upstairs and say the rosary. When I asked him once where he was going, he leaned over and looked down at me through bottle-thick metal-rimmed glasses and said with a grin, "I'm going up to cram for finals."

He gave each of us younger ones a roll of pennies, nickels or dimes when we came to visit, and he always called my brother Walter his "little gentleman," a title so contrary to Walter's usual behavior and so full of trust that Walter always rose to the occasion and conducted himself exactly as expected.

I knew him as a kindly grandfather, but as a younger man bringing up sons, he could be tough. When Dad got into trouble with his father, the punishment given was scales and arpeggios. Depending on the transgression, the practice could last all day, every day, for a week. This combination of forced labor and natural talent began to show, and soon Dad's fingers were flying over the keyboard.

He loved the concert halls and the nightclubs. When he was a student at Boston College, he started his own dance band called "The Burke Brothers and the Gray Towers Orchestra." His brother Fran played bass, brother Billy played trumpet and Dad played piano, did the arrangements and led the band. They played the swing music of the Dorseys, Glenn Miller and Duke Ellington for college dances and performed all over New England. The Burke Brothers also supplied the orchestra for the dance shows put on by the Burke Sisters Dance School.

When the Depression hit in earnest, Walter left school and went out to look for work, but kept the dance band going as "The Burke Brothers Orchestra." He also landed a very lucrative job on the radio selling pianos for the Stark Piano Company and broadcast under the name of "Don Maestro," playing piano and singing over the air. He was making such good money with these radio concerts that when the time came to return to Boston College, Walter chose to stay where he was.

It was this polished young man with the easy smile and the fast finger work that caught the eye of Anne Devine as she made her way down the ramp that afternoon, and though she'd never heard them, it was his band she described as "absolutely marvelous" to her grammar school reunion committee one month later.

The committee agreed to hire the Burke Brothers Orchestra, and Miss Devine, not wanting to be handicapped by a date, astounded her younger brother by inviting him as escort. Dressed to ensnare in a stunning, rust-colored, crepe number with a tricornered hat and gloves, she entered the hall, promptly forgot about her brother, and approached the stage "to listen to the band."

Walter spotted her and left the piano. He went to the edge of the stage and squatted on his heels, where they decided to stare at each other for a while. In the meantime, his brother Fran, grinning from ear to ear, put down the bass to direct the band.

Eventually, Walter left the stage to dance with Anne, which effectively ended any thoughts either may have had about living a single life. He asked if he could take her home; she agreed and ended up in the backseat with the bass drum and the bass fiddle. Walter drove in the front seat with another band member. There is no information regarding how her younger brother got home.

At the end of a five-year engagement, during which time the terrified bachelor often complained that he hadn't yet made enough money to get married and the eager bride-to-be gave him an ultimatum and threw his diamond onto the sidewalk (marking it's exact location even as it flew through the night air and landed), they finally got married in 1940. They had three kids by the time World War II changed the nation's priorities and Dad, noticing a diminishing market for piano lessons and swing bands and concerned about feeding his family, took a job as a heavy rigger at the Bethlehem Steel shipyard in Quincy, MA.

It was not a smart job for a pianist and this error in judgment would cost him greatly. On New Year's night, he went to the shipyard to work the 3:00 to 11:00 shift and as they were unloading a three-and-a-half ton condenser off a flatbed on the tracks, the crane operator, who was still "bringing in the New Year," thought he got the signal to lower it and let it go. My father couldn't get his hand out of the way in time. The condenser broke every bone in his right hand and tore off most of his thumb.

They rushed him to the hospital and to a young navy doctor who examined the thumb lying in the palm of Dad's hand. In shock but still conscious, Dad looked at him and said, "Doctor, I'm a pianist." The doctor was young enough to try anything and, not knowing if it would take, sewed the thumb back on. It did take but Dad would never again have the stretch or the agility to play concert piano or piano in the Big Band sound. The accident at the shipyard changed forever his career and his lifestyle.

Instead of performing in the muted light of nightclubs, he would now play in the early morning sunlight refracted through stained glass. Like his father before him and his father's father, he would master the organ and play church music. He would move from conducting jazz players to building boy's and men's choirs, from wearing satin-lapeled tuxedoes to donning white cotton choir robes, and from the excitement and applause of nighttime performances to the discipline of giving early morning praise.

I cannot imagine his frustration and his sense of loss as he sat down at the organ with a damaged hand. As an instrumentalist, I can't envision what life would be like if something happened to my hands. Some might say, "He did what he had to do" and perhaps they're right, but I think he was a hero. I think both my parents were. And sometimes I wonder if the spark of thought that began the Burke Family Singers wasn't really God's gentle whisper into the ear of a humbled man.

In the meantime, Mother was looking for roses—literally. The war was over, Bethlehem Steel was closing down, and Dad, who had been working inside the office after his accident, was out of a job. One day he got a call from T. Francis, who told him that a Father Greenan in Wakefield, Rhode Island, was looking for a full-time organist and asked if Dad was interested. They now had four mouths to feed, so Dad called the priest and accepted his invitation to go down to Rhode Island, meet with him and check out the facilities.

Dad took a train from the South Station in Boston on a Friday afternoon and that night, as she tucked the four little ones into bed, Mother got the rose idea. She told the kids that she had heard a story about St. Therese of Lisieux and roses. It seems that St. Therese—also known as the Little Flower—promised she would spend her heaven doing good on earth and she would prove her love by strewing flowers. She said her death would be like a shower of roses—and she has been sending roses down to earth ever since. So Mother said to the children, "We're going to see if this really works. We're going to pray really hard tonight and we're going to ask St. Therese to send us a rose if God wants us to take the job in Wakefield."

For the rest of that weekend, the children watched out for the rose. They inspected the mailman when he came and kept looking out the window at the doorstep to see if St. Therese would leave it there. Saturday night came and then Sunday and the little sentries announced the end of each hour's watch with, "Well, no rose! No rose!"

At the end of a long, hopeful Sunday, Mother put them to bed. Dad, who was unaware of the deal she had struck with the Powers that be, came home soon after and opened the front door. He was holding an overnight bag in one hand and a single red rose in the other. He held the rose out to her and was about to say, "Hi, honey" but was cut off in midsentence. He stood there, dumbstruck, as Mother let out a shriek, grabbed the rose and ran out of the room.

She bounded upstairs to the children's bedroom. "Look!" she cried and they sat up and began shouting "St. Therese sent the rose!" over and over again. Dad had followed her up the stairs and was now looking through the doorway to see his wife laughing and his kids hugging each other and jumping from one bed to the other. She explained to Dad what had happened and then he told his end of the story.

"I was very thrilled about the new job. I liked the facilities, and Father Greenan and I liked each other immediately. While I was at the South Station waiting for the train, I saw a flower mart near the boarding area. It was run by a little Jewish man and I went over to him and I said, 'I'd like to buy a gardenia for my wife. It's her favorite flower...' And the little Jewish man said, 'Oh...my gardenias are kind of tired-looking. Why don't you give her this?' and he picked out one red rose—and he wouldn't take any money for it."

And so with all the stars in their proper constellations, with Dad's good feeling about the new job and a rose from St. Therese, our family moved from Massachusetts to Peace Dale.

Peace Dale is a community in the ocean town of South Kingstown, right next door to Wakefield, Rhode Island. In the 1950s it was primarily Protestant and it was easy to spot the few Catholics. We were the families with eight or more children.

There were the Laffeys (10 children), the Fagans (8), the Ladds (10), the Burkes (10) and the Warners (8). The parents of these large families were close friends. They shared the same ideals and beliefs and they were a great support system for each other. Mary Laffey, Eva Ladd, Carol Fagan and Bea Warner were women my mother could talk to and laugh with when others in town looked on her with pity. We five families clung together in this sea of Protestants and what we lacked in numbers we made up for in liturgical events.

The Feast of the Holy Innocents was one of a few liturgical events held every year when all five families gathered to celebrate some particular tradition of the Church—or to start a new one. These get-togethers served a few purposes. They got the children involved in creative worship while teaching them about their faith, they were a great excuse for a very big potluck supper, a chance for the harried adults to visit and they reinforced who we were as Catholic families through our sheer strength of numbers.

Another big yearly event was the St. John's Fire or summer Christmas. On the evening of June 24th we celebrated the birth of St. John the Baptist outdoors with a bonfire, hymn-singing, scriptural readings and, of course, a potluck supper. Begun in the Middle Ages, St. John's Fire was the early Church's replacement for the pagan ritual of lighting bonfires during summer solstice. But to watch us, children descended from the land of the Druids, it was as if Christianity had never arrived. After the "service" led by the adults, we kids tore around the fire, danced barefoot in the circle closest to the flames, whooping and waving our sticks stuck with marshmallows, leaping and spinning as close as we dared.

Who in Peace Dale would unearth an almost forgotten Christian rite begun in the Middle Ages and celebrated today only in French Canada and in some parts of Ireland? I don't know for sure, but I'd place all my available cash on Anne Devine. She was always coming up with new ideas. But the one idea that would change life for all of us didn't come from Mother. It came from Dad.

1959—Our first public appearance

1960—Dad hears something good . . . while Pete and I warm the bench

CHAPTER 3

The Birth of the
Burke Family Chorale

THERE ARE TWO STORIES about what happened during Christmastime in 1958. The first story, written in the newspapers, told by the public relations people and the only one that I ever heard until recently, tells how we first sang together one night after saying the rosary. The story goes that someone said, "Let's sing something..." and so we sang an Ave Maria plainchant, a chant sung in unison and using the limited Gregorian scale of the early Church. When Dad heard the sound we made, he asked us to try singing something in parts. Once he heard the tonal blend and saw how quickly we learned, he began to get an idea. And that was the beginning of the Burke Family Singers— or so the first story goes, and so swear about half the family.

The second story, which I heard only recently from both Florrie and Steve, made immediate sense to me. It felt right.

Dad was aggravated. He was lying on the couch in the living room and just about to doze off when he heard sounds coming from the middle room. Stephen and Florrie were getting ready to go out Christmas caroling. They were trying to learn the "Carol of the Bells" and they were learning it wrong. For a musician with perfect pitch lying in a semiconscious state, this was torture.

He tried to ignore the children's voices, but when he heard them memorizing the wrong notes, any thought of sleep vanished and Walter V. Burke, musician and choir director, got up off the couch. "You're singing it wrong," he said, and went over to the stacks of sheet music piled high on top of the piano, found the music and began to teach them. As he taught the song, he listened to their singing voices. The sound was clear and sweet and on pitch. He noticed how quickly they learned and he began to wonder about the others. Could they sing, too? Was it possible that all of them could sing?

"I want all the kids in the living room—right now!" His call boomed through the house. Something in his voice was different and we came even more quickly than usual. Mother was in the kitchen making supper—alone, now that her help had run off. Unaware of the "doings" in the living room or maybe just happy to have some time to herself, she stayed in the kitchen while Dad tested the range of all our voices, one at a time.

He worked with Stephen first, singing different notes and asking the seventeen-year-old to match them. Then he turned his attention to Marty and on to Florrie and so on, down the line, looking for the tone quality and range of each voice—and checking for duds. All of us could hear pitch and match it. Well, almost all of us.

With his three-and-a-half octave range, Dad took each one of us as high or as low as we could go and when he got down to the last three shaky, little voices, he saw the earnest look in our faces and grinned down at us. Walt was seven, Pete was four and I was six years old. We didn't know what was going on but whatever it was, we wanted in. We sang our hearts out but we just couldn't hold pitches. He leaned down to us. "You're just not big enough yet," he said, and crestfallen, we sat on the couch and watched him work with the others.

He was chuckling to himself and we were caught up in his excitement but none of us knew what he was doing. We didn't know that he was choosing sopranos, altos, tenors and basses until he separated us into little groups, grabbed the sheet music he had been working with and began to teach the different parts.

Marty, Florrie and Annie were now sopranos. John and Jim were altos, Gemma sang tenor, Steve was a bass, Dad was any part he wanted to be and Walter, Peter and I were benchwarmers. Mother would sing tenor—once she got out of the kitchen.

He taught one line of music to the sopranos, then sent them up to a particular bedroom and told them to practice until he called them. He did the same with each of the four parts. After a few minutes, he called everyone back, played the first note for each part and said, "Okay. Sing."

Music. Voices in harmony. They looked around at each other in amazement at the sound they were making. Everyone was singing and grinning. Dad had his hand over his mouth and he was laughing. That was when Mother came in from the kitchen with a pot in her hand and her jaw down to her kneecaps. She just stared at them, wide-eyed. For once, Anne Devine was speechless. They finished singing the line and the place erupted with laughter, applause, hugging and jumping. Dad looked at Mum and his first words were, "Oh my God, Anne, I think we've really got something here." They had something, all right. That night would rearrange our appointment books for the next twelve years.

In the months that followed, the words "flat" and "sharp" were added to our musical vocabulary. We learned about singing in the front of our mouths and how to sing head tones. Dad re-arranged music to suit our voice ranges and taught us to sing "Brahm's Lullaby" in four parts and "Lo! How a Rose Ere Blooming." We learned more Gregorian chant and a canon by Mozart. By the spring of 1959, we were ready to sing for someone, but who?

Our first audience was made to order. For years he had come to our door every day bearing bills and letters. His name was Mr. Gadreau and that morning he looked up in surprise when Steve opened the screen door and said, "Mr. Gadreau, could you come in? We want to sing for you." Steve held the door open to the puzzled mailman, who took his hat off and walked into the house.

Nine people were lined up by the piano and he was invited to put his mail pouch down and join the other three on
the couch. Walter, Peter and I watched his face while the
others sang "Brahm's Lullaby" and the canon by Mozart. At
the end of it, tears came to Mr. Gadreau's eyes. He applauded
and he didn't have a look-at-all-those-kids-oh-isn't-that-cute
smile on his face. He was moved. Our music had touched him
and the power of that discovery was not lost on my mother or
my father.

Dad knew what he had from the first night he heard us
sing, which is probably why he was out of his mind for the next
three days. Mother may not have known squat about music but
she knew a "force for good" when she saw it, and she saw it in
the eyes of Mr. Gadreau. Soon we were singing before meals
and after the nightly rosary. The rehearsals got longer and the
practice more serious. Due to my parents' "liturgical bent," we
changed the sacred music with the church calendar and our
repertoire grew to include the Gelineau Psalms and the works
of Palestrina, de Victoria and Bach.

We were growing along with our repertoire and with
growth came change. In June of 1959 Steve graduated from
South Kingstown High and announced that he wanted to give
the Passionist Seminary another try in September. His first stint
with the Passionists in upstate New York ended after seven
months. That was back in 1955 when training for the priesthood
often began at puberty. Steve was fourteen years old and home-
sick. He left the seminary at Easter and got home in time to get
pimples and hear Elvis Presley wail "Heartbreak Hotel." Now
he was eighteen and he wanted to go back.

It was a mixed blessing for my parents. It meant that we were gaining a priest but losing the bass section. There was no real contest, however, and in September they sent him off on the train. Dad rearranged the music and took over the bass section.

Luckily, that man was not only vocally versatile but could also adapt the music to the boys' ever-changing ranges. The whole sound shifted as John, Jim, Walt and Pete each took their turn into manhood. First, their voices began to crack and they'd clear their throats and look around, confused. Then they'd sing a little more and a few weird low notes would drop out of them. Their voices got hoarse and the embarrassing dips increased until they were singing in octaves with themselves. It sounded like a loud sighing or a rhino in heat.

They hovered in the no man's land between the high and low registers, somewhere between music and hell. We sneered at them. (Well . . . I sneered at them. I sneered at Walt and Pete, that is. Jim and John would have kicked me into next week but Walt and Pete were my size and anyway, it was habit. I sneered at them on a regular basis. It was something I enjoyed . . . like playing tennis.) Dad gently told them what was going on and asked them not to sing for a while and they'd stand there, looking stupid. (Especially Walt and Pete.) Finally, from the four ugly ducklings emerged three great tenors and a resonant bass. Happily, they did this one at a time giving Dad time to teach them all our music in their new parts.

Voices came and went during our years of singing together. Where they went depended on who was calling the boys at the time, God or Uncle Sam. Steve and John joined the Passionist seminary for a while and both John and Jim served in Vietnam, John with the Marines and Jim with the Army.

In September of 1959 Steve rejoined the Passionists in Dunkirk, New York. He came home for Christmas break in time to rehearse and then sing with the others in their first public appearance. The occasion was the annual Feast of the Holy Innocents party. Walter, Pete and I were still not old enough to sing, so we sat in the audience and waited for the show to begin.

When the others began to sing, I looked around at the faces in the audience and saw that everyone was listening—even the kids. And after each song, people were clapping like crazy. We were a hit.

The parents were buzzing about the concert all through the deviled eggs, potato salad, three-bean salad and cold ham and they kept it up during the pineapple upside-down cake and coffee. Dad was huddled in a corner with Paul Ladd, a musicologist whose specialty was Church music and a man whose opinion my father valued. Dad was listening with his head down and grinning at something Paul was saying. What we heard most often was, "What are you going to do with this?" and "Other people should hear you." My parents agreed and so after Steve returned to the seminary, the rest of us started to go out singing.

We sang at convents, P.T.A. gatherings and orphanages. We sang at nursing homes and for a Christmas party at South County Hospital where Marty worked as a nurses' aide. We went to sing wherever we were asked and we sang for free. We loved to see faces light up and we loved the sound we could make.

Back then we called ourselves the Burke Family Chorale, and though we were still three singers (and one seminarian) short of a dozen, Walter, Pete and I did our best to steal the show from our chairs on stage right. The act started when our interest waned and boredom set in, about fifteen minutes after the singing began and if you didn't like the music, you could always watch us. Even if you liked the music, you couldn't help but watch us at least some of the time.

They sat us on chairs that were the metal-backed, folding type with cold, no-give metal seats. Unfortunately, I was not a plump child and the search for relief had me in pretty much constant motion, slouching and draping my skinny self on and around the chair, crossing one leg and then the other while boredom raged with discomfort.

Pete sat to my left. He'd yawn for a while, then take his glasses off, dig around in his pocket until he found his handkerchief and start breathing real hard on his glasses. He'd polish them, hold them up to the light for inspection and if he saw something he didn't like, he'd start all over again. And then there was Walt. His opening number was a real crowd pleaser. He'd wait for pauses in the music to crack each and every one of his knuckles. This was followed by stretching, back scratching and looking over at me or Pete with his tongue curled up under his upper lip in a monkey face which, of course, would crack us up. By then he was usually warmed up for his main act.

He'd pick out someone from the audience, usually an insecure adolescent, and leaning forward in his chair with his elbow on his knee and his head in his hand, he'd look down and stare.

He'd grin and stare and he didn't let up. His victim squirmed, looked up at Walter and then looked away and still Walter stared, his eyes acting like the sun through a magnifying glass on an insect, focusing heat until even the people sitting near the unfortunate person began to look over at him to see what was the matter. Finally, Walter moved on to someone else. Needless to say, our show within the show was broken up as soon as possible. For one thing, Dad wanted Walter Jr. standing right in front of him. Good idea.

Pete and I tried to carry on, but it just wasn't the same without Walt. By April of 1960 I had joined up, leaving Pete to distract the crowd as best he could and according to Mother, he seemed to be doing rather well. In a letter to her seminarian Steve, she writes: "Peter was quite a hit at the Bayview concert. While we sang and edified everyone with a scad of dignified music, he made faces at the audience. He stuck his tongue out at a group of children sitting in the front row. He kicked his feet, wiped his glasses, stretched and yawned, etc. Every time Dad turned to look at him he was sitting as quietly as an angel, which panicked the audience. At one point I thought I'd whispered 'Pete, cut it out!' but evidently the audience heard me and thought it was very funny."

Way to go, Pete. Though my mother writes about it with good humor, something had to be done. He wouldn't be able to sing for at least another year and this sort of behavior couldn't continue. And so my parents, being astute observers of human nature (and government), decided that Pete would straighten out if they gave him a title. He was too young to be able to really do anything but he needed to have a job, a purpose, a feeling that he was a part of this singing group and so Peter became "Official Librarian."

He thrived in his new capacity as guardian of sheet music, and at the beginning of a concert, proudly carried a red suede brief case on stage, ceremoniously handed it to my father, and then conducted himself with great dignity to his chair on stage right. There he sat for the next fifty minutes, calm and self-assured, until it was time to retrieve the case at the end of the first half.

At the end of a fifteen minute intermission, Dad came out on stage alone to introduce us individually. He'd tell the audience something about each of us and we'd come onstage one by one and take a bow. For the final introduction my father said, "And now . . . the most important member of the chorale . . . the librarian, Master Peter!" And on came Pete, hair slicked back, two front teeth missing, eye glasses with wire rims wrapped all the way around his ears, clutching the big briefcase and wearing a wide grin.

John   Gem   Florrie   Marty   Steve

Pete   Sarah Jo   Walt   Annie   Jim

July 10, 1958

CHAPTER 4

Our First Paycheck

ACTUALLY, THAT RED SUEDE briefcase marked a turning point—not only in Peter's behavior but in all our lives. It was deep red and soft to the touch, with rounded leather grips and a patch of black leather on each side embossed with the name "Burke." It was the first of many gifts from our new next door neighbor, Mrs. Halton, and though it was handsome, there was nothing particularly miraculous about it. What was miraculous was that Mrs. Halton hadn't moved down to our humble neighborhood. We had moved up to her wealthier one.

That was in December 1960 and as I look back on that year,

it seems that things began to move fast and furious in our lives; major events and small discoveries that would irrevocably change the way we saw ourselves and others.

1960 began with a concert at Blessed Sacrament convent in Providence. We sang for a teaching order of nuns called the Faithful Companions of Jesus, whom Dad knew well. He sometimes stopped in to the convent for morning coffee after playing Masses. Dad had left St. Francis in Wakefield and had taken the position of organist and choirmaster at Blessed Sacrament Church, at that time a very wealthy Italian parish. For more than five years he had driven the hour to Providence to play daily Masses, funerals, weddings and then back again some nights to direct choir rehearsals.

Often he didn't ride alone. Marty and Florrie, who were now high school age and great lovers of motorcycles and the boys who cruised down to Scarborough beach on them, kept Dad company. My parents decided that their two oldest girls would be much better off with the good Sisters than doing the stroll with the James Dean look-alikes at South Kingstown High. Soon, my sister Gemma joined them and then all three either took the train from Wakefield or rode in with Dad to Providence to attend Saint Patrick's High School.

There the Faithful Companions entertained their all female audience, enthralling them with verb conjugations in Latin as well as in French, transporting them to the heady heights of philosophy and theology and to the lofty peaks of various mental disciplines such as chemistry, biology, history and math.

Not everyone enjoyed the show. The two oldest girls were infinitely more comfortable on the back end of a Harley than in the classroom. On this cold and snowy New Year's Day, instead of enjoying a holiday away from those watchful, wimple-headed eyes on this cold and snowy New Year's Day, it was their turn to entertain the nuns.

Our concert began at 2 P.M. It must have been a short one because there was a second concert slated for St. Margaret's Home at 4 P.M. followed by tea and cookies. Both benefits given that day were a success. The audiences were charmed and the glow of their gratitude warmed us. We took our leave at around 5:30 on New Year's Night, in the winter's early dark. Feeling good and full of cookies, the twelve of us somehow squeezed into the rusty silver station wagon Dad had fondly nicknamed "The Gray Ghost" for the ride back to the cramped house in Peace Dale. It was a fine way to begin the New Year and indicative of the kind of year 1960 would be.

We tried out our musical wings at mostly Catholic functions that first year, taking our heavily religious repertoire to Retreat Houses, the Lion's Club and to quite a few convents. From the beginning we saw ourselves as more than a family singing group. We were an American Irish Catholic family of singers and happy about each adjective that described us. The Catholic Church, delighted with our attitude, our repertoire and our numbers, claimed us as her own.

Smiling, supportive faces greeted us always but I can't help but wonder what those early audiences really thought as they looked at this human xylophone of singers, smiling faces scrubbed or lightly-made up, worn dresses starched and some of the boys' pants cuffs higher than style permitted. Were the parents of this brood unusually courageous or simply out of their minds?

We continued to improve musically but all the gratis performances didn't do much to enhance our presentation. In February we sang for the Retreat League Banquet at Rhodes-on-the-Pawtuxet, a popular dancing and dinner hall. Not only would we be singing in a big ballroom but Governor Del Sesto was going to be there, so we decided to get fancy. We borrowed instruments from South Kingstown High; drums for John, triangle for Jim, tambourine for Anne and our little dinner bell for Walter and used them for "Give Thanks to the Lord for He is Good,"one of the Gelineau Psalms. After the performance, Governor Del Sesto came over to our table to congratulate us and said, "Were my eyes deceiving me or was that a nutcracker the little boy was using to hit the triangle?" It was.

That was one to tell the priests over at Blessed Sacrament rectory and Dad, being terminally Irish, couldn't pass up the chance for a laugh. Although he stopped in occasionally at the convent, he most often had coffee at Blessed Sacrament rectory before and between Masses.

It was at the rectory of this city parish where he became friends with a circle of musician priests, one of whom was the diocesan music director, Father Norman LeBoeuf, an eccentric and talented musician who taught Gregorian Chant. After he heard the family sing, he asked if he could be our business manager. Father LeBoeuf loved the whole idea of the Burke Family Chorale. He appreciated even the early sounds we were making and he thought we should be paid to sing. Mother and Dad, who were barely scraping by and often doing without, listened to him with great interest.

As it turned out, we had a rather short amateur career. It ended in April 1960 with our first full, paid concert at St. Michael's Auditorium in Providence. Father LeBoeuf set it up, we sang it, they clapped loud and long and we went away with our first paycheck of $150.00. With our budget back then, it was a windfall. Anyone who's had more than a few pancake suppers will better understand what it meant to my parents. All of us felt so proud that we could do this; that we could sing well enough that someone would want to pay us. We were also a little amazed.

While Father LeBoeuf was telling people about us and trying to get us more paying gigs, my father decided that the best way to get exposure was to sing at every opportunity, starting with the most obvious. We all went to school, so that's where we sang next.

It was June and the end of my second grade year at Peace Dale Grammar School when my family came to sing in the school auditorium. The parents, students and teachers in the audience were the same ones who sat spellbound through our class's dazzling performance of the *Song of Hiawatha* the previous November. Most of them knew us or knew of us as "that family with all the kids who lived down Sweet Fern Lane and Rodman..." and many parents came out of curiosity.

My voice had developed and now I stood up there with them, sweaty-palmed on a warm spring afternoon and singing for all I was worth. I loved being a squaw in the Thanksgiving play, wearing a headband with a seagull feather sticking up in the back, painting my face and beating on my homemade drum, but this had Hiawatha beat hands down. Standing on this same stage with just family felt entirely different. It felt powerful.

Next, we drove into Providence to sing at St. Patrick's High auditorium. Those Faithful Companions just couldn't get enough of us. The word spread via the nun grapevine, and we branched out to other Catholic schools, thrilling students who otherwise only got out of the classroom for fire drills, hurricanes or heavy snowfalls. Of *course* they loved us! We kids loved them, too, because not just once, but *every* time we sang, *we* got out of the classroom.

My mother took some of that first paycheck and went to the fabric store with her older daughters. Both Florrie and Gemma knew their way around a sewing machine and soon all five girls and Mum wore the same dresses on stage. For the boys, Dad went to a place called "Quirk and McGinn" to rent tuxedos. As time went on, Mr. Quirk and Mr. McGinn must've just loved to see Dad coming.

In the twelve years of professional singing that followed, Dad never bought tuxedos for himself and the five boys. He always rented them—for-month-and-a-half long tours as well as for individual concerts.

Dressing alike gave the act formality and made us look professional. That look came just in time. Our next paid performance was for the white-gloved and well-heeled Catholic Women's Club at the Sheraton-Biltmore Hotel in downtown Providence and Anne Devine, graduate of Notre Dame Academy and the Mary Francis Rooney School, was not going to have her family looking shabby in front of this crowd.

Father LeBoeuf had set this up and was hovering somewhere along the sidelines. We kids were wide-eyed. This place was beautiful, from the plush carpeting and the high ceilings to the rich wall colors and lush fabrics of the long window drapes. Across the lobby were elevators that went to the top of the hotel. From way up there, the whole city of Providence was laid out in lights!

Singing at the Sheraton-Biltmore. As far as we kids were concerned, we had definitely hit the big time. Of course, back then we had no idea what the big time was. We had never even *been* in an elevator—never mind one that went up and down an eighteen-storey building. We didn't want to warm up vocally. Or stay together. We wanted to get on that elevator and *stay* on that elevator, up and down and up and down. Dad was holding us youngest three still with the sheer strength of the "don't-even-think-about-it" look in his eyes.

We sang and the Catholic ladies loved us. After the concert, punch was served with cookies and little sandwiches with the crusts cut off and shaped in bite-sized triangles. Walter ate dozens of these and then approached the priest in charge.

"Father, my cummerbund is too tight. Do you mind if I take it off?"

"Well...I don't...uh..."

Unfortunately, this exchange was overheard by one of my older sisters who went over, smiled at the priest and whispered something—I don't know what—in Walter's ear. As near as I can figure, it was a death threat of some sort. Walt excused himself and moved away, cummerbund intact.

I walked over to the food table just in time to spot Jim

filling his tuxedo pockets with the little triangle sandwiches. He caught my eye and grinned. Not a word was spoken, but we both knew that he would now be sharing those sandwiches he was saving for the ride home.

Having successfully manuevered the heavy ladle from the punch bowl across the white linen tablecloth and into my cup without spilling a drop, I was ready to enjoy a fourth cup of punch with my tenth cookie when I saw that I was about to be accosted by an older woman who looked like trouble. Her face had "agenda" written all over it even as she bore down on me. Vulnerable and alone, I swallowed the food in my mouth, stood my ground and waited. It didn't take her long. She began by telling me what a pretty little girl I was. "Thank you," I answered politely, antennae up and on full alert.

"It must be hard work to do all that singing. Do you practice a lot?"

"Yes. We rehearse a lot," I replied. She was up to something, that was for sure.

"Do your parents make you sing?" she grinned down at me, feral eyes sharp and eager. Ah! So there it was!

"Oh *no*! They don't *make* us! We *love* to sing!" I smiled guilelessly up at her, meeting her shrewd gaze. I may have been only eight years old, but I was my father's daughter and had watched and listened enough to know who this woman was—and she knew that I knew. After a moment, she moved away and I went to seek out family.

1961—Our first television show on WJAR-TV, Providence, RI

CHAPTER 5

"Doors and Radiators in Every Room"

SHE WAS THE FIRST to ask a question like that but she wouldn't be the last. Throughout our career, there were some people who just could not believe what they were seeing. Not many, but a few who, courageous souls that they were, invariably approached one of us three youngest kids after a concert to get "the real story," "the dirt." They asked if we were being coerced to sing and did we *really* get along that well and were we *really* that happy or was that just part of the show?

Of course we were that happy! We got out of school to sing.

We were all together, which almost always meant laughter. People smiled at us and clapped for us. We got to eat out in restaurants. Soon we had some brand new clothes and new shoes. Granted, rehearsals could sometimes get a little dicey. And there was that time when Jimmy showed up in the family room after a half-hour rehearsal break wearing his full football gear, helmet and all, in case Dad decided to throw furniture.

Jim purposely waited until after we had all gathered to make his bulky entrance. Dad happened to have his back to us while he looked for music on the piano. He turned, tense and determined to drill more notes into us, saw the hole in the line where Jim should have been standing, opened his mouth to say, "Where the hell is Ji..." when he spotted Jim making his way to his place. He nudged his way in, stood there and grinned up at Dad. There was a moment of silence and then Dad started to laugh. We all joined him and the tension was broken.

The tension was broken—for a little while, that is. In rehearsal, it was never gone entirely. It wasn't easy music we were singing. Eventually we would sing in up to nine parts and twelve languages, sometimes bringing in linguists to help with pronunciation. This music was difficult to learn and then tougher to sing on pitch and a cappella and Dad was exacting—and yes, sometimes we wanted to strangle him. He didn't let us get away with anything and his ear for pitch was maddening. I will never forget the day he introduced us to Jacob Archadelt's sixteenth-century madrigal "Il Bianco e Dolce Cigno." I'm sure none of us will.

I could tell from watching his face as he sang the melody to us the first time that he loved this song. Interpretation was going to be important because he wanted us to sing it as beautifully as he heard it in his head. We listened carefully. He told us that the song was about how the swan sings before its death, and then he taught each of the four parts their first line of music, which happened to be the title of the song—and that's as far as we got for the next three hours.

The meaning of the song began to feel more and more appropriate. We were going to die trying to learn this song. Steve started to count how many times Dad stopped us because someone sang a wrong note or came in at the wrong time or was flat or was sharp or was too loud or breathed in the wrong place and he counted to 104. It wasn't just the constant stopping that set our nerves on edge, it was the *way* he stopped us. At first, he'd say "Stop!" and tell us who was doing what wrong, but after a while he'd just bang a discord on the piano to stop us. Fingernails on a chalkboard were nothing compared to this. We were ready to kill him but we sang it again and again until the very last time when he looked around at us, smiled and said, "Yes. That's it."

You could fool an audience some of the time but you could never fool his ear. That was what judged our sound, not the smiles in the audience or the applause. He held a musical ideal up to us and it was in his ear. It was a constant challenge and one that had nothing to do with the audience. It was between him and us. He'd never lie about what he heard when we were off so when we were on and he told us, we believed him. We learned how to use our voices and as our trust grew, we became more pliable, like the horizontal curve on a TV set that he could adjust higher or lower with the slightest move of his hand.

Dad was not a flamboyant director. He directed close to his chest and during a concert, he'd point to or lock eyes with one of us, gesture up or down and then give us a stop sign when the pitch was where it should be. Eventually, we began to hear what he heard. There were times during later concerts that, at the end of a song and with his back still to the audience, he would look at us, grin, blow his pitch pipe softly and say what his ears had all ready heard, "Perfect pitch." Then he'd turn to the audience and lead us in a bow, all of us grinning out at them as we bent at the waist.

But those concerts came long after the one for the Catholic Women's Club, years after the wonder of watching the city lights from the top floor of the Sheraton-Biltmore Hotel.

As promised, after the reception on the main floor, we got to ride all the way up on the elevator. Eighteen floors! The view from the large windows was beautiful. Even my sophisticated, city-wise older sisters couldn't keep the thrill off their faces. Marty tried not to show it but a pent-up giggle popped out and gave her away. The lights from the roof caught the snowflakes as they fell and we watched in wonder at all the ground lights spread out below us.

We felt triumphant and full of hope. It was December 8, 1960. John F. Kennedy, a Boston-Irish Catholic, had just been elected President. Mother's sister Ellen, founder of "Execu-Tours" of Boston, was invited to accompany Rose and Eunice Kennedy on their campaign "teas" throughout the country. Later on, Uncle Jack and Uncle Jim, both lawyers, headed to

Washington to work in this new administration. The era of the large Irish-Catholic family was at hand and we gladly ushered it in! Our time had come. Looking out through the window, we saw our city. And it *was* our city. We had left Peace Dale and had been living in Providence for one whole week.

We made the short trip back to our new home and piled out of the car. I looked up at it again. I still couldn't believe we lived here. Besides Dad and Mum, none of us had seen the new house until the day we moved.

And what a day that was. Dad locked the back door to the house in Peace Dale and walked around it one last time checking the windows while we waited in the car. We were packed like sardines in a tin can, all staring in the same direction but alone in our separate thoughts. It was a quiet car. Finally Dad got in the driver's side and we were off. Once we got into Providence, he decided to take the scenic route to the new house.

He drove with a grin on his face and not a word out of him, past the Tudor mansions and tree-lined Blackstone Boulevard and then up the hill on Doyle Avenue through a very wealthy, quiet neighborhood, with us sitting there bug-eyed and wondering where and when he's going to stop. These houses were old and solid and beautiful. It couldn't be around here.

He took a right onto Morris Avenue, maples and oaks everywhere and wide, well-paved streets, past the synagogue and then looped back around onto Doyle and continued up to the top of the hill. I could see the sign for Hope Street and Sugarman's Funeral Home on the corner when he finally pulled the car over and looked at us, still grinning. Great! Were we moving into the Funeral Home?! *Where was the house?* Sometimes his flair for the dramatic made me crazy.

He was enjoying this, that was obvious. He pointed across the street and we let out a collective gasp. No problem with enough oxygen in that car. None of us were breathing. Chuckling, he jangled the keys in front of us, got out of the car, crossed the street, walked up the steps and across a long, wide porch with a roof supported by four thick columns like an honest-to-God Southern mansion. He unlocked a massive wooden door that had a brass knocker. We followed him up the stairs and saw that the key worked. He opened the door, reached over and turned on the light.

We all looked up. From the ceiling hung a chandelier, lights hidden in circles of crystals, shimmering layers of cut glass and refracted light that tapered down like an upside-down Christmas tree. Dad laughed as he watched us, his eyes full. He didn't say anything and after he opened the door, he just stood by it and gave us all a sweeping gesture with his arm as if to say, "...After you..."

Then we raced through the house. Marty and Florrie held hands as they ran together, laughing and crying. Annie grabbed me in passing and whispered, "Doors and radiators in every room! We must be rich!" We were knocking into each other, flying up and down the stairs.

I systematically bolted through every room in the house, beginning with the first floor and worked my way up until I found an excellent hiding place. It was behind a sliding door built into the lower section of a bookcase that had been left in the bedroom at the end of the hall on the third floor. I got into it, slid the door closed and waited. Annie was the next one to slide the door open and I scared her silly. We both screamed, then I slid the door closed again before she could get her hands on me. I stayed in there for a while. I needed a small, safe place and time to think about how big this house was.

Laughter, shrieks of pleasure and the sounds of running feet filled the empty rooms. Names were called out and responded to from faraway places. There was a full cellar and three floors of rooms to run in! Seven bedrooms! Four bathrooms! There was a den built three-quarters up with oak paneling and the top quarter with stucco to reflect the light from the front window. This den had a fireplace with a mantelpiece and built-in oak bookcases that stood on either side of it, enclosed with doors made of glass cut in small diamond shapes, held together with strips of lead and framed in polished oak.

There was a formal front sitting room, a reception hall, a family room upstairs with another fireplace, a formal dining room and a big kitchen. A butler's pantry connected the two eating rooms by swinging doors. Two different sets of stairs connected the first floor with the second. Wall-to-wall carpeting covered the wood floors in the front rooms, then traveled up the wide, front stairs to cover the second-floor hallway.

We had no furniture for this house. We had one couch, a small, carved-up kitchen table, some chairs, a turntable, a TV set, three double beds, some army cots and bunk beds. This was a fourteen-room house. This was insane.

Enter Mrs. Halton, next-door neighbor and proud Irish mother of two grown sons and both of them Dominican priests.

She was the color of winter: crisp sky blue eyes set in a soft, wrinkly face topped with long snow white hair wound and pinned up on the back of her head. She was tall, trim, wore well-made tie shoes, no-nonsense clothes in grays or gray-greens and tweeds and could be seen gardening from the time the snow melted until it fell again. Watching her through the wire fence that separated our two back yards and then later working knee-deep in dirt alongside her, she passed the madness on to me and I thank her for every backache and every pair of filthy jeans.

Mrs. Halton was a smart woman and it didn't take her long to figure out that we were finished moving in and without the help of North American Van Lines or any other van lines, for that matter. So Mrs. Halton decided to get in line.

She joined the long line of generous people who had helped us along the way when I was growing up. I don't know why. We never begged. I don't think we even asked. These people just showed up with a basket of apples or a box of clothes. They were just there. My sister Florrie had made reference to them years earlier. When she was a child, she came home from school one day and told my mother that some little girls in her class had teased her, chanting, "Your family's poor, your family's poor!" My mother started a slow boil but kept the anger from her voice and asked, "What did you say to them, dear?" to which Florrie replied, "I said, 'No, we're not! We're not poor! How can we be poor when people give us everything?'" How can you argue with such flawless logic?

Now came Mrs. Halton, but this was no bushel of apples she was offering. After waiting a suitable time and sure now that there would be no van arriving, she called my mother and complained that she'd gathered so much furniture over the years, and even with her living alone in it, now that her priest sons had moved away, the house was so full that she was having difficulty moving around for heaven's sake and could we use any of it before she sent it off to St. Vincent de Paul's?

The woman must've emptied out her house. What arrived in ours was more than just usable furniture. These were antiques, sturdily-built, beautifully carved, polished wood; two matched four-posted twin beds with a carved acorn design on the headboard and at the top of each post, a tall china closet, a buffet or bureau for dishes, a big mirror to hang over the buffet, matching high-backed, over-stuffed chairs covered in a woven brocaded cloth, a formal upholstered couch and only God remembers what else. They were like nothing we had. It was furniture that fit this house, classy and rugged, and she just gave it to us.

Mrs. Halton was generous but always practical and sometimes not terribly subtle. Consider the time she announced that as a graduation present for Marty and Florrie, who had finally escaped the watchful eyes of the Faithful Companions, she was going to have the outside of our house painted. She saw what needed doing and used any pretext to get it done.

The truth was that we couldn't really afford this house. Dad had seen it, fallen in love with it and was somehow going to make it work. Incredible by today's standards, it cost $19,000 and for Dad, it was a very big financial leap. The budget meant being able to meet the mortgage payment and maybe heat the place—period. It didn't include furniture and I don't think it covered upkeep like roof work, furnace repair or exterior painting. Later on, finances would change, but during that first year in the new house my parents gratefully accepted Mrs. Halton's extraordinary "graduation present."

It didn't take too long for the tide to turn financially. We had been in our new house for less than a month when we did our first television show. "Columbus National Bank presents 'Christmas Carols' by the Burke Family Chorale on WJAR-TV..." It was all very local, but if they wanted to, anybody in Rhode Island could turn on the TV set and see us. Steve and John, our seminarians home for Christmas, stood out in the black floor-length cassocks of the Passionist Order. There was no doubting who we were, that was for sure.

Some people first learned about us through the TV show, but a lot of people were finding out about us through word of mouth. Rhode Island is a very small state. Dad's "sing anywhere/sing everywhere" policy helped, too. But primary in getting the word out were the newspaper columnists who took an immediate and lasting interest in us. A month after the TV show, our picture appeared on the cover of *The Rhode Islander* magazine, part of the *Providence Sunday Journal*, with a four-page story and photo spread.

This was a very big break and the work of Ruth Tripp, winner of the 1960 National Music Critics Award. She titled her article, "A Dozen Burkes Love the Sound of Music." There. It was out. And it didn't take long. *The Sound of Music*, based very loosely on the story of the Trapp Family Singers, had just opened in Boston. The Trapp family's singing career had ended in 1956 and here we were, a large family of singers doing a very similar type of repertoire. Like it or not, the association with and comparison to the Trapp family was almost immediate and would last throughout our career. As a matter of fact, on the last page of Ruth Tripp's article, below a close-up shot of John and me singing at WJAR, is an advertisement for the show with a picture of Mary Martin hugging the Baroness Von Trapp. Coincidence? I doubt it.

The very first article written about us back in May of 1960 made the connection between us and the Trapps. Paul Ladd, writing for the *Providence Visitor*, declared that "This lovely family has made such an impressive beginning that, inevitably, comparisons will be made between it and the Trapp family. They are different. Their vocal style is not German, they are Irish and American, and look it, and they will probably be appreciated by Americans more than the Trapps were."

Whether we were appreciated more than the Trapps or less is impossible to say, but it is true that our vocal and performance styles reflected two very different cultures. The Trapps were extremely controlled on stage. In fact, the Baroness once wrote that while performing a "Jodler" (one of the mountain calls from the Austrian Alps), she took a deep breath and inhaled a fly. Rather than make a coughing sound on stage, she turned purple and choked quietly until she finally swallowed it.* If that had happened to one of us on stage, there'd have been gagging, coughing, and backslapping. There would surely be a pause in the program, an explanation given by Dad and there would certainly be laughter.

---

* *The Story of the Trapp Family Singers* c. 1949 by Maria Augusta Trapp, J.B. Lippincott Company, Philadelphia, New York, p. 199.

Though it was impossible to sing this type of music without discipline, there was a spontaneous quality to our singing. Our individual personalities were obvious on stage. Our sound was bright and bold, and my father's gift for humorous storytelling and ad lib gave our stage presence a much looser, more informal quality. The Trapps, on the other hand, had a very pure, controlled sound. They sang in covered tones and were cohesive enough to sound like one voice. We were more rambunctious. However, there were enough similarities in the two sounds that when Hedwig von Trapp heard a tape of us singing, she said, "Why, it's like my family all over again."

Pete with poison ivy—Waterman Lake, 1961

CHAPTER 6

We Got It for a Song...

1961 BROUGHT MORE CONCERTS advertised with radio spots and newspaper articles, our first brochure set up by Father LeBoeuf, red curtains for the kitchen and no new furniture, a repertoire that now included songs in eight languages and a summer house.

Remember the expression "I got it for a song," meaning you got a real good deal? Well, for a Lithuanian song, we got the use of a summer house at Waterman Lake. In Harmony, Rhode Island.

Father Martinkus was the pastor at St. Casimir's, a

Lithuanian church near the State House in Providence. He came to hear us sing and approached my father after the concert.

"Would you come and sing at Saint Casimir's? We have no money to pay..."

By that time, we were mostly getting paid to sing. Singing, we discovered, put a good-sized dent in the mortgage payment. Besides, we had to pay not only the tuxedo people, Mr. Quirk and Mr. McGinn, but now there was Mr. Phillips who rented out the small, portable Conn organ that we used when there was no piano in the hall.

Dad was explaining all this to Father Martinkus, who nodded his head as he listened and told Dad that most of his parishioners were refugees who came over to this country after great persecution in Lithuania. They were poor and most couldn't speak English. By the time he'd said, "They'd really love your family...," my father was ready to book a date. Then Father Martinkus said in his strong accent, "Oh wait! I know! I have a summer house at Waterman Lake. What about trade? Would your family like to use it for one month for the concert?"

Dad, who was no stranger to the barter system, laughed, and they shook on the deal. We learned two songs in Lithuanian for the concert and though verbal communication was tough, the audience smiled a lot, clapped like crazy, and some of them cried when they heard their own language sung by a bunch of Irish people who were probably murdering words right and left.

Then came the other part of the deal—a month in paradise! No chores except to sweep the sandy floors and make sure you made your bed and hung up your bathing suit and towel.

There was no TV, but you could get up as early as you wanted to and sneak out of the house, sit on the front lawn and watch Jimmy fish for bass and pickerel or you could walk off with some hot dog rolls and a bamboo pole and catch sunfish.

It was a simple, not-too-fancy, mostly summer community: a bunch of cottages nestled around the lake, with a little beach where a lifeguard watched the children wade while the teenagers hung out on the raft anchored farther out in the water, and the older people sat on the shore trying to read while the sand flew around them. Dogs weren't allowed but still found their way onto the beach and were mostly ignored until someone complained.

One dog in particular seemed to have the right of entry onto that beach. Her name was Honey, which was the color of her coat. She was a long-haired mongrel and she was one weird dog. This dog could smile. She could smile on command. We'd say "Smile, Honey!" and Honey would. Honey's whole back end moved from side to side as she looked up expectantly, her stretched mouth exposing pointed teeth in an appalling grin as she waited to be petted or given Cheetos. She'd eat anything but she loved Chee-tos.

Honey was a major source of amusement for the Waterman Lake teenagers—of which I was an aspiring member. The other source of entertainment was the juke box at the Community House. That summer I logged in quite a few hours milling around that coin-operated music machine with my sister Annie, singing "A-hab the A-rab" and "My Boyfriend's Back," trying to look cool, dancing a little and eating the red silver dollar penny candies that were sold at the concession stand.

Still a child but caught in the pull of oncoming adolescence, I fluctuated between watching the boys and trying to pick up Annie's dance routines, to attempting to catch what I thought was a very cute little chipmunk by blocking off all its exit holes except for the one where I stationed myself, hand outstretched and ready to grab my future pet. Luckily, Jim spotted me and did some explaining about chipmunk teeth.

There is one more image that stands out in my mind about that play-filled month. It was the first and only time that I ever saw my father swim.

He'd just come back from playing morning Masses in Providence. I'd never even seen him in a bathing suit and was struck momentarily speechless at the sight as he came out from the cottage with a towel in his hand, looking hot and ready to cool off. He was very overweight and usually stayed inside when it was warm. As he passed by me I asked, "Where ya goin'?" "Swimmin'," was all he said.

I watched him cut through three backyards then wade to the raft where a diving board was mounted. He knew I was staring and grinned at me right before he ran the length of the board and dove expertly into the water. Open-mouthed, I watched him surface and begin to swim, the weight he carried gone. He was so graceful, moving in rhythm with the easy power of a young man. He swam without stopping clear over to the other side of the lake and I just stood there and watched thinking I'd never seen anything so beautiful.

The month ended too quickly, but going home to Doyle Avenue was no great cross to bear. A lot of us had settled in new schools and had already made friends. During that fall of 1961,

Steve and John were still in the Passionist Seminary in Dunkirk, New York, though Johnny would return home before the year was out and Steve would follow near the end of 1962. Marty and Florrie had just graduated, but Gemma was still at St. Patrick's High School and Jim, Anne, Walter, Peter and I were enrolled at Holy Name Grammar School, just a few blocks away from home. Even Mother went back to school. After a twenty-year break, she took a part-time job teaching speech at St. Sebastian's Grammar School.

Besides our school and home activities, there was a concert schedule that continued to grow. We auditioned for the music faculty at the University of Rhode Island and were invited to sing at Edward's Hall. This was a different type of audience for us. In addition to singing for university students and faculty, it was the first time that the general public bought tickets to hear us and we were nervous. The university was in Kingston, just a jump away from Peace Dale and all our old neighbors.

The old neighbors had seen us off stage. They knew a lot about us. Many had been at St. Francis Church the Easter morning we all marched in for Mass, the five girls bouncing down the aisle in banana curls topped with an intriguing style of Easter bonnet.

Everyone stared, but it was Mother Albeus who first figured it out. Grinning, she leaned over to the nun next to her and said, "Look at the Burke girls. Aren't those doilies on their heads?" They sure were. The latest thing in mantillas. Doilies with plastic flowers woven in them. Truth was—there was no money for new Easter hats so Mother invented the "flower and lace" look and then sold the concept to us. After Mass, Mother

Albeus told Mum how much she admired her ingenuity. God only knows what everyone else thought that morning, but we girls were delighted.

These old neighbors had seen us before, all right. And before they saw us, they heard us coming. It was our car. The fender was held on by a wire attached to the gas tank cap. Mum wrote: "It's such an adventure to ride in that car—with every left turn there is a series of crunching sounds as the fender rubs the tire. People used to look up in alarm but now they know . . ."

Between our means of transportation and our various fashion statements, it would seem that we hadn't kept a low profile in Peace Dale. Would the now gowned and tuxedoed Burkes be welcomed back near the place where Walter once strolled around wearing nothing but an old ski hat and a smile? We needn't have worried about the hometown crowd or the professors. The place was packed and they gave us our first standing ovation.

We came home triumphant to our new neighborhood and our new neighbors. Mrs. Halton, who lived in the house on our right, was only one in a cast of many distinctive characters who lived on Doyle Avenue. On the corner to our left and behind us stood two massive houses on a big lot. Like their occupants, the houses were a matched set. Both were as big, if not bigger than ours and looked as if they had been built around the same time. They were both yellow with white trim and were connected by a private paved walk. The long, wide front porches gave them a

Southern look and the elegant old ladies who traveled back and forth from one house to the other, leaning on their canes, only enhanced the effect of stately decline.

They were spinster sisters and heiresses to the Gilbane Oil Company. Each lived in one of the yellow houses; that is, one sister occupied a few rooms in each house. Most of the rooms were closed off. The Gilbane sisters were ancient but there was nothing feeble about their mental capacity, especially when it came down to a good game of Old Maid or Rummy or any of a dozen others. These old ladies were card "sharks." You could set your watch to the sound of one of their canes tapping along that private walk. Two o'clock—let the games begin.

On warm summer afternoons, they often dragged a card table out to one or the other's front porch and there they'd sit— in old high-backed white wicker chairs, drinking lemonade or hot tea and playing cards for hours at a time. Gemma joined them and Annie, too. I sat in on a few games when I got a little older, but it was tough going. The games were complicated and I swear they were making up rules as they went along. So I mostly sat and watched, mesmerized by the snapping sounds, the flying cards and the occasional cackles.

The Gilbane sisters were fun afternoon entertainment but they couldn't compete with the evening performances given by the Waldbauers. They were a Hungarian husband and wife team of concert pianists who lived a few houses down the street. Mr. Waldbauer was on the Brown University music faculty and Mrs. Waldbauer was teaching at the New England Conservatory of Music. They had one precocious and probably very talented daughter, Katy, who came to our house some afternoons to join me in a formal tea, served by Mother on miniature blue and white china with a plate full of date crumble. This elegant display was brought upstairs on a tray and served on a card table with a white linen tablecloth—probably in an effort to civilize me. Katy and I both ate and drank little teacups full until we were sick.

Two grand pianos filled the Waldbauer front living room. They faced opposite walls with their keyboards side to side. On hot summer nights, the Waldbauers opened their windows wide before they began to play and the neighborhood was treated to Bartok, Chopin, Bach or Beethoven. I often lay out on their front lawn, watching the stars and listening to the sweet, intense sound pouring out their windows.

It was a very musical block. When we weren't singing and the Waldbauers weren't playing their pianos, you could often hear the sound of a flute. That was Mr. John Burgess. He lived across from the Walbauers and played first flute with the Rhode Island Philharmonic Orchestra. He had a daughter, Leslie, who was my sister Annie's best friend. When they weren't defacing the sidewalk for a serious game of hopscotch, they were making up new dance routines—primarily tap, but sometimes they got real creative with modern jazz. It was a sad day for Annie when John Burgess agreed to play flute with the Philadelphia Orchestra and they all moved away.

It was a sad day for me, too. I had to find another flute teacher, and I'd had enough trouble getting the first one. The flute I now played was a rental. It was handed down from Leslie, who discovered that instrumental ability and interest are not always genetically passed, to Annie who had talked Dad into taking over the rental but was soon bored with it, and finally passed to me. Or rather, I grabbed it. It was an unofficial takeover. Dad was about to return it to the rental place but he couldn't find it.

When he learned that I had it, he told me, "Oh, you're going to quit just like everyone else in this family."

"Oh no, Dad, I'm not!" I pleaded. "Give me one month. Rent it for just one more month and I'll teach myself. I'll practice in the cellar so you won't even have to hear it. Just one month. You'll see. Okay?"

Poor guy. I couldn't blame him, really. He had already paid for flute lessons, violin lessons, ballet lessons, piano lessons (for three), trumpet lessons, saxophone lessons, drum lessons, oboe lessons and still he remained the solo instrumentalist in the family. No one played anything. Everyone had quit. This was a distinct disadvantage in being the ninth child. History preceded me. Finally, I convinced him that I was serious about it.

I really was serious about it. Even before I'd gotten hold of my first flute, I had a reputation in the neighborhood for my musical improvisations. I'd blow into anything I could find. I preferred penny whistles but an ocarina would do, and if those got stepped on or lost, there were always milk jugs or soda bottles. If Mr. Burgess lulled the neighbors to sleep on a Friday night, I was sure to wake them up at 7:00 on Saturday morning, strolling up and down the alley behind our garage, making up melodies or doing my best to imitate bird sounds. They must've loved to hear me coming.

When the month was up, I presented myself to Dad, who had just come home from playing Masses and was sitting in the kitchen with Mother. With flute and lesson book in hand, I told him I was ready to play for him. Quickly picking up my mood, he got serious. "Go ahead," he said and waited quietly for me to begin. I'd put in a lot of drafty cellar hours to get to Lesson Sixteen in the book and now, sitting before him, it felt like not nearly enough hours. I wanted this real bad. The sound was shaky but it was there. I wobbled through every note that I knew how to play beginning with the lowest, which came out as mostly breath. Then I played "Rigadoon" by Purcell and "Silent Night."

When the audition was over, it was my turn to wait. A moment later, he turned to my mother and said, "Well, Anne, she seems serious. I think she should have lessons."

"Thank you, Daddy." I hugged him real hard, breathing in the familiar smell of Old Spice. As I closed the door behind me, I let out a whoop and danced all the way to my room.

Dad, Mum, Jim, and Buck Spurr

CHAPTER 7

Buck Spurr

SINGING TOGETHER WAS BEGINNING to get us into places. We were asked to sing at Jordan Hall in Boston and for a radio program put on by the Passionists. Booking agencies were beginning to contact us for concerts in and around Boston. They were referred to Father LeBoeuf, who told them that we were "class" and that he didn't want us "sandwiched between a ventriloquist and a juggler." Life is funny. Just a year later we would appear on the Mike Douglas Show with Shari Lewis and "Lambchop" and then later on the Ed Sullivan Show with that Latin mouse, Topo Gigio. So much for not appearing with voice-throwers and dummies.

The arrival of 1962 brought more opportunities to sing away from home, and although the expansion was exciting, it was clear that handling our career was becoming too big a job for Father LeBoeuf, who was already very busy as diocesan director of music. His efforts locally had been a great help and had given us a wonderful start but soon we would need some full-time assistance.

People were talking us up and, as they usually do, would-be agents were making promises for a cut of the action. The Flora Frame Agency, for one, wanted to book us for twenty-five percent of the fee. Another guy from a big New York agency came to the house, heard us sing and pulled out a contract right then and there. Maybe that was the way they did it in New York, but it was exactly the kind of slick maneuvering that Dad wanted to avoid.

This was unchartered territory and Dad was understandably cautious. Years earlier, on the night of his injury at the Bethlehem Steel shipyard, he was promised that the medical bill would be paid in full if he just signed the form they put in front of him, a form that released the shipyard from any liability—even though it was later determined that there was insufficient lighting in the yard and that the crane operator was far from sober that New Year's Night. Dad didn't have the money to pay the medical bill so he signed the release form. It had been a mistake and one that he would not repeat. Besides, signing this document affected not only his life, but the lives of all his children. The man from New York was politely but firmly shown to the door.

The doorbell rang again. This time it was a young man from the Lordly and Dame Agency in Boston. He stood on the porch and told Dad he'd recently been down to the University of Rhode Island to book a van Cliburn concert and Ruth Tripp was there. He said the two of them got to chatting and she said to him, "You might be interested in something here in Rhode Island. There's a family... they're quite good. They sing madrigals and polyphony and the classics and some folk songs and gospel... and they live in Rhode Island. There's a mother and father and ten children, five boys and five girls." He said he laughed and told her, "Well, that attraction must be sponsored by Planned Parenthood" and then this guy chuckled. My father stared at him for a long moment, grinned, then laughed outright and invited him to come in.

His name was E. Lawrence Spurr but everyone called him Buck. Buck Spurr. He was twenty-eight, an only child, and he liked to do magic tricks. He also loved a laugh and soon became famous in the family for his one-liners designed to put the listener off balance. There were two that he often used as exit lines. One was "I'll see ya later"—(pause)—when you're better dressed" and the other was "Don't think it hasn't been fun"—(pause)—"because it hasn't." His exit lines became ours, a running family joke. Buck Spurr was the right fit for us and he was patient enough to build my father's trust over months of defining how they might work together.

His role would be one of personal representative. He

would be the buffer between us and the industry. Dad told him that we were a family and that he didn't want people coming to our door. So Buck acted as a screen. He would talk to these people, pull deals together and then present them to my father. Then Dad, with Mum's input, would decide whether we'd do a particular gig. Buck booked our television appearances and individual concerts and worked with other agents to set up tours.

That was just the professional side of the relationship. The other side was strictly personal—he had no brothers and sisters so we decided to adopt him. Dad acquired an advisor and Buck gained an extended family and an audience for his magic tricks.

This was a magical time, our own Camelot. It was the short and precious few years of in-between: after the younger ones had grown enough to catch up with the interests of their older brothers and sisters, but before marriage called the older ones away. John and then Steve had come home from the seminary, having decided the priesthood wasn't for them, and now the twelve of us roamed the many rooms of the Doyle Avenue house, laughing, singing, fighting, growing, competing and living hard and close together.

In the summer, Gemma or Florrie would borrow the station wagon and a carload of us piled in and headed off to Scarborough Beach in Narragansett or to Second Beach in Newport, both about an hour away, for a day of swimming and sight-seeing (boy-watching). In the winter, after a heavy snowfall, we'd all bundle up and trudge out into the quiet night, down the middle of the hilly East Side streets, lined up like the Rockettes, singing anything from four-part polyphony to four-part "Goin' to the Chapel," pushing cars out of snow drifts, throwing each other into the snow, and pelting the passing plows with snowballs. Sometimes we walked past Brown University and slipped into the Rhode Island School of Design cafeteria and then down we went, flying down the Angell Street hill on borrowed plastic cafeteria trays, hanging on for dear life with only the street lights to guide us.

We had a lot of laughs together and we seemed to set each other off. Buck felt it sitting around the kitchen table and so did the priests who came for dinner or an impromptu lunch. They were drawn to the humor and the power of us all together just as we were drawn to be with each other. It was always that way. Dad used to say to Mum, "Anne, if you get any two of these kids together, it's an instant party."

What was not a party, however, was Saturday morning chores. Our roles at Doyle Avenue were defined in black and white, and as much as I wanted to join the boys outside doing the yard work or washing windows, my job was inside with the girls. I got to clean the third floor.

The third floor was where the five boys lived and had their own bathroom, God help me. They didn't have to make their beds or pick up after themselves because no one went all the way up there anyway and it was all mine, like it or lump it. I definitely lumped it, but I learned how to clean.

Girls cooked, cleaned, sewed and did the laundry. They didn't putty windows. I envied those who did, and as soon as my housework was done, I hung around them that did, offering to help and getting in their way until I was grudgingly allowed to use a putty knife and was gradually elevated to sidewalk sweeper, hedge-trimmer, and then to not-a-half-bad raker and finally accepted as being "handy outdoors."

On Saturday mornings that house was scoured from top to bottom, inside and out—but mostly inside and mostly by the girls. The cleaning was divided by floors; Marty and I would take the third floor, Gemma and Anne did the second, and Florrie and Mum did the first. Every now and then the jobs were switched except, for some reason I always seemed to have the third floor. Once in a blue moon, the boys were told to clean the cellar. It was usually a painful, daylong affair that they avoided at all costs. The laundry room was down there. It was known as "the pit"—and the piles of laundry that rose and grew from the cement floor were left alone to breed and multiply for as long as we could stand it, and we seemed to have quite a tolerance.

Dad came home from Masses around noontime and yelled up to the second floor to tell us to turn down the stereo, which inevitably blared Ray Charles singing "Sweet Georgia Brown" or "Stella by Starlight." If it wasn't Ray, it was Stevie Wonder wailing harmonica to "Fingertips," or an album called "Scandinavia" by Claus somebody, or one featuring a French chorus called "Sixty French Girls Can't Be Wrong." It was an odd combination, but our music-to-clean-by choices seemed to slant either toward soul or foreign languages. To our way of thinking, the music had to be loud enough to inspire all the housecleaners, no matter which floor they worked on and, of course, you had to be able to dance to it, even while vacuuming.

The music heard on Saturday afternoons was radically different than that played in the mornings. Afternoons were often slated for rehearsal and happily, there were more reasons to rehearse. For one thing, the head of the Boston Catholic archdiocese had found out about us.

Cardinal Cushing listens in the Donnelly Theatre—Boston, 1961

CHAPTER 8

The Whist Game

RICHARD CARDINAL CUSHING WAS a man of many talents, not the least of which was a gift for gab and the ability to reach out to many different types of people. He was the son of Irish immigrants, born and brought up in South Boston. As a young man, he was torn between going into politics or the priesthood. He decided on the priesthood and by the age of forty-eight had become the youngest archbishop in the Catholic Church serving in the second-largest archdiocese in America.

During his fourteen years as Archbishop of Boston, he proved his skill as an organizer and fundraiser by acquiring land

and building new churches, schools, hospitals and other social institutions. He was well known for his work raising money for the missions, and because his ecumenical spirit endeared him to non-Catholics and Catholics alike, he soon became a major player in Boston politics as well as in religion. Years earlier, young Monsignor Cushing had sought out the late Joseph P. Kennedy with a fund-raising appeal, thus starting a friendship with the Kennedys that would eventually see the aging Cardinal standing by the Catholic president at his inauguration, and later sadly presiding over his funeral.

The man was powerful. He was also a character. The *New York Times* called him "utterly without pretense," while the local papers quoted an associate who described him as "utterly unsubtle." He had a quick wit and strong opinions, and was often in the center of controversies. Before he died in 1970, he had raised nearly $300 million for the work of the Church. He loved to tell and to hear a good story and he knew everybody. He was also a holy and generous man; a natural "master of ceremonies" who loved to bring people together to raise money for good causes—and we were just the kind of act he was looking for to help with his next benefit.

The Cardinal had invited the Dominican Sisters of Bethany to come and work in the Boston area. They were a European order and their apostolate was the rehabilitation of women in and out of prison. Money was needed to get them started, and so the Cardinal decided to have a benefit at the Donnelly Theatre. Like Ed Sullivan, another Irish master of ceremonies, the Cardinal enjoyed the variety shows of his day and imitated that style in his benefits. Along with the Burke Family Singers, the Cardinal engaged the services of a "special quartet of priests," a team of Irish dancers, and other entertainers.

He had heard of us, but this would be the first time that Cardinal Cushing would hear us sing. We were excited to meet this man and Mother had given us a brief but thorough course in ecclesiastical etiquette. We would later discover that the Cardinal was uncomfortable about people kissing his ring and would often clasp his hands together over his head to avoid it. But he could see that it was important to us—especially to Mother—and was gracious enough to put her pleasure before his embarrassment. When it came my turn, I managed to genuflect on one knee while keeping my back straight, my shoulders back and lean forward to kiss his ring without falling over. Kneeling, I was so close to the ground that the six-foot tall Cardinal had to bend at the waist and still reach down to let me take his hand. I took his hand but I wasn't thinking holy thoughts. I was wondering if there were a lot of germs on his ring.

When he and Dad met, the two emcees quickly recognized one another and there was an instant respect and admiration between them. Mother was already sold on the Cardinal. She had heard long ago about this man who never forgot to single out her father in a crowd and call him by name. How proud Sergeant Devine was that the Cardinal would remember a Boston cop and call out "How-ah-ya, Jack?" in front of everybody as he passed by. It was a small thing, but Mother had heard much more about the goodness of this man and she was awed by him. For his part, the man in red adopted us on the spot.

He was so pleased with the sound of us and the idea of us that he decided we'd make a great hit at the Boston Garden with Jimmy Durante for the upcoming Columban Sisters' benefit show on the last Friday in November. So the Cardinal contacted Buck Spurr about using us and asked if Buck would put together the rest of the supporting cast for the show.

Jimmy Durante with Sonny King and Eddie Jackson would be the headliners and they'd do about forty minutes. Before they came on, there would be about an hour-long show to warm up the audience. It was a typical variety style show. Besides us, it included a couple of comedians, the Italian tenor, Angelo Picardi, Tony Bruner's Orchestra and others.

What an opportunity. Jimmy Durante was a legend. According to *Webster's*, a legend is "a notable person whose deeds or exploits are much talked about in his own time." That's the right word for Jimmy Durante. The man created stories wherever he went and the Boston Garden show was no exception.

For one thing, although the Columban Sisters were considered one of "the Cardinal's Charities," the Cardinal himself had nothing to do with getting the sixty-nine-year-old Jimmy Durante to fly to Boston from Las Vegas to do a freebie. According to Buck Spurr, getting Durante was the work of one Sister Bernadette.

A year earlier, Jimmy Durante was playing at Blinstrub's Village, a big supper club in Boston where all the stars played, and it was there that he was first approached by Sister Bernadette and another Columban sister. I doubt they caught his show but Sister Bernadette and her companion did go backstage and knocked on Durante's dressing room door. Durante opened the door and when he saw that it was two nuns he said, "Oh! Come in!" and they did. Then Sister Bernadette said, "Mr. Durante. We would like it very much if you could do a benefit. We're building a new novitiate . . . and a special hall . . . and we'd very much appreciate it if you'd help us raise the funds."

And he said, "Fine, Sister. I'd be glad to do that. Do you want to have the party here while I'm in Boston this week— and I'll come out and make an appearance . . . or something?"

But that wasn't quite what Sister Bernadette had in mind.

"No," she said, "We wondered if you'd do a concert for us?"

"A concert?! Well, I'll have to check my book and see. Can I get back to you?"

The next day Jimmy Durante pulled up in front of the Columban Sisters convent in a limousine and knocked on their door. "Jimmy Durante's here!" they whispered one to another and soon all came down and gathered in the sitting room.

Jimmy sat down. "I've checked my book. I can do the engagement for you sometime next October . . . the last week in October."

"What night?" queried Sister Bernadette.

He said, "Well, I have Tuesday and Wednesday available."

One of the Sisters returned to the room with the convent calendar and Sister Bernadette thumbed through it.

"Oh, we can't do it on those dates. We have a whist party scheduled for both those nights. Could you come . . . ?" and they named a couple of other dates. No, he couldn't. He was booked to the year 2000 and they preferred a card game to a gratis performance by the great "G'night, Mrs. Calabash, wherever you are!" Schnozzola!!

He finally said to them, "When I get back to the West Coast, I'll have someone call you and we'll try to arrange another date." Always good for his word, he had someone get back to them and the date of November 30 at the Boston Garden was chosen. It would be a year and a month after the whist game.

So, after a night flight from Las Vegas, "the legend" arrived at Logan Airport at 8:30 on a cold Friday morning in November. He was greeted by about 150 people. Alan Frazer from the *Boston Record American* and other top columnists from Boston's newspapers were there. Jess Cain, the morning man at WHDH radio, Bob Kennedy from WBZ-TV, and lots of photographers and clergy (including Sister Bernadette, I'm sure) sat down to a breakfast reception at the Logan Airport Hotel. Everybody who was anybody in Boston was there, including the Kennedys and all the rest of Boston's prominent politicians. It was a mob and they were there because they all loved him. I missed the breakfast but Buck Spurr was there and he told me about what happened next.

The photographers wanted to get in a picture of Jimmy Durante for the afternoon editions with a caption that would read something like "Durante in Town for Catholic Benefit" and the story people were smelling around for something to write when one of them looked down at the ham and bacon in front of him, got an idea and called out:

"Hey, Jimmy! You're in Boston . . . it's Friday . . . what about all that?!" and he pointed to the meat on his plate.

Durante looked down, slapped his forehead with the palm of his hand, feigning horror, and then yelled, *"Gimme Dick Cushing on the phone!"*

A grinning waiter brought a phone up to the head table and the room hushed as they all turned to watch and listen. Nobody said a word.

"Dick? Jimmy Durante . . . Yeah! I'm here . . . Yup . . . Howwah ya? Good . . . Tuhnight. I'll see ya at the Gahden? . . . Yup . . . Oh Dick? . . . Well, I gotta little problem here. Listen, they brought us in a lotta *sau*-sage n' *ham* n' *ba*-con and every-thing . . . Now . . . What? . . . Oh, good . . . Great, thank you . . . Thank you very much."

He hung up the phone, grinned at everybody, and bellowed, *"Immediate dispensation for everybody in the room!"*

The place went crazy. They all knew it was coming but they waited for him to do it. It was classic Durante and that's just how Jess Cain told it on the radio the next day.

At the Boston Garden with Jimmy Durante, 1962

CHAPTER 9

It Was a Small Thing...

DURANTE WAS THE CONSUMMATE showman. He may have appeared to be a wild man but he was always in control. When the photographers would say, "Give us a smile, Jimmy!" he'd put his nose up, cock his head to one side, and turn on the charm. Jimmy could really light up a place! He could light up people, too. We watched him light up Boston Garden's electrician.

There was an afternoon rehearsal scheduled, and as was typical, we were there an hour early. Dad hated surprises. We were so early that the doors were locked. We knocked and waited and finally Dad went to a pay phone and called the Garden. The electrician opened the door. He was excited, and as he led us down to our dressing rooms he said, "You know, I've been the electrician for the Boston Garden for over forty years, but I've never met Jimmy Durante." Then he said, "Gee, I'd love to get an autographed picture of him." He was wistful as he said it and most of us agreed politely and didn't think much more about it, but my brother Jimmy had filed that little piece of information.

The hour was soon over. Our places on stage were marked, the lights were focused, the piano was in place, and we were about to head back to the dressing rooms when we heard the loud wail of police sirens. Was the place on fire? No, it was just Jimmy Durante arriving in a limousine with a police escort. What an entrance! The cops were having a good time. We all were.

When we met him, he took the fat cigar out of his mouth and looked around at all of us in wonder.

"*Dis* is one *fam*-ily?! *Geez*! So many *kids*!" he said, "and is *dis* their *beau*-tiful *Mudda*?!"

Dumbstruck, we all just grinned at him except for Dad who came right back with, "Yes, this is my wife, Anne. She's the producer of our show!" and then it was Jimmy's turn to laugh.

This guy was bigger than life. I never saw so much energy. He was all over the stage. But it was a directed energy. He took control of the space and led a very brisk, quick rehearsal, going over who was going to do what when. We kept our eyes open, our mouths shut, and we paid attention. The orchestra had been playing and we were so tuned in that some of us jumped when he suddenly bellowed,

"Stop da music! Stop da music! Where's da electrician?!"

The music stopped all right and the electrician came running down the middle aisle, looking like he was beginning to have a real bad day. The guy was all upset.

"Is there something wrong, Mr. Durante?" he stammered.

By this time, he had walked onto the stage and Durante quickly put his arm around the guy's shoulder and yelled again.

"Where's da photographa? Get me da photographa!"

We realized then that someone had whispered in Jimmy's ear, and as we began to laugh the electrician got this big dumb grin on his face. Jimmy snapped into a pose with him while the guy was still grinning and the thing was done. This was more than an autographed picture. This guy could now show the world that Jimmy Durante was a personal friend of his. It was a small thing. No, it wasn't.

We left the garden to have a nap and a light supper. No one slept, and after a very geared-up, joke-cracking hour at a sandwich shop, we were back in our dressing rooms. We had arrived according to schedule and, with all that nervous energy confined to a small space, could now look forward to tormenting each other for the next two hours.

Florrie and Gemma sat down to do their own hair and make-up while Marty did hers and then mostly everyone else's. She enjoyed it and she was good at it.

Marty was used to taking care of us. As the oldest girl, she didn't have a lot of playtime growing up. There was too much work to be done. She was our second mother and had fed, changed, clothed and cleaned us younger ones regularly. She was ten when I was born. Come to think of it, I was probably her first doll. So when I was ten and she was twenty, it was the most natural thing in the world for it to be she who stood over me and told me not to blink while she pulled at my eye with one hand and applied eye liner with the other.

Some of us were ready to go while others waited for a dab of V05, pancake makeup and the rest of it. John was checking out his profile in the mirror, Steve was reading, Annie was putting on clear nail polish, and Pete and I were watching Jim and Walter get a little rough with the "slap game," until Dad told them that the game was over and they'd need to find a quieter way to hurt each other.

The slap game was a test of reflexes that, like the game of "chicken," involved bluffing. If you weren't fast enough, you got your hand slapped, and if you flinched for no good reason, you got your face slapped. The strength of the slap was left to the discretion of the slapper. In general, however, the slaps began with light taps and grew harder as the game progressed and the element of revenge increased. If the slappee succeeded in moving his hands apart quickly enough to avoid the slapper three times, then they switched sides. Fun game. Mother loved it. By the time Dad put an end to it, Walt looked as though he wouldn't need any blush. His cheeks had a nice rosy glow.

Walt was quietly inviting Jim outside the dressing room for a little more, but Dad caught it and told them to stay in the room. That was one thing about Walter. He'd never quit. No matter how big his opponent was or how bad a beating he'd already taken, Walter would beg for more. When we later toured the U.S. and Canada, Walter, who sat between Jim and John in the lead car, would see most of the country at an odd angle for he was often either in a headlock or being squeezed thin by Jim and John, who periodically threw their larger body weights toward the center of the backseat where Walter lived. Of course, Walter had fearlessly provoked them to this madness, and as soon as the bigger boys eased up, thinking "he's half-dead; he's got to quit now," Walt would jump up laughing, eyes wild, and would go on the attack with a fierceness that was dumbfounding.

Jim and John couldn't figure it out. It didn't seem to matter to Walter that they were bigger and stronger and could easily defeat him. For those of us in the second car, it was like watching a movie on a wide screen and seeing the same scene repeat itself. Mother watched in horror from the front seat. "Oh God, They're gonna kill him!" she'd moan, and it really did look that way. Mostly we saw the backs of their heads, but sometimes Walter's head would twist in such a way that we could see his face. It would be red and contorted, like he was about to cry. That was when Mother would call on God, and eventually the older boys would stop squeezing him.

Setting Walter free was usually a mistake, and soon we'd see Jim and John look at each other in disbelief as Walt, having delved into his innermost self and come up with a fifth wind, would rise up, raining blows on them until they were forced to retaliate. We'd all be laughing in the second car, except Mum, who could only shake her head and exclaim, "Do you *believe* that kid?!"

Dad believed. He had watched Walter for years and was now watching him put his arm around Jim. They looked like the best of buddies as they headed toward the dressing room door to slap each other silly out in the hallway. Dad had just called them back when there was a knock on the door. Walt opened it and we all turned to see Eddie Jackson, one of Jimmy Durante's sidekicks. He was holding a coat. He looked over to my Mother, grinned sheepishly, and said:

"Jimmy ripped his jacket on a nail backstage and I figured the mother of so many children would have to be carrying a needle and thread. Do you? Would you mind stitching it, Mrs. Burke?"

"Surely!" said Anne Devine, and took the coat with a flourish. Eddie left and Mother closed the door and sat down to sew. A few minutes later her laughter broke the silence. We all looked over and she said, "I've just been thinking about Peace Dale and the years of sewing sleeves and knees of corduroys and sock heels, and then I thought, 'What in heaven's name am I doing here at the Boston Garden sewing Jimmy Durante's jacket?!'"

Soon Eddie was back for the coat. He looked at it with admiration, then grinned and asked Mum if she'd mind traveling, to which my father answered, "Yes, she would," and everybody laughed. Eddie thanked her once more, and we didn't see him again until Durante yelled for him and he strutted onstage.

*   *   *

They packed 16,000 people into the Boston Garden that night. The place was sold out and as it got closer to eight o'clock, we went beyond nervous. We were more like numb. We could hear them out there. There were stairs leading up to the stage on the wings and we lined up on them and waited. Dad wanted us to run onstage in New York-show biz style. It was the first time we'd ever done that and I figured I'd be the one to fall on my face before I reached my spot. Or maybe I'd just keep going and jog over to the other wing. I was thinking this would be a workable plan if I could just get my legs to stop shaking. The performer on ahead of us was a singer and had just begun to lead 16,000 people in a sing-along. The sound was terrifying. I looked down and my eye caught a thin yellow trickle of water slowly working its way down the steps. Someone up ahead of me had lost control. I whispered, "Hey! Who wet their pants?!" and a voice hissed, "Shut up, Sarah!" and then we got our cue to run onstage.

We all made it to our places and then looked out at a sea of black. We could hear them all but we couldn't see a thing past the footlights. The thunderous clapping ended and it got very quiet. This was really different. It was like throwing your voice and yourself out into a great void. We stood closer together and Dad tried to calm us with his eyes.

The microphones brought our little voices to every part of that large house. It felt as if the audience was leaning forward, listening intently and politely. We couldn't see them watching us with interest. We could only feel it in the silence and then in the roar of the applause.

We sang our five or six songs and then ran offstage, which I noticed was much easier than running on. Jimmy Durante came on after us and the place went crazy. When the audience finally calmed down, he told some jokes and did a few numbers on the piano and they were loving it. He talked some more and then suddenly he yelled into the mike,

"Where's Eddie? Get Eddie Jackson out here! C'mon!" and Jimmy started to rev up the band and they began playing "Won't You Come Home, Bill Bailey."

Jimmy ignited the crowd, but they didn't need it. They knew what was comin' and they were ready for Eddie. By this time the band was wailing and finally, out came Eddie Jackson, strutting onstage with a top hat and a cane like a high-stepping drum major coming on to a football field and the crowd was screaming. Eddie worked the stage—all the way around it while Jimmy cheered him on, yelling into the microphone, *"C'mon Eddie! Give it to 'em, Eddie! Go ahead!"*

It was the wildest thing to watch. Everybody in the audience knew that, at some point, Jimmy was going to call Eddie out on stage and they knew what Eddie was going to do once he got out there. Eddie's strutting was a showstopper and it worked every time. The audience waited for it. It was part of the reason why they had come. These guys had been doing this for years and you could feel the love of the audience for them. The air was thick with it.

Before the night was over, we got a picture with Jimmy Durante. Pete was in the Men's Room at the time and was almost forgotten until someone noticed and Walt ran off to get him. When they came running back, Jimmy Durante grabbed Pete from behind, then made like he was looking all around for him, calling out, *"Hey! Where's* da little guy? *Where* is ee?! *Oh! There* ya ah! *Geez!* Ya so *little*, I *thought* we *lost* ya! I *thought* ya *fell* through da *crack!"*

The photographer caught us all just at that moment. We were all laughing. It was a small thing. No ... it wasn't.

Dad with pitchpipe in hand

CHAPTER 10

Le Sommeil—
The Sleep of Death

THE BOSTON GARDEN APPEARANCE marked the beginning of a new phase in our singing career. Life went on but it was altered somehow. It was like taking a long road trip. There you are, sitting in the car, marking the miles you've passed and measuring those to come, when it suddenly occurs to you that you are rolling on rubber at 65 or 70 mph and you have no idea, really, how you are doing this, but you remember learning someplace that a day trip in this vehicle would have taken a covered wagon at least two months' hard ride.

Our career was like the car that was suddenly taking us fast forward. Dad was behind the wheel and Buck Spurr was riding shotgun. We were about to rid ourselves of that rusty, jury-rigged contraption we called a car and in less than a year we would "see the U.S.A. in a Chevrolet." Two Chevrolets, to be exact. Two identical brand-new maroon Chevrolet station wagons with *Burke Family Singers* printed on the front doors. Pretty sleek. People could learn our name and occupation if they could read fast enough. They needed a quick eye, though, because these wagons were in motion. In less than a year we would be headed on the road for our first concert tour, but a few things happened first.

First, we had to sing at Holy Name Grammar School. It may not be marked as the route to success on any other entertainer's map, but paying our dues to the School Sisters of Notre Dame was clearly a prerequisite to our becoming celebrities. They were teaching the youngest five of us, and if it is not wise to bite the hand that feeds you, it is certainly foolhardy not to entertain those who give school assignments in advance so you can get out of school to travel. Dad understood this and booked a concert at Holy Name as soon as possible.

It was just nine days after we had sung for 16,000, and now here we stood in a line before our classmates and their parents to sing again. We also stood before our teachers; Sister Winifred Marie (who took no nonsense), Sister Assunta (who took even less nonsense), Sister Dennis (who was young, energetic and laughed easily), Sister Mary Vincent (the little old, sweet one with the wispy voice who taught Pete in first grade) and dear Mrs. Grundy (who had a dimple and a tic in her left cheek that we third-graders felt compelled to mimic—well, that this third-grader and her best friend, Dolores "Tay" Taylor felt compelled to mimic). They sat quietly before us—waiting. The program read:

HOLY NAME
presents
A CONCERT OF CHRISTMAS SONGS
by
The Burke Family Singers
Walter Vincent Burke Conducting
THE AUDITORIUM
HOLY NAME SCHOOL
Sunday, December 2, 1962
at
Eight in the Evening

PROGRAM

1. Non Nobis Domine—William Byrd
2. O Come, O Come Emmanuel—Chant Mode I
3. Ave Maris Stella—de Victoria
4. Adeste Fideles—18th Century English
5. Carol of the Bells—Ukrainian
6. Jesus Falls Asleep—Czech
7. The Christmas Nightingale—Swiss
8. Bring Your Torches, Jeannette Isabella—French

9. I Sing of a Maiden—15th Century English

INTERMISSION

10. Medley of Christmas Spirituals   arr. Wm. Lawrence
    1. Behold That Star
    2. Mary Had a Baby
    3. Go, Tell It On the Mountain
11. Le Sommeil de L'Enfant Jésus—Gevaert
12. Angels We Have Heard On High—18th Century
    French
13. Little Jesus (arr. Peloquin)—Czech
    (Anne-Marie, Walter Jr., Sarah Jo and Peter)
14. Shepherds Hearing Angels Sing—Czech
15. Coventry Carol—12th Century English
16. The Spinning Top—Russian
17. O Come, Little Children—German
18. Silent Night—Austrian

The opening selection was the musical prayer sung at the beginning of each and every concert we ever sang, and my parents meant it. The few Latin words were sung in parts and repeated like a round. They were "Non nobis, Domine, non nobis, sed nomini tuo da gloriam" meaning "Not to us, O Lord, not to us, but to Thy name give glory."

It was not the usual way to begin a concert. We walked out on stage, found our places and gave Dad our complete attention. The audience became still as soon as they saw us. Silently they waited. Dad sounded one note on his pitch pipe and the sopranos began to sing, followed in a moment by the altos, then the tenors came in and finally, the basses added their notes and the music began to swell and move, the volume rising and falling off like a balloon catching air currents until it came to a stop, soft and simple. It was very dramatic. When it was finished, Dad turned to the audience, explained the meaning of "Non nobis" and then we began the rest of the concert. No matter how our programs changed and grew, "Non Nobis Domine" was always the opening song.

There is one other song on this early program list that I'd like to mention and that is the French song "Le Sommeil de l'Enfant Jésus." It is a song we never should have learned. Translated, it means "The Sleep of the Child Jesus" and it became famous among family members because it put some of us to sleep—literally—as in "out cold" and temporarily unconscious. People fainted more often while singing this song than I care to remember. If the floodlights were too hot or the Colorado air was too thin or your cummerbund was too tight or you were fighting the flu and holding on to your balance with sheer willpower, using every shred of self-control you had left and this song was up next, forget about it, you'd be down for the count.

But my father loved "le Sommeil," as he called it. He loved its slow and somnolent mood. He especially liked to draw out those already long, sustained notes until the whole thing became One Big Sleep. Just how long can you sing without taking a breath? A long time—or so my father thought—and a sustained note sung softly could be held that much longer. Keeping the note on pitch added to the challenge. These ideas seemed to fascinate him and he continually tinkered with the tempo, slowing it down from soft slumber to stately funereal to death march. We were all learning things. I discovered that, for short intervals, it is possible to sleep and sing at the same time. The sustained notes were the reason the sopranos and tenors dropped like flies. Florrie in Greeley, Colorado, Marty in Edmund, Oklahoma, Peter in Tryon, North Carolina, Walt in Morristown, Tennessee, Florrie again in Cookville, Tennessee, Gemma in Perry, Georgia, and even Mother was quickly led to a chair in Fayette, Iowa. The song was a killer.

No one swooned during "Le Sommeil" at the Holy Name concert. We held those notes as long as they deserved—and then some. The School Sisters of Notre Dame were pleased. It was now clear to them that we would be getting out of school in order to do useful and worthwhile things. So when the request came just ten days later for a few days' absence, the good Sisters were willing to give us our assignments in advance.

For the first time, we would all be going away together and sleeping someplace other than home. Though this was only a four-day trip, plans were underway for a real tour to the Midwest in the coming Fall, so Dad and Mum went out and bought twelve suitcases. They were identical except for the colors: the boys' were gray and the girls were going with powder blue. Each of us wrote our name and address in Magic Marker on the inside top of our suitcase, and to make sure there'd be no mix-up, Jimmy put a couple of stickers with grotesque *Mad* Magazine-type characters around his name and address.

Jimmy was fond of these gruesome stick-ons and for a while he put them up everywhere. They were the size of baseball cards and each had a title and a picture. "Laughing Larry" had wild bloodshot eyes and two mouths that roared with laughter and sprayed spittle. Besides Larry, there was Jittering Jervis, Creeping Carl and Oozing Ozzie, to name a few. They became his calling card and he posted them in the most interesting places—even on the underside of the third floor toilet seat... target practice. And lucky me, the bathroom was part of my cleaning domain. Lucky for Jim, Dad hardly ever went up to the third floor. They were sick-looking stickers, but no one mistook Jim's suitcase for theirs.

The next question was, now that we had our own suitcases, what should we put in them? Mother decided that most of the answers lay on the shelves of Zayres and armed with a cash amount known only to her, she took Marty and headed out to shop.

Twelve open suitcases greeted her when she got back. They were laid out in the front hallway with names and addresses written in styles that ranged from perfect Palmer method to near-scribble. Mum, however, was not daunted by the numbers. She and Marty had been on quite a spree and after helping them bring in all the bags, we sat around and watched as she emptied them.

I looked down at my suitcase, at my own tube of toothpaste, my blue brush and comb, the new underwear, socks, pajamas and a powder blue headband that, for nearly a year, I only took off for the time it took to brush and braid my hair. (Jimmy commented that it was the only thing holding my brains together. I told him his were warped by those stickers. Then we grinned unpleasantly at each other.) Every single thing in that suitcase was mine, almost all of it was new and it wasn't even Christmas. Before we left town, Mother bought a light green velveteen jumper for me, a white puffy-sleeved blouse to go under it and a new pair of black velveteen shoes and black knee socks. It was my first brand-new dress and, though I was never overly fond of dresses, I felt I was now ready for Manhattan and our debut on network television.

With the cast of The Sound of Music—*Mark Hellinger Theatre, NYC, 1962*

CHAPTER 11

"I'll Have The Usual"

TODAY WE THINK NOTHING of turning the television on and watching a show broadcast simultaneously throughout the country, but in 1962 it was a big deal. Back then they called it a "nationwide hookup." That meant that anyone in the country who owned a TV set and had decent eyesight could spot the scab on the shin of my left leg peeping out of the top of my kneesock. This made an impression on me.

We were to appear on a thirty-minute show called *Look Up and Live*, which aired on CBS on Sunday mornings. It was sponsored by CBS Public Affairs and the National Council of

Catholic Men. cbs put us up at Loew's Midtown Motor Inn (also called The City Squire) at 48th Street and 8th Avenue during the hotel's opening celebration.

We stepped through the revolving doors and into the lobby of the hotel and saw our first New York showgirls—and they saw us. Before the boys could really gawk, Dad told them to "mortify their eyes." Jim didn't get it but Steve and John, the ex-seminarians, understood immediately and lowered their gaze. The contrast was so startling that for a moment the two groups of women just stared at each other. They were heavily made-up and lightly dressed, low-cut and leggy with spike heels and they looked—knowledgeable.

We couldn't have looked more different. Mother wore a royal blue coat with a white fur collar and her hair the way she always wore it; parted down the middle with two braids pinned across the top of her head. The five girls wore handmade, knee-length, forest green, woolen capes with brown leather trim at the neck and arm slits. The same dark leather covered three big buttons on the front. We wore matching green pillbox hats and short dark leather gloves. My hair was in braids and my sisters wore theirs in buns at the back of the neck. Jackie Kennedy would have been proud. Mother and the older girls wore some make-up, but not enough to hide the shiny excitement of seeing New York City for the first time or the shock of seeing the women who now stood before us.

They had taken us by surprise but we had also caught them off guard and for a moment they stared at us as if they were remembering something. Then the manager spotted the capes and approached saying, "You must be the Burkes! Welcome to the City Squire!" The publicity people followed, along with the photographer who wanted a picture of us with the manager of the hotel, Sam Levy, and the showgirls. Everyone stood together and smiled.

What a hotel! Everything was brand new: the uniforms of the bellboys, bell captain and parking valets, the smells of the carpeting and the vinyl of the deep red booths in the coffeeshop to the right of the front lobby. Elegant vases packed with fresh-cut roses stood in front of the lobby's two large mirrors and wreaths of evergreen decorated with red velvet bows hung along the walls.

The whole front side of the hotel's first floor was made of glass and gave a full view of the street. Sitting in a booth in the coffeeshop, you could see everything. You could get an education looking out that window.

One morning while I sat with my sisters having breakfast, we saw a woman out on the street who had suddenly decided that she was no longer interested in wearing clothes. We were chatting and keeping half an eye on the street, so we caught her first dance move. Using a street sign as her prop, she put on her own little show and proceeded to strip down to what God gave her. I was stupefied. The older girls instructed Annie and me to concentrate on our oatmeal and toast which, as the crowd began to gather, got tougher and tougher to do. Finally a policeman showed up and soon after, a police van arrived and took her away.

New York City was a crazy place and the Loew's Midtown Motor Inn was right in the middle of it. When you'd had enough of the view from street level, there was a whole bank of elevators to take you up to your room. Or you could ride to the roof and sunbathe by the pool. This area was the domain of José, the handsome wolf in pool attendant's clothing who tried to get somewhere with Marty *and* Florrie *and* Gemma. In his enthusiasm, José had forgotten Rule #1 from the Handbook on Clan Loyalty—It is never wise for a suitor to choose more than one sister. In our family, that was the recipe for getting nowhere fast, so it wasn't long before José was left to jog in place with his folded towels and his tan.

Had José been smart enough to single out just one of my sisters, he wouldn't have gotten much time with her anyway. Our dance cards were pretty much filled for the next four days beginning with the time we got there.

After pictures were taken in the lobby, we went to check in at the front desk and ran into a snag. Management had seen no problem with booking rooms for us on two different floors. They hadn't met Walter. Now that they had, it was too late to do anything about it. It was the grand opening and the hotel was booked solid. Mum and Dad and the five girls would have two rooms on the fourteenth floor while the five boys shared a room on the sixteenth floor. All those floors, the telephones, the elevators and Walter free to roam hallways unchecked. It was a scary thought. Steve and John were told to keep an eye on him, but Walt was slippery.

We checked in to our rooms, freshened up and then hurried out to a 12:15 audition at the William Morris Agency. They were setting up a new concert division and we wanted to see if they'd like to work with us. We didn't stay long. Buck had told us that whatever we wanted to show them, we had to do it in fifteen minutes or less, so we sang a couple of numbers, smiled when they applauded and then went back to the City Squire for lunch. The people at William Morris seemed to be interested, but when Buck spoke with them later they said that, though they thought our music was beautiful, it was a little too high-brow for what they had in mind. They were also concerned that it was too religious.

Back at the City Squire, Walt and Jim discovered the carpet's static electricity almost simultaneously. The wall-to-wall carpeting made it possible to get nailed from any direction. It was Freeze-tag with a jolt and if you knew what was good for you, you looked out into the hallway before you got out of an elevator—a conductor could be waiting on the other side. The younger set quickly got into the spirit of trauma-giving and the older ones were ready to strangle us. Luckily, we could run farther than they wanted to chase us.

Then, just as things began to get quiet, down the hall came Hans Brinker from Hell. It was Walt, swaying from side to side like a hockey skater with his hands behind his back and a wild grin on his face. He hadn't had his growth spurt yet but his shoe size had exploded and the shock he was building up on those big feet was substantial. A hasty retreat was the only sensible plan.

Fun and games ended promptly at two-thirty. Dad promised Walter that something nasty was going to happen to him real soon and this news seemed to slow Walt down considerably. The next appointment was for three o'clock at CBS Studios. There we had a three-hour script conference with producer Chalmers Dale and director Joe Chromyn of CBS and then a run-through. Dad was relaxed in front of the camera. He ad-libbed so easily that they told him that he didn't need to use a TelePrompTer and he could just go ahead with a general script. By the time we left the studio, we were all clear on what we'd be taping the following day.

Dad and Mum made sure we were fed, watered and had a good night's sleep. They knew the next day would be a long one. Before bed, we did spend time calling each others' rooms and speaking in strange dialects. The front desk must have loved connecting all those extra calls. Even Dad got in on the act and when he called with an Italian accent saying it was "room service," Marty didn't have any idea who was on the phone. Dad had always been good at accents. Years earlier when he was out selling cars, Mother could always tell where he'd been by how he talked when he got home. He picked up the dialect he heard, whether it was Italian, Canadian French, Irish or swamp Yankee.

The phone calls back and forth continued for the rest of our stay at the City Squire—so did the accents. John, Florrie and Gemma were so confident with their French skills, in fact, that after breakfast the next morning, they played the part of "Three Parisians On Holiday" window-shopping their way past the jewelry stores on Fifth Avenue while saying short but snappy French phrases like "Ecoutez! Oh! C'est grand!" with the compulsory "Mais oui!" response. Fortunately, no New Yorker was polite enough to engage them in conversation.

While the "Parisians" toured Fifth Avenue, I enjoyed a solitary breakfast, setting in, as I did so, the pattern and the menu that I would come to expect. Dad had given each of us a dollar to spend on breakfast in the coffeeshop. We could go to breakfast anytime we wanted, alone or together, and we could order anything we wanted as long as it did not cost more than one dollar. I contained my excitement. I was being treated as an adult and was determined to take this new freedom seriously. And for some crazy reason, there was this waitress who decided to play along.

I initiated the routine on the first day by telling her that I would be coming down to breakfast at 9:30 every morning and that I would like a small orange juice, hot oatmeal with cream and a corn muffin. She brought these things to me with an amused smile, along with the bill, which I studied carefully. I left a tip and she was still grinning when I thanked her and took my leave.

I headed for the same booth the next morning, eased into the warm red vinyl and watched her approach. She carried no menu. When she stopped at my table, I looked up at her and said, "I'll have the usual." A hint of amusement played around her eyes but she kept a straight face, turned and came back with the same breakfast. She was enjoying herself. I was in heaven.

When I arrived the third morning with three of my sisters, she passed menus to them and then, with great dignity, asked me if I would like "the usual," to which I haughtily replied, "That would be fine, thank you." My sisters stared at each other, then at me and then at the waitress. She said nothing, smiled blandly at them with pen poised and waited for their order.

From two in the afternoon to seven o'clock that evening, we taped the half-hour, coast-to-coast show on a set built to look like a living room. Dad narrated and told stories and at one point he introduced each of us. We sang eleven songs. I couldn't believe how long it took to tape eleven songs.

The first song was "Wondrous Love" and judging from the look on Dad's face at the end of it, we had sung it beautifully. First try and it was a keeper! After the last note, we held our breaths and looked up at the sound booth. That was when one of the men wearing headsets said, "Okay. I think we've got a good level now. Do you want to try it again?" We looked at Dad. He grinned at us and answered "Sure" to the soundman. This was obviously not a concert. The song was over when *they* said it was over.

We sat and waited a lot. We played tick-tack-toe and hangman. We tried to stay fresh, both vocally and physically but it was impossible to contain our energy for all that time. The heat didn't help. The television lights were hot enough. Add a fireplace with a real live fire burning in it and the temperature climbed even higher. We quickly learned to leave the "living room" set whenever possible. It was cooler on the working side of the camera, so while Dad worked on playback with the technicians and the girls sat with Mother and watched or talked quietly, the boys visited with the cameramen.

Soon the CBS people were trying to laugh quietly at Jimmy's Walter Brennan and John Wayne impersonations, Johnny's imitation of the James Brown slide and Steve's jokes. Buck was not far away with his magic tricks. He was always half kid brother, half agent and for our crazy family, it seemed to be a very workable combination.

Between the sotto voce antics, we tuned in to Dad's direction and when the last scene was shot and the sound man said, "That's a take" on the final song, the CBS crew surprised us by applauding. We would see these guys again two Christmases later when the CBS trucks pulled up to Maria von Trapp's lodge in Stowe, Vermont, for four days of taping. By then, we'd know them well enough for a good snowball fight.

That night we had dinner together at Barney's on Lexington Avenue and the next day we went sightseeing in New York. We not only saw the sights, we became one of them. The green capes and the boys' matching red wool overcoats drew stares from passersby. A photographer traveled with us snapping pictures and, just in case we didn't attract enough attention, Dad decided to sing in almost every place we stopped.

We sang at the Christmas carousel at Lever Brothers Plaza and again across Fifth Avenue at Rockefeller Plaza. The doors were open at Carnegie Hall so we sneaked in and Dad asked the cleaning ladies, who were sweeping around the seats, if they'd like to hear a song. They loved the idea and sat down while we got on the stage. We sang "Santa Lucia" for the two Italian ladies who got teary-eyed and clapped like crazy. Then we sang an Irish song for the one with the brogue and she was proud of us. They clapped and we bowed. Then Dad turned back to us and whispered, "Now you can honestly say that you sang at Carnegie Hall!"

We sang on the steps outside St. Patrick's Cathedral and were taken by surprise when a woman approached and asked if we were the Burke Family. That was the first time that had happened and we were feeling pretty nifty by the time we returned to CBS Studios for some still shots.

We sang again during the photo session and during one carol were suddenly joined by two very capable voices. They belonged to Nancy Dussault and Donald Cook, who were playing the lead roles in the Broadway production of "The Sound of Music" over at the Mark Hellinger Theatre. We sang a couple of songs together and they invited us to come see the show that night. My parents thanked them for the invitation and said we'd try to be there, but we knew there was no way they could afford to buy twelve Broadway theatre tickets.

When we got back to the City Squire later that afternoon, there was a message for Dad at the front desk. A Leland Hayward had called and wanted Dad to call him. Buck heard the name and his eyes lit up. "That's the producer for 'The Sound of Music!'" he said. Dad went up to his room to return the call and we all piled in and stood around listening to his side of the conversation.

After the initial pleasantries, Dad said, "Oh, we'd love to!" That was when some of us started jumping up and down like pogo sticks while others Twisted and Jerked and Boogalooed their way around the room. John did his J.B. slide, swung into a tight spin, then went down on the carpet in a split. He pulled himself up using legs only and then went into the Funky Chicken—all this while Dad tried to talk on the phone.

Most of us had never seen a stage play, much less a Broadway show. The place was packed, but they still managed to put us all together in a line of seats up in front. We could see everything and the show was just great. At intermission someone came over to us and asked if we'd stay after the performance to meet the cast. That was just fine with us and when it was over, we sat in our seats and waited until the place cleared out.

The theatre was nearly empty when the curtain opened again and the cast stood there. We applauded and then came up on stage to greet them. The "von Trapp" girls wore brocaded velvet dresses that were just beautiful up close, the boys wore lederhosen, and they all wore lots of makeup. One of them spoke up and asked "if a real singing family would sing for us who have to pretend for each performance." Do bears live in the woods? Was Dad a musician? Of course, we'd be happy to sing for you.

When I think about it, Dad had quite a thing going. The only instrument he needed to carry was the pitch pipe in his pocket. He had weaned us off sheet music early on in the re-hearsal process and had taught us to sing a cappella music. He had also taught the altos, tenors and basses to pick up their starting note by memorizing it's relation to the soprano's first note, so now he only had to blow one note and his wife and his ten kids would break into four-, five- or six-part harmony. It was a helluva deal.

We started to sing and people waiting for taxis drifted back into the theatre to listen. We sang three or four songs for the cast and then they sang for us. A photographer showed up and wanted to get a few shots. He arranged our positions for the picture and then backed up a few paces. Someone said "Smile!" someone else said "Say cheese!" and then the smallest actress who looked to be about seven years old said, "Say money!" and broke into a smile that looked like pure sunshine—except for something in the eyes. I looked down at her in horror. So this was showbiz. Suddenly, it felt way past my bedtime.

Before we left New York the next morning, we auditioned for the Ed Sullivan Show. A man named Jacques André listened to us. He didn't think we were too religious. He talked to his boss, Ed, and Ed told him to call us and ask if we'd like to appear on his show just three months later—on March 24th—and would we sing something Irish seeing as it was close to St. Patrick's Day. Dad fumbled through our calendar, looked for that date, and bit his lip. We were booked to sing at Bishop Fenwick High School on March 24th. It was a very local little gig. So which was it going to be, integrity or opportunity?

Dad mopped his forehead with the pocket handkerchief he always carried and told the Sullivan representative that he was awfully sorry but we were booked on that particular date. He said we'd be real happy to sing on his show at any other time. Jacques said he'd have to check on another date and they hung up. My brother John, then a student at LaSalle Academy, wrote about Dad's reaction in a required autobiography. He wrote: "My father almost went through the roof but this other engagement could not be helped." Eight months later, when Dad was convinced that that chance was dead and buried, we got another phone call from the Sullivan people.

After the Sullivan audition we went back to the City Squire and gathered up our things. It was time to go home.

One more elevator ride down to the lobby. The bell captain looked like he was going to weep with joy as he watched Walter smile winningly at him and then run to the revolving doors one last time. Dad shook hands with some of the desk personnel and promised we'd be back. It was a promise he'd keep. The girls wore the green wool capes and pillbox hats and could be spotted easily—even from José's lonely perch on the roof. The coffeeshop waitress didn't wave good-bye and neither did I. We were far too dignified for that sort of display, so we just grinned at each other.

At home, 1961

CHAPTER 12

Friends in the Press

WE GOT HOME ONLY a few days before Christmas and there was a lot to do. We baked the Christmas cookies, sent out Christmas cards, decorated the tree and entertained the press.

There were a few Boston and Rhode Island reporters who were particularly interested in supporting our singing career by making us a household name. Alan Frazer was one of them. He had a daily column in the *Boston Record American* (which later became *The Boston Herald*). He wrote on the arts and entertainment and about who was doing what to whom in Boston and the rest of New England. After the Durante show, he adopted us.

He told the people of Boston anything and everything he could about us. Sometimes it was so trivial that it was funny. For instance, in one of his columns entitled "New Picture For the Birds," he stomped on the newly released Alfred Hitchcock thriller and then added: "Speaking of birds, the Burke Family Singers of Providence, R.I., have two new parakeets and have named them after the Boston firm that acts as their agents: Lordly and Dame." He must have gotten that from one of us kids because I don't think my parents planned on that little item making press.

After the New York trip, Alan Frazer went to lunch with Dad and Buck and then devoted his next column to us. "Burke Family Inspires New York" was the headline and in it he gave a detailed account of our doings.

Another friend in the press was Ruth Tripp, who wrote articles and reviews for the Rhode Island papers. She came to our house with a photographer and then wrote a very warm article with a photo spread.

The 1962 Christmas season was capped off with a six-page feature article about us in *Sign Magazine*, a national Catholic magazine put out by the Passionists. Someone had found out about the Saint John's Fires we lit every June 24th and titled the story "The Family That Celebrates Christmas Twice a Year." We had carried the tradition over from Peace Dale but the picture of the Providence city blaze shows a very tame little campfire in comparison to the wild, heathen-dancing, country conflagrations that I recall—then again, I was closer to the ground in Peace Dale.

Whoever wrote this article did their homework. Not only was the Saint John's Fire photographed, but there also was a picture of the last year's Feast of the Holy Innocents party when The Big Five (families) and their zillion kids gathered at Doyle Avenue. There was a picture of us singing around the Advent wreath and another of us singing for Cardinal Cushing. It was a great article. It was a great year and 1963 would be even better.

The new year blew in quietly. We got back into going to school and just being kids again. We enjoyed winter sports on weekends and on weeknights when our homework was done. Unfortunately, with the amount of homework the nuns gave us, it was often dark outside by the time we finished. This didn't stop us. We'd bundle up, boot and scarf ourselves until we looked like the Pillsbury Dough-children, turn on the floodlights in the back yard and play snow games such as tackle, pigpile, body-slamming and hurling.

This last one was a favorite among the older kids. Hurling was science, really. It was the study of centrifugal force using small projectiles and snow drifts. The older kids grabbed us younger kids by the hands and began to spin in place, quickly pulling us off our feet until we became a flying Y, arms stretched to the limit and spinning faster and faster. When we were whirling at top speed, the older one let go. The object of the game was to see how far the screaming little bundle could fly through the air before it reached the snowbank. I have no idea why we let ourselves be flung, particularly when the older ones were often a little short of the mark and we landed on the hard-packed stuff. It just shows you what little kids will go through in order to play with the big kids.

On weekends, we often snuck into Brown University's Meehan Auditorium for an hour or two of ice-skating. We tried to get in for the time slated as "University Skating," which was for faculty and staff and their families. These lucky souls had passes. We weren't members of the University family, but for some reason they often let us in if we wore our capes. I don't know why they let us in at all except that maybe we were beginning to become known in the area and the capes were very recognizable. Or maybe they let us in because we just kept showing up and begging.

Every once in a while we couldn't get in, which, of course, made getting in *very* exciting and special. The boy behind the glass hit a button that released the gate and, keeping a dignified I-do-this-all-the-time look on my face, I boogied through to the other side, found a place to sit and laced my skates in a hurry so I could get out on the ice in case they changed their minds. I noticed that there never seemed to be a problem getting in when my sister Gemma was with us. It was easy to see that guys would do most anything for Gemma. The reason was simple, really. She was gorgeous.

Another weekend activity was Sunday dinner: a large, semi-formal affair centered around the dining room table that often ran on for more than two hours. Sometimes a priest showed up or Buck might sit in, but most of the time it was just us. Mother got to work on our table manners and our conversational etiquette, Dad got to sit at the head of the table and survey his wealth and everyone got a chance to speak. It was a good way for Dad and Mum to see how each of us was doing.

Dinner began at around twelve-thirty or one in the afternoon when Dad came home from playing Masses at Blessed Sacrament. Mum and the rest of us walked to an early Mass at Holy Name or, if we were running late, we piled into the car and drove the five blocks to church.

After Mass, Mum and the girls put aprons on over their dresses and started the peeling and chopping and put the meat in the oven. These were not meatloaf dinners. On Sundays, we had ham basted with pineapple, cloves and brown sugar, or chicken, pot roast, turkey or lamb. Having such a bounty of food was still new to us and I felt so wealthy on Sundays.

I hung around with Mum and the girls in the kitchen until it was decided that perhaps I was old enough to use a peeler without shaving my fingers off. Carrots were easy. Potatoes took longer but I eventually found my way around them. However, when it came to peeling winter squash, I was happy to hand the peeler over to someone with a surer hand. Slipping and sliding around a smelly orange slime that stuck to my hands was not my idea of a good time.

Last was not least on the Sunday menu. Every week Mother or one of the older girls (usually Florrie) managed to come up with a killer dessert.

Hasty Pudding, Peach or Blueberry Buckle, Bread Pudding with Hard Sauce, Tomato Soup Cake, Date Crumble, Rice Pudding with Pineapple, Strawberry Shortcake with freshly baked biscuits and real whipped cream. One dessert in particular stands out in my memory. It had a layer of graham crackers on the bottom, chocolate pudding, another layer of graham crackers, then vanilla pudding. The whole thing was covered with whipped cream. The graham crackers got soft as they chilled in the refrigerator. I could have eaten half the pan all alone.

Soon the aroma from the oven drew the boys into the kitchen and they'd compliment the cooks, try to steal a taste and generally get in the way. Shooing them away did no good. They'd hang around on the periphery, lean in the doorways making wisecracks and telling jokes. That kitchen was a hub of activity and laughter on Sunday mornings and you just wanted to be around it all.

The dining room table was set with a white linen tablecloth. To the right was a card table with its own tablecloth set for the four youngest, Annie, Walt, me and Pete. We insisted on our own salt and pepper shakers, butter dish, and our own candle that we'd try to blow out by enunciating our "p's", such as, "*Peter!* Will you *please pass* the *pickles!*" At first Mother was thrilled by our perfect pronunciation. Then she noticed all the "pah" sounds coming from the card table and the smell of sulphur floating over as we struck fresh matches. A warning look from her and a glance from the head of the table was enough to keep our candle burning smoothly.

"Comin' through!" cried a cook, moving butt-first through the swinging pantry doors and turning into the dining room with a steaming platter. With so many bodies moving through those swinging doors, we soon learned it was a good idea to call out a warning. Before the Early Warning System was in place, we looked a lot like the Three Stooges.

These Sunday dinners would continue with all of us at the table for about the next six years and there was no excuse good enough for not being there. As the older kids began to fan out, they sometimes tried to get out of Sunday dinner. "We have a concert Saturday night so I want to go out on a date on Sunday afternoon, okay?" Not okay. Instead, another chair was added to the table. Must have been real relaxing for the guy or girl who came to dinner under twelve pairs of watchful eyes.

I loved Sundays. I thought they were fabulous. Of course I was eleven years old and happy as a pig in mud to be around my family. I hadn't yet developed a lot of separate interests or learned the phrase "but-everyone's-going-to-be-there." Actually, in my family, that line didn't get you very far anyway. "We *are* everyone" was the usual response.

Rockingham Race Track—Salem, New Hampshire, 1963

CHAPTER 13

"Don't Think It Hasn't Been Fun..."

I N THE EARLY PART of March 1963, Buck and Dad decided it
was time for us to put a few songs on vinyl. We'd start small by
making a low-cost 45 rpm record that we could sell after concerts and on the upcoming fall tour. If they sold like hotcakes,
then we'd contact a label company and see if they were interested in doing something bigger. It was the Buck/Walter min-
uet. Buck took a turn in a new direction and Dad followed up
with a very cautious two-step.

Buck contacted a jazz producer friend of his named Fred

Taylor, who had a jingle factory in Boston. Fred would later set up his own jazz clubs in Boston, Paul's Mall and The Jazz Workshop, but at this time he was doing recording projects and was very adept at finding the right place and then rigging equipment to get the right sound on a tight budget.

We found ourselves in the basement of the Bradford Hotel in Boston. There was no audience here and no hot lights—only us and Buck and Fred, the reel-to-reel tape recorders and the microphones. We could relax. We sang for a while, took a break, and Buck went out for sandwiches. On the way out the door, he turned back and said, "Don't think it hasn't been fun—" *"because it hasn't!"* we all shouted back before he could get it out. His mouth made a perfect "O" and all of us cracked up. We could still hear him laughing down the hall.

A black man came in after the break and Freddie introduced us to him. His name was Howard McGhee and he was a jazz trumpeter. He had just put out a new album and was in town playing at one of the clubs for Freddie. While we had been eating our sandwiches, Freddie had phoned Howard and told him he was taping this singing family, and instead of sitting around in his hotel room, why didn't Howard come on over and hang out. So Howard did.

He had a gentle face, a nice smile and eyes that looked like they'd seen a lot of life. When he heard us sing Dad's arrangement of "Wondrous Love," those young-old eyes filled with tears. Later on, he'd be laughing. He was all warmed up and so were we. It was a good afternoon and Fred Taylor was getting it all down on tape.

The 45 was given the title "Equinox" after a mountain in Vermont that my father loved. Besides "Wondrous Love," this hi-fidelity little recording played one of Dad's personal favorites, "Le Sommeil de l'Enfant Jésus" (also known as "The Big Sleep") which took up nearly an entire side, and "Carol of the Bells," "The Spinning Top" and "Hospodi Pomilui."

These last two were novelty numbers. "The Spinning Top" was a real tongue twister set in a very fast round that literally imitated the sound of a big, old-fashioned, hand-pumped spinning top. Dad jokingly introduced it as "our miracle song—it's a miracle if we finish it together." The other song, "Hospodi Pomilui," Russian for "Lord, Have Mercy," was sung seventy-five times—very quickly. Written in five parts and used in Russian liturgy, it started strong, gradually got down to a near whisper in the middle and then built up again to a big finish.

Singing these songs was like riding a bike. Once you learned how, you never fell off, and yes, I suppose they were show-off songs. Audiences were always amazed by them and many people bought the 45 record after a concert because these novelty songs were on it.

Though we were identified more and more often as "singers," we were a family first and like every other family, we saw our share of accidents and scuffles. The only difference between us and most other families was that the effects of our day-to-day living were in full view of the public.

On St. Patrick's Day of 1963 we had two concerts booked in Massachusetts. In the afternoon we sang for the Carney Hospital Volunteers over in Dorchester and that night we sang for the Knights of Columbus in Wakefield. There was an article in the

Wakefield paper the next night titled "Inviting Burke Family Gives Warm Vocal Show." The opening line was "The melodic, stirring sounds of a dozen Burke family voices resounded sweetly—like a chorus of angels—through Memorial High auditorium last night. . . ."

We may have sounded good but we must have looked pretty raggedy. The columnist, obviously enjoying the "family angle," then describes Peter as appearing "with blotches all over his face which Dad explained to the audience was not measles but the result of an accident in the kitchen when Pete decided to soak a hot grease-filled pan under the cold water faucet . . ." Next, he wrote that "Walter Jr. was sporting a 'shiner' which he passed off as the result of a run-in with another youngster." "Then," the writer continued gleefully, "before the Burkes got halfway through their repertoire for the evening, Dad discovered his brand new pitch pipe wouldn't play A-flat."

What a night. It was the only time "Don Maestro's" pitch pipe ever let him down.

Dad always carried his pitch pipe in the right pocket of his tuxedo jacket. When the applause ended from the previous song, he'd take it out of his pocket and blow one note softly. The audience could usually hear the beginning note on the pitch pipe. That night they watched Dad's back, saw his shoulders rise as he inhaled and his right elbow bend as he brought the pitch pipe up to his lips and blew. No sound. Dad blew again. You could hear a pin drop but you sure couldn't hear that note. Some of us began to grin nervously which, of course, the audience saw immediately. They also watched Dad take a deep breath and lean into the pitch pipe to blow even harder. His shoulders shook a couple of times and that was the end of all composure. We were all laughing and so was the audience.

There was not an A-flat to be had in that auditorium, it seems. Either that or Dad decided that the mood was totally blown because we "replaced the scheduled number with a gay Italian tune." We may have been organized as a concert chorale singing primarily unaccompanied classical, sacred and folk music, but we were also a bunch of kids—kids with splotches and shiners, who burst out laughing—even on stage. No doubt about it, people who came to hear us could see that we were a family—with all the knocks, scrapes and giggles that go with it.

The next family accident, however, put the Burke Family Singers out of commission for three months. I claim credit for that one. Without benefit of a bungee cord, I went flying—straight down thirty feet and broke my thigh in two places. Naturally, I was with Walter at the time.

It was a Sunday afternoon in the middle of May. School was almost out for the year and the weather was looking good for tennis. Full of pork roast and strawberry shortcake but determined not to succumb to "the flarves" (a family-invented term used to describe the lure of sleep after a big meal), Walt and I eased away from the dinner table and went up to the third floor to get our tennis rackets.

We found our rackets but couldn't come up with one tennis ball between us. The more we searched, the more we wanted to play. There had to be at least one stinkin', rottin' tennis ball somewhere in that house. We checked every crevice from top to bottom. We even waded through the laundry room. Nothing. We moved out to the back yard and checked around the gardens, the garage, behind the lilac bushes and under the picnic table. Maybe a dirty Dunlop or a Wilson was hidden there where the grass grew longer. We didn't care if it was dog-chewed or had no bounce. We just needed something to hit.

Our determination became a kind of madness. We weren't asking for anything real big. Just one tennis ball. We checked the hedges on the sides of the house and looked behind the big bushes by the front porch—and came up empty. Leaning on our rackets, we sat on the front steps and tried to form a plan. It seemed at the same time our eyes focused on the building across the street. We looked back at each other and grinned. Why hadn't we thought of this before?

Across the street from our house stood the Ladd Observatory. It was a three-storey, ivy-covered, red brick building that housed a giant telescope under its silver dome. It was owned by Brown University and built on a plateau that was about half the size of a football field. On some starry nights, we'd watch the round roof turn and open up to the sky and know that Professor Smiley was in there watching the stars. Contrary to his name, Professor Smiley was a frowner. In fairness, that could have been due to us noisy kids.

Professor Smiley mostly worked at night—which meant that the Ladd Observatory was usually deserted during the day and the early evening. The raised level lawn was available for playing football, freeze tag or no-net tennis. A single tennis player could use the side of the building as a backboard. And what happened when you shot it up too high? Simple. It landed in the gutter and you never saw it again.

Walter and I were still grinning as we jogged across the

street to the Observatory. We'd lost tennis balls up there before and we knew lots of other kids had, too. Those gutters had to be packed with them. Now we just had to find a way up.

We circled around to the back. The thick, old ivy vines that grew up along the side of the building proved strong enough to carry our weight and up we went, Tarzan and his little sister, Tarzana, to the small roof above the back entryway. The next roof was out of reach—unless I gave Walt a boost and then he leaned way over the edge and pulled me up. Tarzana's legs were a little shaky but we made it up there. Now we only needed to get over to the other side and up to the higher roof; the slanted metal one with the white fence that separated the edge of the roof and the gutter.

We didn't wonder why there was a white fence two-and-a-half stories up. We should've, but we hardly even saw it. We were too busy looking down the incline, past the railing to the gutter. Sure enough, it was packed with a line of white and yellow tennis balls. It looked like a sports store down there. Some of them were brand-new. We were set.

So why did I listen to Walter? It was greed and the challenge, I suppose. He had that crazy look in his eyes and the grin, and the next thing he said was, "I'll race ya..." and down we went, at full speed down the roof. I was ahead of Walter. The fence came up fast and I got up on my toes to lean over it and reach for the gutter and the balls. Unfortunately, momentum was not on my side. Enthusiasm had gotten the better of me and I just kept on going.

I spent five weeks in traction at Rhode Island Hospital, followed by six weeks in a plaster cast that began at my waist and finished at the toes on my right foot. I couldn't sit up. It could have been a lot worse. If I hadn't done a half-somersault on the way down I would have landed on my head instead of my feet.

My head did hit a rock. When I came to, I couldn't help but notice that my body didn't look right. My right leg had taken a sharp right turn at the thigh. I began moaning "myleg, myleg, myleg" over and over again like a wind up toy. I paused in my soliloquy long enough to vomit strawberry shortcake all over myself and then took up where I left off. The smell of strawberry shortcake stayed in my hair for the next three weeks.

It's very difficult to get away from your hair, I discovered—especially when you're pinned down in traction. There was nothing to do but breathe. Finally, the hospital decided I was safe from pneumonia and allowed my sister Marty to wash it out. That afternoon was one of the highlights of my life.

Walt went a little crazy when he looked down over the edge of the roof and saw me laying on the ground with one leg in an impossible position. He kept yelling, "I killed her!" and "the image, the image!" until somebody slapped him or medicated him or told him it wasn't his fault. (Which, of course, it was. He was older than me so everything was his fault.)

A neighborhood boy saw what happened and ran over to our house and rang the bell. Mum answered the door and he cried, "Oh, Mrs. Burke! Mrs. Burke! Something terrible's happened! Sarah fell from the Observatory!"

"Jesus, Mary and Joseph!" Mum cried, her legs turning to jelly.

She was heading out the front door when the neighborhood boy grabbed her arm and said,

"Oh *no*, Mrs. Burke! *You* can't come! You can't *see* it!"—at which point Mum was sure I was dead.

When they finally cracked open the cast nearly three months later, my leg was chalk-white and flat and skinny. The skin felt rubbery. It wouldn't bend. It looked like a dead person's leg. I stared up at the doctor in horror. He said, "Oh, it looks fine!," told me to exercise it and handed me a pair of crutches.

I received a good amount of sympathy at school and by the next scheduled concert, on September 13th, was walking without crutches. Dad was the one who really deserved some sympathy. We had no health insurance and the hospital and doctor bills were staggering. Could we "sing away" these bills? Maybe. Gradually. The Cardinal was no help. He had asked us to do another benefit on September 15th at the Rockingham Race Track. The exposure was fabulous, but at this point, we needed our *own* benefit.

Whatever else could be said for Cardinal Cushing, one thing was for sure, the man had style. This may have been a benefit, but that didn't stop him from sending two very large limousines to come pick us up. He had said to Dad, "Don't worry about getting there. I'll send a couple of cars over for you."

A couple of cars? Each one of these babies was about a half a block long, black as night, and so shiny that we could look at any part of the finish and see that our eyes were bugging out of our heads. This was way beyond cool. Dad couldn't keep the grin off his face and Mum was checking around ever-so-subtly for any signs of movement from the neighbors—a curtain or a screen door—and she wasn't disappointed. Gowned, tuxedoed and exuberant, we entered our carriages and set off.

Rockingham Race Track was in Salem, New Hampshire, about two hours away. Once we got over our haughty superiority, we slid the glass partition aside and began telling jokes to the chauffeur. We sang non-program songs like "Put On Your Old Grey Bonnet" in three-part harmony, and some barbershop. The chauffeur kept his eye on the road but loosened up and started talking, too. I don't know about the other car, but we had a great ride. I felt fabulous. There was nothing better than being with my brothers and sisters, listening to everything while I looked out through the tinted glass and watched the people in other cars crane their necks to see who the big shots were in those two black limousines.

The benefit was for the Kennedy Foundation for Retarded Children and we sang outdoors on a raised platform with a tent behind and above us in case it rained. We were joined on the program by Robert Horton, who played "Flint McCullough," the scout in the TV series, *Wagon Train* and who, my sister Annie swears, was wearing Coppertone's Quick Tanning lotion that afternoon. I thought it might be a bad color makeup but Anne says otherwise. Maybe she's wrong, but it is exactly the type of thing Annie would notice. Mr. Horton also made a name for himself in my family by hunkering in real close to my mother and putting his arm around her during the photo session after the show. Dad didn't take it very well. Nobody did.

Also on the show that afternoon were The Step Brothers, who were friendly and funny. We all loved watching them tap—especially my brother Johnny and my sister Annie, who looked like they were trying to memorize every move.

And of course there were a couple of appearances by the

much-loved Cardinal Cushing. At one point, he made quite a bit of money auctioning off pictures of himself, and then later he came on again and gave a rather long speech. When he finally finished, the master of ceremonies walked to the microphone and said, "I want to thank the Cardinal for one of the nicest weekends I've ever spent!" and the whole crowd, including the Cardinal, roared laughing.

At the end of our performance, the Cardinal presented me with a Raggedy Ann doll that was as big as I was. A doll. Just what I always wanted. I looked over at Annie and saw Walt and Pete smirking. They'd get theirs later.

We sang a few more concerts during September and when October came, we packed our twelve suitcases, locked up the house, got into our two maroon Chevrolet station wagons with "Burke Family Singers" painted in script on each front door, and left for our first tour. The day before we left, we received a Western Union telegram from one of the "Big Five" families back in Peace Dale. It read:

MAY THE PRAIRIES EMBRACE YOU   MAY
THE ROCKIES ECHO YOUR JOYOUS SONG
BON VOYAGE   —JOE AND MARY LAFFEY

Their warm send-off had a grounding effect on us. It connected the old world with the new and reminded us of our strong roots.

Our first tour in SONGS and CREDO, 1963

CHAPTER 14

"May The Prairies Embrace You"

WHAT AN ORGANIZATIONAL FEAT! Twelve people in two cars was relatively simple—three in the front and three in the back and three in the front and three in the back. But then there were the twelve suitcases, garment bags for tuxedoes and garment bags for gowns, a small suitcase for makeup, heavy metal stands for two sets of lights (three to a stand with one blue in the middle and two pinks on either side). And there was Jimmy's rod and reel and my flute, an iron, a borrowed 8mm movie camera, seven homemade cloth book bags filled with books, notebooks and assignments for the next five weeks, two cardboard boxes full of our 45 records with Equinox on the label and, of course, the red suede briefcase with Dad's two pitch pipes and all of the sheet music.

On the morning we were to leave, the *Providence Sunday Journal* photographer came to the house to take pictures for an article that would come out the next week. The title of the article was "Burke Family Tours," and in it, Ted Holmberg wrote that he went to "visit their home on Doyle Avenue." I thought "Great, why don't we let everyone know that our house will be empty for the next month or so . . ." but in 1963, it was not an issue. We were never robbed.

We could, however, still lose things. The problem was we didn't have a clue about packing on that first tour. Six suitcases, made of glorified cardboard and covered with a thin vinyl, were strapped to luggage racks on the top of each station wagon. The second car's six suitcases were crowned with the small square makeup case and then strapped from the top. This upped the stakes considerably, especially when one reflects upon some basic laws of physics coupled with the fact that this was back in the days when 75 mph was the standard highway speed limit.

Sure enough, two days later Gemma's suitcase flew off the top of the car somewhere between Mentor, Ohio, and Vincennes, Indiana, and she spent the rest of the five weeks sharing clothes with her sisters. It being 1963, however, the banged-up suitcase with Gemma's name and address written on the inside was mailed back to Doyle Avenue, contents intact.

On this first tour three priests arrived to see us off. My parents had asked these friends to come and bless us and the cars that would take us to unknown places thousands of miles away from home and anyone who knew us. Father Norman LeBoeuf wore the thin white stole and read from the book. Father Joseph Murphy stood on his right and held the holy water and Father Joseph Leo Flynn, the Passionist priest and the oldest friend, the one who had known Dad as a boy, just stood there in his black fedora and his black wool coat and grinned down at all of us as we sat in the cars. They blessed us, doused us with holy water and off we went.

Dad drove the lead car which we called SONGS because that's what was on the license plate. He shared the front seat with Marty and Florrie. John, Walt and Jim rode in the back. Dad and Mum decided to split up—one to a car—so that if there was an accident, there'd be one parent to take care of the rest of the family . Steve drove CREDO (Latin for "I believe"), named after the license plate on the second car. He sat with Pete and Mum in the front while Gemma, Annie and I sat in the back. (The kids with the shortest legs got to sit in the middle and straddle the floor hump. That would be Marty, Walt, Pete and me.) These cars were not just vehicles with Vanity plates and they were more than the sum of their occupants. These cars had personalities. CREDO was known as the sane car or the intellectual car. Anyone who *was* anyone rode in CREDO. We read, played word games, listened to public radio or slept. Though the people in the lead car, SONGS, thought we were drugged-out, boring deadheads, we knew we were composed and relaxed yet always open to any intellectual stimulus. We were far more civilized. We listened to Paul Harvey.

The others—the nervous wrecks, the crazies—rode in

SONGS. The only thing they read were maps. They were the twitchy, high-strung types who had "freeze-outs" in 40 degree below zero weather: a process that involved opening all the car windows, sticking their heads out and screaming while zooming down the Canadian highway, all the moisture in their nostrils freezing instantly on contact with the arctic air.

It was from SONGS' open rear window on a highway out West that Jimmy's newly acquired stadium horn was heard. The blast, which nearly caused Dad to drive off the road, was immediately followed by an amazing cattle stampede that we could easily see from the road. Frightened by the power of it but laughing uncontrollably, we also watched Dad's car swerve as he turned around to yell at Jim. Happy Trails. There must have been some law about causing stampedes so we felt real lucky that no other cars happened to be on that stretch of highway.

The personalities in the lead car seemed to have more physical energy than we who followed. There was the time down South when SONGS suddenly pulled over to the side of the highway. CREDO followed and the next thing we saw was John bolting out of his door and running like he was being chased. Sprinting along the edge of a wheat field, he kept running until he was just a speck on the horizon. He told Dad that he *had* to get out of that car *now* or he was going to *lose* it. He must've sounded like he meant it because Dad pulled over. Nervous types. And then there was "The Squeeze Play," shown in Cinemascope through SONGS' rear window. SONGS and CREDO, so alike and yet so different, set out on this first Midwestern tour with Dad and Steve as drivers, Mother as keeper of the daily log and Florrie as navigator. Florrie was not only lead soprano and soloist but she was also a damn good map reader. She would guide us on all the tours, through big cities and small towns, across America and Canada, with only one or two wrong turns. She smoothly led us to our first destination, which was KYW-TV in Cleveland, Ohio for an appearance on *The Mike Douglas Show* with John Payne, Dick Gregory and Farley Granger.

Mike Douglas was warm and friendly. Besides being a talented singer, a good showman and very skilled at running his talk/variety show, he was also gracious and unpretentious. He seemed like a happy guy. He clowned for our movie camera like he was a member of the family. We liked him immediately and it seemed that the feeling was mutual because he invited us back twice more to be on his show.

The Mike Douglas Show was shown live in Cleveland and taped for twenty-five other outlets. There was a studio audience and an applause sign that lit up to tell them when to clap. The sign flooded the audience area with light at the end of a song. Then it flashed. I was fascinated. Didn't these people *know* to clap at the end of a song? Maybe they needed it for the biting humor of Dick Gregory, a black stand-up comedian who would eventually quit joking altogether and become a full-time civil rights activist, author, politician, lecturer, entrepreneur and father of his own ten children.

Unfortunately, I don't remember much about meeting Dick Gregory or Farley Granger but John Payne, who looked very sharp in his pinstripe pants and cowboy boots, was a big hit with the family, especially with the boys. Jimmy was whispering excitedly to Mum that John Payne was a great trapper and woodsman just as ten-year-old Peter sidled up to the group and, striking a conversational pose, flattered Mr. Payne with intelligent questions like, "Didn't I see you on TV with a girl riding in a car?"

Packing for our first tour, 1963

Iowa State University, 1963

CHAPTER 15

Gemma Has A Bad Day

THE NEXT DAY WAS not a good one for Gemma. Her suitcase blew off the top of the car in the morning and that afternoon we drove off without her. We stopped for apples and
cider and left her in a near-by gas station. When she came out
of the ladies' room, we were gone. You'd think that someone
would have noticed. You'd think that I would have noticed
that she wasn't sitting next to me. I didn't. It's strange but actually, this happened more than once on the tours. There you
were, cruising down the highway after a nice lunch and you
lean over to talk to the person next to you and suddenly

realize that you can lean farther than you could before because their seat is empty.

We circled back to pick up Gem, who was now clearly discouraged, and then headed off again toward Detroit for an afternoon concert at Rosary High School. After the concert and a standing ovation, we were approached by many young people who asked if we would sign their autograph books. We were surprised and a little awkward about it at first, but soon discovered that this was to become the pattern after concerts from here on. Mother and Dad and the older kids kept an eye on us younger ones, especially during the after-concert receptions, to ensure that we'd continue to be able to fit our heads into the cars—and because they never knew what would come out of our mouths next.

During one reception Mother beamed as she heard a girl say to me, "You sang beautifully and I could understand every word!" Gratified, Mother listened to my poised response. "Thank you," I replied, "That's because my mother used to be a teacher of addiction." The girl laughed and said, "Addiction to what?!" just as Mother, chuckling, joined us. I had no idea why they were laughing until Mum explained.

On tour, there were concerts and then there were the mealtime performances. We had supper that night in McBride's Restaurant in Dowagiac, Michigan. Dad's "sing everywhere" policy was still in effect and if there were no plates of food on the table, out came that pitchpipe. Our Filipino waitress cried when she heard us and said, "I come from a family of eleven children and I haven't seen my brothers and sisters in so many years..." Music hath power, all right—and Dad had his pitchpipe.

We made a scene everywhere we went. And it wasn't just the singing. We created quite a stir simply by walking into some of these small town restaurants. For one thing, there were twelve of us. We took up at least three booths—and one more if we wanted to spread out. And there were times when Dad and Mum decided it would be nice to sit alone and talk—sort of get to know each other again. We all thought this was a good idea.

We stood out because we all looked alike. The fact that very few of us were shy only added to the effect. We were always so glad to get out of the cars that it was often a very energetic group that entered these small establishments. Our traveling clothes were usually different, but the boys' jackets were all the same and so were the girls' capes, which made for impressive entrances and exits. In Vincennes, we walked into a restaurant and heard a child say, "Here comes the Zorro family!" In Cleveland, someone wanted to know if we were Girl Scouts and further west, we were asked if we were from Ireland because all the girls wore their hair in braids.

The posters helped with the recognition factor, too. There we were, taped to the window of a restaurant or to the glass under the cash register. The posters were part of the work done by Jay Russell and Associates, our new Press Representatives from Boston. As artist representative, Buck, along with Dad and Mum, gave the Jay Russell people information about the family that they then rewrote and formatted into three or four standard press releases.

These blurbs, along with an 8 by 10 glossy, would later be sent off to the local newspapers ahead of our arrival. The newspaper simply chose one and then filled in the location and the dates of the performance. Letting the public know we were coming seemed to be our job. Reviewing the performance was entirely in the hands of these reporters and very many of them rose to the occasion.

Buck Spurr with the Lordly and Dame Agency and Jay Russell and Associates were not the only ones holding up the track on which this train rode. Credit for setting up and booking the Midwestern tours goes to a tour group called Pryor-Menz Concert Service out of Council Bluffs, Iowa. They were wonderful people who made sure we had a clear, well-planned itinerary and gas credit cards so we could fill the tanks. They made motel/hotel reservations for us when the schedule was tight or if it was wiser to get them in advance and they arranged for a paycheck to be waiting at different locations along the way. They were typical of the many caring Midwesterners we would meet on tour.

We also worked with Alkahest Attractions, who booked us in the South. Later, we learned how poor planning can affect a tour as we set out with Overture Concerts, who booked us in Canada and thought nothing of asking us to drive 950 miles in two days and then sing a concert that night.

Planning. It was all in the planning. We were little kids traveling in close quarters for many hours at a time. Even with good planning and occasional stops for sight-seeing, there were times when we wanted to kill each other—anything so there'd be one less body in the car and a little more leg room.

*   *   *

We reached Vincennes at five o'clock, in time to sing a concert at the University that night. The next day we drove south through the rest of Indiana, Kentucky and Tennessee and then west to a concert in Arkansas. We had never driven through a time change before and when Eastern Standard became Central Standard, giving us an extra hour of travel time, we felt like we were getting something for nothing.

As we drove south, it gradually turned to summer again and we took off our fall sweaters. The trees now had leaves and it was hot enough to think about ice cream.

We were amazed at the food prices. Outside of Evansville, Indiana, steak was sixty-nine cents a pound. Restaurants sold B.L.T.'s for fifty cents, roast beef sandwiches for thirty-five and in McKenzie, Tennessee, the Dairy Queen was selling hamburgers for twelve cents each. Mum kept her notepad in the glove compartment and jotted down anything that struck her. Road signs were often recorded: signs like "CATCH BRAGGING SIZE BASS AT OTTER LAKE, KY." and "STEWART, TENN COUNTY JAIL—VISITING SUNDAYS 1–4 P.M."

We stopped for a cup of cherry cider, passed a barn on fire and reported it and then stopped for lunch in Dover, Tennessee, where we got our first taste of barbecue pork, black-eyed peas, hush puppies and racial hatred, Southern style.

Right after we sat down, the father of the restaurant owner came over and introduced himself.

"I see you got Rhode Island license plates. I'm from Rhode Island, too. Yep. Come down here thirty years ago and now I own two aluminum plants."

Dad and he talked for a bit and I didn't pay too much

attention. When the hush puppies were ready, he brought them over, sat down and began to talk some more. Everything was fine until he started talking about "niggers" and showed us his guns behind the counter.

"Self-defense, of course," he said, "No trouble 'round here. They keep in their place. There's a little room out back for them to eat and everything. We've had to shoot some, of course." Mother wrote: "The children are deeply shocked at his sincerity."

"Deeply shocked" hardly comes close. I couldn't believe my ears. This was another kind of education altogether. It wasn't really even hatred. It was much scarier than that. It was his calm assurance, the matter-of-fact certainty that what he was dealing with here was simply a lesser form of life. He wasn't worked up or angry. That's what was so horrifying about his words. Sister Dennis, my new 6th grade teacher over at Holy Name Grammar School, could never have explained about this kind of racism. No one could've taught me about ignorance and hate as well as that old man did.

Singing down south

CHAPTER 16

A Different World

WE GOT ON THE road again and crossed the muddy Mississippi River into Arkansas. Our next concert was at A M & N College in Pine Bluff and on the way there we passed balls of cotton blowing along the road, small towns and farmlands of strange red clay dirt and our first cotton fields. We got out of the car and felt the white, downy fibers. So this was where my underwear came from. We began to see one or two-room shacks along the side of the narrow highway. Some looked like they were falling down—but the smoke coming out of the chimney told us that people were living there. Some had TV antennas. We watched two sharecroppers use a skinny mule and a pulley to load cotton onto the back of a flatbed truck. In the distance we could see mansions dotting the fields of soybeans, tobacco and cotton—magnificent structures with stately columns and wide porches.

We stopped at the J & M Restaurant on Route 79 in Clarendon, where we sang for our White River catfish and rainbow trout with hush puppies and coleslaw. After a song or two, Dad sidled over to two state troopers who were sitting at the lunch counter having coffee.

"How's business?" Dad asked.

Grinning, one said, "Well . . . we got a couple of runners."

"Runners?"

"Yeah. Two men escaped from the prison in Pine Bluff. They stole a twenty-year-old horse, rode him 'til he wouldn't go anymore and then they stole a car—and that ran out of gas." His buddy chuckled. "One of 'em is from around here . . . we're waitin' and watchin' the woods." It sounded like a movie.

We left the troopers to their coffee and surveillance and began the last leg to Pine Bluff. Passing the rice fields and huge factories of the Riceland Rice Company near Stuttgart, Arkansas, we finally reached Pine Bluff and checked in at the (unbeknownst to us) all-white Holiday Inn. It was twenty minutes to six. We brought the suitcases, gowns and tuxedoes up to our rooms and began to prepare for an eight o'clock concert. Dad called the college to tell them that we had arrived and to get directions to the auditorium. That phone call was the beginning of a very interesting evening.

We found out we were singing at six instead of eight P.M. as our itinerary said so we threw on clothes and raced to the campus where we were in for another surprise. This was an all-black college. I mean there wasn't one white person on the entire campus. We were it. And my oh my, didn't we stand out. So *this* is what it's like to be a minority. It was a very different perspective indeed. And from the way they looked at us, it was obvious that they were not accustomed to having white people come and sing for them. I think they were as surprised as we were.

Segregation was the rule down here. It was 1963. This was the year that water hoses were turned on the demonstrators in Birmingham who wanted to register to vote and it was in August, just two months before this concert, that two hundred thousand had gathered in Washington, D.C., to hear Martin Luther King give his "I Have A Dream" speech at the Lincoln Memorial. Churches were being bombed. The wheels of change were beginning to turn, but just barely, and the slow grinding movement of those big old rusty parts was a sound to put your teeth on edge. Tension was high. People didn't know how to act. Our concert at their black college was the very type of integration that many of these students had been working for—and yet it was clear that our presence made them feel uncomfortable as well as pleased.

It was homecoming weekend and there were many people on campus, but attendance for the concert was low. We sang the first couple of songs with little or no response from the audience. They hardly clapped. It felt so awkward that I wanted to jump out of my own skin and just get out of there. We were already rattled by the change in schedule and now we picked up their discomfit. They weren't being malicious. It seemed that they weren't sure how to react—either to us or maybe to the type of music. We, on the other hand, had grown used to a very specific audience reaction. We were used to heartfelt applause. What were we doing wrong?

Whatever we were doing, it wasn't working—so Dad decided to take this bull by the horns. He looked at us, smiled pleasantly and said, "Dixie," which was one of the final songs in the second half. He was switching the program and he *never* did that. The applause that followed was thunderous. I don't know if it was just the song, "Dixie" or the fact that white people from the North were singing it to this particular group, but the place went crazy. Still on the piano, Dad followed it up with a medley of Negro spirituals: "Behold That Star," "Mary Had a Baby," and "Go Tell It On the Mountain." Dad had the solos and was using us as backup. He'd certainly found something to do with his nervous energy and he was wailin'. For the rest of that concert, I saw nothing but white teeth out there in the audience. It was so different. From the front to well past the middle of the house, just rows of smiling white teeth.

At the intermission, some people came backstage and began talking with us. That was unusual, too. People normally waited until the concert was over to talk with us but this whole night was topsy-turvy. People were energized. They were excited about what was going on and so were we. I met a little girl about my age at the break. Her name was Corinne Wilkins. She and I got to talking and I asked her if she liked to write and maybe we could be pen pals. Dolores "Tay" Taylor, my best buddy and companion in crime back at Holy Name Grammar School, was black, but this little Southern girl was very different. It was like a foreign country down here. She thought I was sure strange, too. We decided to trade addresses after the concert.

We walked on stage to sing the second half and looked out to see that the audience had doubled. Word had gotten out at intermission that there were nice white people from the North who had come to sing for them. The lights went down and we sang the second half of the concert plus three encores. It was a great night, and then the weirdest thing happened.

The house lights went up at the end of the last encore, the applause died down and the audience just sat there. Nobody moved. We stood there and we didn't know what to do. It got so quiet. We didn't know if they wanted another encore or if they were waiting for us to make the first move or what—but everyone froze. It began to get real uncomfortable. Even Dad seemed glued to his spot. Seconds ticked by. Still no one moved.

Nearly a full minute had passed and the tension was really getting to me when I spotted Corinne sitting at the end of the second row. I decided to end the lesson in group dynamics and did the unthinkable. I broke rank. The eyes of the entire auditorium followed me as I walked away from my family, across the stage and down the steps to talk with Corinne. Everybody in the place was in a daze, my family included. It was not until she and I began to speak that the spell was broken and people started to move again. It was one of the strangest things I've ever seen.

Finally, everyone began to mingle and the volume reached a nice comfortable level. It was a night of discovery. We weren't like the white people they knew and they weren't like the black people we knew. We were all talking up a storm and no one wanted it to end. Some of the students invited us to come back the following night for part of their homecoming festivities, something they called "Stunt Night," but we had a concert in Searcy the next night and had to say no. Marty and Florrie then said, "Why don't you come back to the Holiday Inn with us for some coffee and dessert?"

At first, the students looked blankly at them but when they saw that it was a sincere invitation, one of them said to Marty, "We're not allowed to go in there." The girls looked confused. "We could be shot if we were seen talking to you in public." We didn't really get it before, but we were beginning to get it now.

We checked out of the Holiday Inn at nine-thirty the next morning and drove to the main drag in Pine Bluff for some breakfast. Feeling good and ready for food, we got out of the cars and as Dad and Steve plugged the meters, we noticed people staring at us. We were used to that. We knew there were a lot of us. We were our own mob scene—but this stare was different. It was hostile and the message was clear. Their faces said "Who do you think you are?" and "Get out of town." Some had stopped on the sidewalk and were just watching us. Word had gotten out around here, too, and these white citizens of Pine Bluff were not at all pleased about last night's concert.

Dad led us into the restaurant and we sat down, hoping for a fast breakfast followed by a faster exit. The place was empty except for us. There were two waitresses having coffee with the cook behind the counter. We found menus behind the sugar dispensers in the booths so we studied them and waited for one of the waitresses to come over. And we waited. And waited some more. There were still some people watching us from across the street. They'd talk to each other and then look over. They weren't wielding two-by-fours and yelling but it was nerve-wracking enough.

Dad whispered, "I'll order for everyone. Don't look out the window! And where the hell's that waitress?"

More than ten minutes had passed. We had had plenty of time to decide what we wanted to eat. And still they drank their coffee with their backs toward us and chuckled with the cook. They never once looked over at us. It seemed like the waitresses were doing their best to convince us that we were not sitting there.

A couple more minutes ticked by. Dad was beginning to tick, too. "Can we have some service over here, please?"he finally called out. Twelve pairs of eyes looked to the counter. Now it got quiet. One of the waitresses, a gum-chewing dyed-blond, slowly picked up her pad and pencil, sauntered over to Dad's booth and stopped nearby, leaning on one hip, bored but resigned. She never looked up from the pad.

"Yeah? Whaddaya want?"

That did it. Dad came back with, "Not a thing! C'mon kids, we're leaving!" He was mad, but he was afraid, too. We all were. The people on the street were still standing there watching us as we drove away. We had a late breakfast that day—in a different town after a long ride.

We were heading toward Searcy, Arkansas. I had Corinne's address and began my first letter. There'd be a letter waiting for me when I got home. Corinne and I would be steady pen pals for the next two years.

"...Softly...now sing o-o-o..."

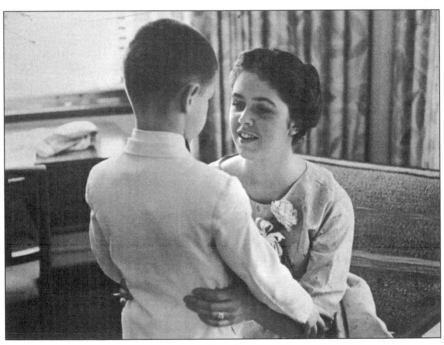

Backstage, Donnelly Theatre, Boston, 1961
Florrie giving sisterly assurance to Pete, who
for the first time was "in the singing line"

CHAPTER 17

Halloween Was
Hard To Drive Past

WE PULLED INTO SEARCY around noontime on Saturday and checked into the Noble Motel to rest before the concert at Harding College that night. Mother did some checking and was appalled to find out that there was only one Catholic Church with one Sunday Mass at ten o'clock. That was too late for us. We had to drive 360 miles that day in order to get to Shawnee, Oklahoma, and sing a Sunday night concert at St. Gregory's College.

But Mother was not easily discouraged. She somehow

turned up another Mass in Searcy—a six-fifteen A.M. Mass at the Morris School for Boys, an institution run by the Franciscan Brothers. So after singing a successful concert Saturday night at Harding College and having a late night sandwich and piece of pie in the motel restaurant afterwards, we fell into bed and were woken by a gentle rap on our room door at the crack of dawn. It was a quiet ride to Mass. Just us and the singing birdies shared the dusty road, but we weren't half as happy as they sounded.

We got to Mass on time and after the service Dad thought it'd be nice if we sang some songs for the boys and the Brothers. So what else was new? We sang three songs and they invited us to share breakfast. We felt a lot friendlier after the food. Some of us even talked.

On the road again by eighty-thirty, we drove all day and finally arrived at the Kickapoo Motel around 5 that evening—in time to lie down for ten minutes. Just as I was sinking into a deep sleep, Marty woke me and I quietly pulled myself out of bed. When we got to St. Gregory's, we saw that it wasn't a concert hall. It was more of a "gymatorium" filled with two dozen Mexican Benedictine Sisters, many priests and brothers and the entire student body—all of them college and high school boys. It was great to sing for kids our own age and I noticed that my four sisters were particularly rejuvenated by the enthusiasm of the crowd.

One of those cute boys thought that a souvenir would help him remember the wonderful night of music. So he decided to unscrew the "SONGS" license plate from the front of the lead car and walk away with it. We discovered that it was missing the following morning when the boys took the car to get haircuts. Dad notified Father William at Saint Gregory's, who promised he'd get right on it.

Our next stop was the Huckins Hotel in Oklahoma City, just forty-five minutes away. Reservations had been made in advance and SONGS still had the back license plate, so we decided to get on the road. (At that time, the state of Rhode Island required a front and back license plate, but many other states didn't and we figured we could make it to Oklahoma City without creating too much attention.) More Equinox 45 records had been shipped and were waiting for us when we arrived at the hotel. So was Terry McGovern, a teacher, with the SONGS plate in his hand and a big apology.

"Boys will be boys," my father said, glancing over at Walter, who returned the look, his soap-shiny face and fresh crewcut imitating the picture of innocence.

We headquartered at the Huckins Hotel for the next couple of nights and sang concerts in nearby Edmond at Central State Teachers College and at the Ladies Music Club in Oklahoma City. The first one was hard to sing because of bad acoustics. We couldn't hear each other sing. And the second one was hard because we couldn't hear them applaud. The members of the Ladies Music Club wore furs and jewels and gloves, which they kept on. Mother wrote: "The restraint of the woman's club is uninspiring."

Turns out they were much more enthusiastic than they sounded and warmly treated us to a lunch of chicken a la king and avocado. Mother thought it was a beautiful lunch, but the rest of us weren't too sure. We had never eaten avocado and now courtesy demanded it. The ladies were watching. So was Mother. Gem took one taste, leaned into me and murmured, "Oh my God, this is like sucking mud!"

It was October 31. Halloween night was just a few hours away but there'd be no dressing up and going out this year.

We got on the road again and drove northwest, all afternoon and into the night, past the early evening trick-or-treaters in the little towns: all the children zigzagging across the streets, carrying bags and wearing capes or black pointy hats and grease paint or tripping on their white sheets, everyone out, allowed to roam the streets after dark, take candy from strangers and scare each other silly. Halloween was hard to drive past. We still had our makeup on, too, but it was the wrong kind.

The next year was no better. We spent that Halloween traveling from Lamoni, Iowa, to Council Bluffs. The radio said they were having contests in Kansas City—$1 a pound for the biggest black cat and your weight in jelly beans for best costume. "How far is Kansas City?" I wanted to know. "We're not going that way" was the reply. In Peru, Illinois, children were painting the store windows with water paints and a prize was going to be given for best picture. Sorry, but we were headed west to North Dakota.

The year after that, we spent Halloween traveling south from Fort William, Ontario, toward our next concert in North Platt, Nebraska. The radio in Ontario said that Canadian children don't say "Trick or Treat" like we do. They say "Shell out, shell out, the witches are out!" I was practicing quietly in the back seat—but then we drove out of Canada.

It was 1966 before we had a Halloween for ourselves. Maybe that's why we went so crazy.

Jimmy started the whole thing—days in advance. He decided we should capture the attention of the entire neighborhood with a sound effects tape that he would make and then crank through our powerful stereo system and out the open window of the second-floor family room. Jim was the handyman of the family. He could fix things and he was real good with wires.

Using two reel-to-reel tape recorders, microphones and experimenting with sounds taken from various household items, then overdubbing and playing the tape on slow speed, he was able to create something that really made you sit up and take notice. When Dad was out of the house, the girls competed individually to see who could produce the most blood-curdling scream. It was good that Dad was nowhere around. He wasn't big on screaming. There were no cheerleaders in our family. He said we had better things to do with our vocal cords.

Marty's scream was fabulous. She won it hands down. Accompanied by thumps (a baseball bat on an overstuffed chair cushion) and low moans, it was agreed that, without a doubt, Marty's scream on slow speed was the one that could make your toes curl.

After the tape, things started to escalate. Everybody wanted to get into the act. On the morning of Halloween, we turned the first floor into a maze of cobwebbed, dark walkways. There were bowls of horrible-feeling stuff that you had to touch in order to pass through and there was bloody Peter, hardly breathing, waiting in the dark with an arrow through his head and a flashlight under his chin that he'd turn on when anyone approached.

Steve and John raided the laundry room and made a life-sized stuffed dummy that they hung from the elm tree in the front of the house. They used a real hangman's noose, stuck it in the heart with a very large butcher knife and then the two of them had a fine time with a bottle of ketchup. It was hung high enough so that if you had your head down and weren't paying attention, a swinging shoe could easily brush past your head in the dark. Most of the kids who came by that night were much too jumpy to miss it and gave it a wide berth.

As the undisputed Master of Gore, we all deferred to Jimmy's expertise and eagerly carried out his ideas. Jimmy would have made a great theatrical director. By late afternoon, 205 Doyle Avenue had been transformed and a lot of us were applying a different kind of make-up, using jet black, powder white and blood red.

Alfred Hitchcock's "Psycho," now six years old, had already become a movie classic and Jimmy thought he'd bring one of its characters to life, so to speak. He dressed Walter up in one of Gemma's wigs, a frilly old dress, a shawl and a blanket for his knees and sat him in a rocking chair out on the flat second-floor roof. Walt had the perfect grin and he just sat there all night long, rocking back and forth and humming to himself.

That flat roof made a great stage. It was the topside of the long front porch and the only way out to it was through the family room window. Jimmy went over that windowsill I don't know how many times that night. He had given himself an amazing makeup job, made a hump for his back, stuffed his torn clothing with fabric to make muscle lumps and when he spotted a group of children across the street, he'd fly over that windowsill, grunting and scuttling over the length of the roof like a monkey, leering down and drooling and trying to speak. The kids screamed and granny's shoulders shook with laughter.

Two witches opened the front door. My crazy white-haired mother took out her upper bridge revealing a jack-o-lantern smile, let down her hair, dressed in black and cackled just like the real thing. When she poked a little trick-or-treater in the stomach or squeezed an arm and said, "Hmm . . . I think we can fatten you up!" they smiled or giggled but you could tell they weren't too sure. A few said, "You're Mrs. Burke . . . right?" and then she'd grin and say, "Right!"

I was the junior witch and helped pass out the candy. I couldn't imitate that cackle if my life depended on it. Mum was good. We scared a couple of very young kids but mostly all of them were screaming and laughing and having a helluva time.

And there were a lot of kids. We didn't know where they all came from but the word had gotten out, and more than five hundred kids showed up at Doyle Avenue that Halloween. A cop showed up, too, at around ten o'clock. The porch was full of kids, the sidewalk was congested and cars had pulled up on both sides of the street. We were getting close to shutting it down when this lone ranger pulled up. Jimmy hit the switch on the reel-to-reel so we could hear him clearly when he said to my Mother, "You ought to be ashamed of yourself for causing all this." Mother tried to explain that we didn't mean any harm. He huffed a little more, said something else to her about scaring little children and then drove off.

The guy must've just moved to Rhode Island a week earlier from, say, San Francisco. He didn't have a clue. He had no idea who Mother was. He found out soon enough.

She asked all the kids to please go home, closed the front door, covered her face in her hands and cried. We all looked at each other. Everything had changed so suddenly. Florrie tapped Gemma's arm and the two of them left quietly by the back door, took one of the station wagons out of the garage and drove off. They came back about twenty minutes later. Florrie was grinning and she had a wonderful story to tell.

After spreading joy to all of us on Doyle Avenue, Officer Krupky toodled down Hope Street with Florrie and her considerable navigational skills on his tail. He pulled into the parking lot of Brown's Meehan Auditorium to see if there were any wrongs he could right in that vicinity—when suddenly, he spotted this very attractive young woman who sidled up to him charmingly, eyelashes batting and asked him a procedural question.

"Good evening, Officer."

("Well hello there! What can I do for you, little lady?")

"Um . . . I was wondering, Officer, is it permissible for a citizen to ask a policeman for his badge number—and if they do, does he have to give it?"

"Well . . . yes." He still didn't get it.

"That's good, because I'd like yours!"

He gave it to her. She then explained the relationship between her and that white-haired lady he had just humiliated. She also explained who we were. Both cars pulled out of there in a hurry. Krupky was headed for the police station to do some fast explaining and Florrie was headed for the nearest pay-phone. She got to the desk sergeant before he did.

He and another officer drove up to the house the next morning and Krupky delivered a very sincere apology to my mother. What a night.

Two lessons can be learned from the Halloween of 1966:

1. Try to avoid letting a concert schedule keep your children from celebrating Halloween for three years in a row; and
2. Never, *ever* mess with the head witch.

Jim being Jim—WPRI-TV Thanksgiving Special, 1965

CHAPTER 18

A Voice Whining
In The Wilderness...

WE PULLED INTO THE Holiday Motel in Alva, Oklahoma, at eight o'clock that night and ate a late supper at the motel restaurant. Dad reminded us that tomorrow's concert at Northwestern State College was at ten-fifteen in the morning, wake-up time would be at seven A.M. and there'd be no watching horror movies on TV tonight. Bela Lugosi and Boris Karloff would have to get along without us. A capacity crowd of college students and townspeople greeted us the following morning and we were ready for them. Mum wrote that the concert was another huge success and that Dr. Martin, president of the college, was moved to tears. Mother loved to see people cry.

We had four days to get to our next concert in Greeley, Colorado, and we were ready for a rest and some sightseeing. We headed west around two in the afternoon and it wasn't long before we saw our first tumbling tumbleweed dancing across the highway. There was something so happy and carefree in the way that it bounced along, like it was daring you to chase it, to catch it. CREDO couldn't resist the call and decided to bring a ball of it home. Steve signaled to Dad to pull over and then got out the car himself and went running along the edge of the road after the tumbleweed.

Watching Steve race down the road in such a whimsical pursuit struck me as oddly out of character. He was usually more serious. When he wasn't driving the car, he had his nose in a book. On that nose was a pair of black-rimmed glasses, a little too big for his young face, which made him look even more studious. Steve was a psychology major and he was on the Dean's List at Providence College. Being on that list meant that he could take an unlimited number of cuts from classes. He was eager to stay on it. We were eager to have him stay on it. He had a beautiful bass voice and he was a safe driver. Besides, we liked him.

It was great watching him go after that tumbleweed. He looked like an idiot with his tie flapping over his right shoulder as he ran. He finally cornered one, then gingerly picked it up, brought it back to the car and carefully passed it to Annie in the back seat. The experiment lasted about another ten minutes.

By then Annie was covered with prickles so we pulled over again and out it went, bouncing away behind us.

Next we pulled into Dodge City, a cluster of old, single-storied, flat-roofed storefronts that looked like every Western movie I'd ever seen. Steve, John and Jim were jumping out of their skins. They couldn't wait to get out of the cars and see Boot Hill and stroll through the swinging doors of the Long Branch Saloon.

Steve stood looking at the mounted guns of Bat Masterson, Wyatt Earp, Billy the Kid, Pop Clanton and Doc Holliday. I was fascinated by the open grave, the jail and the hanging tree. Jim and John staged a running gun battle outside the Long Branch Saloon using their fingers for guns. Walt made a beeline for the nickelodeons, sat down and began pumping his feet like a madman and all the boys, including my father, had to do their own John Wayne swagger as they pushed open the swinging doors of the Long Branch and stepped out into the sunlight.

We followed the Santa Fe Trail into Garden City, Kansas. It was Mountain Time here and the land was so flat and the horizon so free of buildings and even trees that the sunset that night was simply gorgeous. It went on and on, every shade of yellow, pink, orange and red as far as the eye could see.

Mother laughed when she saw the sign "Boats repaired" and said, "Where do they sail 'em?" to which Steve replied, "They're probably prairie schooners." Sometimes the CREDO wit would have us smirking uncontrollably.

The Santa Fe became the Navajo Trail as we crossed into Colorado the next morning. We began to see cactus by the side of the road and lots of sheep ranches. This was the land of the ten-gallon hat. Ten gallons of what, I wanted to know. I never did get a clear answer. It was later on that morning, outside La Junta, Colorado, that Jimmy used a stadium horn to "talk to the animals" and nearly blew Dad off the road in the process. Man, those cattle could run!

On the way to Greeley, we passed through Colorado Springs and Denver. Mum was crazy about these cities with the mountains in the background and the wonderful air. Colorado mountain air was wonderful all right, as long as you weren't new in town and standing on an outdoor stage and needing a lot of it in a hurry. The air was thin and stingy. Combine it with "Le Sommeil de L'Enfant Jésus," the Sleep of Death, and you've got trouble.

Somewhere in the second stanza Florrie tried to suck up enough air to sing those long high notes and she sagged to the floor, down for the count. Steve and Dad sat her on a chair, gave her some water and gradually she revived. She sat out the next few songs but was up again to finish the program with her solo in "America the Beautiful."

We sang two encores and sold thirty-eight records that night. We were becoming a professional-sounding singing ensemble. Program repetition was teaching us to tune into the audience as well as one another and apart from people falling down on stage occasionally, our performances were starting to show some real polish.

It was around the middle of the tour and we had found our stride and were running nicely together. The tension associated with a new undertaking was gone now. We knew we

could do this thing called touring and we were enjoying ourselves. The next morning as we drove north to Kearney, Nebraska, we laughed easily at the antics of the tumbleweed
blowing in front of the cars. Gemma read Steve's psychology
book to him out loud as he drove and when we stopped for
lunch at the Brown Jug Hotel in Julesburg, Colorado, Mother
wrote that "the children and Walter are in very funny moods
and there are many laughs."

One of the things they were all laughing about was Jimmy
doing an imitation of me drugged out on Dramamine. They
all thought his staggering toward the booth, weaving and bob-
bing and finally falling into it while trying to open his eyes and
focus was hilarious. I laughed, too. You couldn't help it. He was
so funny. I noticed, however, that his act didn't include my pre-
Dramamine period; that is, all the time I'd spent vomiting into
a large peanut butter tin. That was not funny. Motion sickness
is no joke and I seemed to be the only one with the consistently
screwy equilibrium. So I slept a lot. So what.

He wrapped up his act by dropping his head back and snoring in midsentence a couple of times and then (happily) the
food arrived and we could concentrate on that for a while. But
Jim was in a rare mood that afternoon and after we had eaten,
he went into this strange character he called Crying Loon. He
took the name from one of the Indian characters in the TV series "F Troop" but that was where the resemblance stopped.
Apart from the name, this character of Jim's was completely the
result of the workings of his own weird little mind.

Crying Loon was a voice whining in the wilderness. When
asked, he carefully stated his earnest views on nature, the state

of the planet and on the loon, in particular. He did this in a plaintive voice that always made Mum cringe and laugh at the same time. It was pitiful and grating and had a splayed, smooth quality to it, like the underside of a frog.

C. Loon, as he was known in scientific circles, was most comfortable with a question/answer format and was usually interviewed by either John or Steve. (This interview method of comedy was familiar to all of us after hours of listening to, laughing with and imitating Carl Reiner's interview with Mel Brooks on their "2,000 Year Old Man"album.) The setting for these interviews was often in a restaurant after a full meal and then only when Jimmy was in the mood. John or Steve would roll up a menu or a napkin to use as the microphone and tentatively ask Jim, "Is Crying Loon there?" Sometimes the answer was "no" and other times a cloyingly sweet voice responded and the ad lib interview would begin.

Steve and John's provocative questions lured Jim into some very funny inventions. He was quick on his feet and gave outrageous answers to questions on family, politics and just about anything else without cracking a grin. The two older boys often tried to get Jim to break character and start laughing but they rarely could do it—even when Jimmy had us crying from laughing, he stayed in character. That was the thing about Crying Loon—he was so sincere.

This particular afternoon Crying Loon was asked to give his thoughts on the state of Colorado. He was expounding on the beauties of the flatland, the various flora and fauna and then he got into the mating rituals of the Colorado puce-juicer.

"The what?!"

"The Colorado puce-juicer. It's a small reddish-gray bug pe-culiar to the mountain ranges."

There was no point in looking this bug up in the diction-ary. It was so rare that only Crying Loon had ever even seen one. He continued.

"Imagine my excitement at spotting *two* puce-juicers in their *extraordinary* mating dance!"

"Can you describe this mating dance?"

"Well . . . it involved a back-and-forth swaying motion cou-pled with elaborate antennae display and a heavy exchange of sputum shot from one to the other at distances of no less than three feet!"

"Sputum? You mean that the puce-juicers *spit* at each other?" chortled the incredulous interviewer.

"Oh yes," intoned Crying Loon, serious as ever, "from amazing distances until they were both covered in slime." Jim was out of his mind. Just to hear him pronounce "puce-juicer" in that gratingly sweet voice was enough to send us falling out of the booth.

When Jim wasn't the one fooling around, it was Steve or John, Florrie, Marty or Walt taking center stage. We had learned to amuse ourselves while we waited—and we did a lot of waiting. We sat waiting for the food to come and then for the bill afterward. We stood in place and waited for the lights to be adjusted and then we waited for makeup and then waited to sing. We waited for sound technicians and photographers and cameramen. We waited in the cars while Dad went into motel offices to dicker for the best price—and most often, we waited for each other because there were a lot of us and some were slower than others.

By the time we toured, we kids had been playing together for years and had become quite used to and adept at imitating and cracking on one another's foibles, personality traits and quirks, in general and in particular. Nothing was sacred and not one of us was exempt from the keen observations of the rest of us—and believe me, this was a very sharp group. There was no place here for the thin-skinned and as for those who needed an attitude adjustment, they got it—and sooner rather than later. We nudged and prodded each other, often with laughter and sometimes not so gently. But not all wounds are bad. Some of us learned how to laugh at ourselves.

Promo shot for Christmas special, 1965

Thanksgiving special—WPRI-TV, 1965

CHAPTER 19

Git Along Little Dogies

TWO MILES OUT OF Julesburg and the Brown Jug Hotel lay the Nebraska line. "Puce-juicer," mumbled Steve, chuckling softly to himself as we drove into the Cornhusker State. We stopped at a reptile ranch to see a bobcat, coyotes and rattlers, alligators and a black bear that drank as many bottles of Yoohoo chocolate milk as the tourists wanted to buy.

After singing a nine-thirty concert at the State Teachers College in Fort Kearney the next morning, Dad had us sing for the hotel kitchen help while we waited for lunch. He could draw that pitchpipe as fast as any gunslinger.

After lunch, we headed north to begin the 620-mile ride to Mayville, North Dakota. We had a concert scheduled for the following night. Git along little dogies. Over the rolling hills of northern Nebraska, past the neat, orderly farms and full corn-cribs, the fields of squealing piglets and sows and the fields of silent plowed lines, we drove further into this great wide bread-basket. On into South Dakota and the miles of wheat, barley and sorghum; waves of harvestland and prairie grasses hissed softly and changed colors as we watched another slow incredible sunset.

We found a motel in Watertown, South Dakota, at ten o'-clock that night and it was a pretty good guess that by that time, Walt had been squeezed to near-lifelessness at least once. Sitting in the car and waiting while Dad went to see about motel rooms seemed to be a particularly harrowing time for Walt from what I could see sitting in the second car. While the cat was away, the two beefy mice on either side of Walt leaned in, pinched, pummeled and pressed him to their breasts with carefree abandon. Their caress was never uninvited, however, and just to prove it, we watched as Walter got himself free only to leap into the fray again, arms flailing.

Dad cut a deal with the motel owner. Two double beds and a roll-away cot for the girls and the same for the boys. Mother and Dad had a room to themselves and were able to get away from us every night on tour. They must have loved it. We all fell into bed that night and the next morning we pulled out early and drove about seventy miles before stopping for breakfast. Seventy miles. That must have been an agreeable little ride.

We finally pulled into the only restaurant in a one-horse

town called New Effington, located on the northeast tip of South Dakota. It was flat coming in and flat going out, just a few small buildings on the one road that made up this no-frills town. There was something cut-off and desolate about the place. It was clear that these buildings were important, not just for what could be bought and sold in them, but because they were an excuse to gather. They were the *only* place to gather. As we stepped into the small restaurant, it looked like anyone who didn't have to be out in the fields was more than happy to sit in here near the jelly donuts, drinking coffee and talking.

There was one old-timer who looked like he could use a good cup of coffee. He sat on a swivel stool at the counter, watery-eyed, shaky and unshaven. He wore stained overalls, a dirty, worn-out railroad cap and watched us all walk in like he was seeing a vision. A bunch of fresh and rambunctious, very hungry youth descended on the place, and he, along with the other eight to ten patrons, the cook and the waitress, paused in whatever they were doing to watch.

We could have been from Mars. They were that surprised and that curious. Fortunately for them, Dad didn't suffer from Midwest reticence. He had no problem talking to anyone at anytime. He needed no lead-in. They just had to say "Hello" or "Good morning" back and he was off and running. He could give total strangers a brief but full synopsis of our life in a flash. And, hey, before you knew it, he was pulling out that little silver disc he kept in his jacket pocket.

We had ordered breakfast and could smell our food being prepared. We squinted at him. He grinned back at us. His eyes said, "We have to sit here and wait for the food to come anyway—so why don't we sing something and give these nice people a treat? C'mon." Can eyebrows really dance? His did—just before he said, "The Kerry Dance" and blew a note. He gave our food-starved brains a moment to grab hold of our first notes and then raised his hand to direct us in fourpart harmony.

Dad sure knew how to pick 'em. There was the old guy, tears streaming down his face as we sang,

> *Only dreaming of days gone by, in my heart I hear;*
> *Loving voices of old companions,*
> *stealing out of the past once more,*
> *and the sound of the dear old music,*
> *soft and sweet as in days of yore.*
> *Oh, the days of the Kerry dancing,*
> *Oh, the ring of the pipers' tune;*
> *Oh, for one of those hours of gladness,*
> *Gone, alas, like our youth, too soon!*

Why didn't Dad just keep his hands out of his pockets? The poor old conductor was a mess! We sang another song and then one more after we ate and he followed us out and hugged us and asked us not to go. Some of the townspeople looked away, uncomfortable by his display of affection, but I wanted to watch him, to memorize his face: the taut red cheeks and wrinkles around the eyes, like a broken Santa smiling and frowning just a little as he tried to control himself, eyes full of tears and waving good-bye as we drove away. I turned around in my seat and watched him as he stood there, wide open and still waving until the dust hid him from view.

*   *   *

As we drove through Fargo, North Dakota, Peter thrilled us CREDO riders with his latest discovery. "Hey, they even have little kids around here!" he declared. Annie, Gemma and I just looked at each other. So did Steve and Mum up in the front seat. Another planet heard from. Peter was nine years old and it was obviously a safe little world where he lived. I'm not exactly sure *where* this world was, however.

This is the same kid who at age six, when asked what he wanted to be when he grew up, had seriously answered, "I'm going to be an elephant—but a *good* elephant and if one of you is good, I'll let you ride on me!" Can you imagine what we could do with a kid like that? He was just begging to go for a ride. We mostly kept him out of dangerous traffic but every once in a while, when he'd give us an opening as wide as the Grand Canyon, we just had to pull up to the curb, where he eagerly waited, and say, "Hey Pete! Want to come along? Hop in!"

Mother tried to set him straight on the fundamentals of breeding as they applied to humans in North Dakota (not wanting to overwhelm him, she kept it simple) and by the time we reached Mayville, fifty miles later, Pete was almost clear on the principle that if you see a bunch of big people in an area, there's a pretty good chance there's gonna be some kids not too far away.

After a concert in Mayville, North Dakota, we headed south, returning to Fargo for breakfast and then over the Red River into Minnesota. Soon we were enjoying another mid-day dose of Paul Harvey on the radio. On this broadcast Mr.

Harvey was quoting a man who complained about the smog in London. He said, "It's the only place in the world where people are awakened mornings by sparrows coughing." We all just loved that one. Mother opened the glove compartment and grabbed her pad so she could write it down. It was near the end of Mr. Harvey's broadcast, and as usual, as soon as he was finished, a chorus of CREDO voices imitated his unique sign off, "This is Paul Harvey, . . . good—DAY!"

After successful concerts in Winona and St. Joseph, Minnesota, we headed for Cornell College in Mt. Vernon, Iowa. On the way there we stopped at the Sac and Fox Indian Settlement and School, and Dad, who was never one to pass up an opportunity for spreading goodwill or having an impromptu cultural exchange, spoke to the principal. Before long, we were singing in each of the school's three classrooms. Two grades shared each room and all of the children were very shy. After we sang for the fifth and sixth graders, they sang a sweet soft song for us in their native language. That was the thing about singing. We could go into just about anyplace and say, "Hello. We're a family of singers from New England and we're driving through here on tour. Would you like to hear a song?" Who was going to say "no" to a song?

We got back into the cars and made the short trip to Mount Vernon where we booked three rooms at the 30-30 Motel. The concert was in King's Chapel on the Cornell College campus and the mostly student audience was great. One woman came up to Mother afterward and said, "I cried when I heard you. So many years ago I sat in this same seat and watched the Trapp family."

Our final concert of the tour was in Dubuque, Iowa. The school was Clarke College, founded by a group of Irish nuns, Sisters of the Blessed Virgin Mary (BVMs), who came over to Dubuque in order to establish a school for Young Ladies in 1843. It was aimed at "broad and thorough training of mind and character, and for intellectual excellence, religious and moral discipline, and the arts of womanly accomplishments."

Clarke College was a place I would remember. There was a love for learning, a spirituality and a warmth in that Catholic women's college that stayed with me, stored someplace in the back of my young brain. Twenty years later, when I was 31 years old, I would again walk off the stage of Clarke's Terence Donaghoe Hall, this time alone and with a BA diploma in hand. Better late than never.

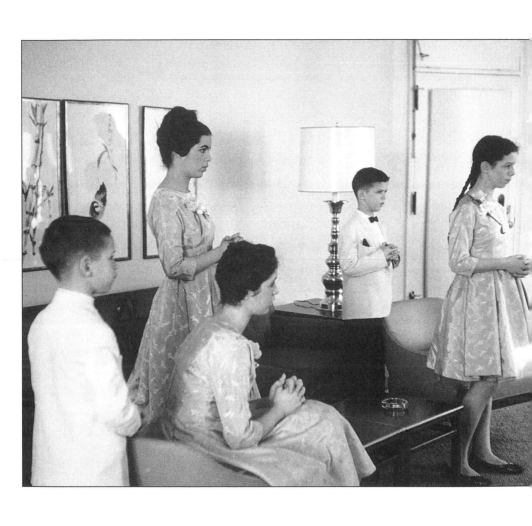

CHAPTER 20

"The President's Been Shot"

SEVEN THOUSAND MILES AND eighteen states later, we turned toward home. It took four days to drive from Dubuque to Providence and it was just five days after we got home that President Kennedy was shot in Dallas.

I was sitting in the sixth grade classroom of Holy Name Grammar School when the announcement came over the intercom. "The President has been shot." That was all we knew. We sat there stunned to silence. This wasn't supposed to happen. Some kids were crying but most of us were too numb and then the voice on the microphone began to say the rosary and every classroom answered her "Hail Marys" with the second half; our "Holy Marys" echoing down the corridor, baby voices to near-grown-up voices streaming out of the open classroom doors, highs and lows blending together, "now and at the hour of our death" bouncing off the polished wood and the bricks in the high-ceilinged hallway.

After the rosary, a TV set was wheeled into our classroom and instead of watching the NASA astronauts circle the Earth, we now watched Walter Cronkite give us the news as soon as he got it. "This just in..." and as he read the bulletin we all dreaded, his face seemed to visibly age. Those of us who heard his words that day would never be the same. In one moment, we Americans had lost our innocence and the loss was irretrievable.

After that, they sent us home and I remember being glued to the TV set for the next four or five days, watching the grief and grieving. Don't miss any of this, I thought to myself. These are historic days. The long black polished boots pointing backwards on the riderless prancing horse, the sound of its hooves clicking on the city street and that particular drumbeat, the one I can still hear, sounding over and over again in 4/4 time,

> tap tap tap roll   tap tap tap roll
> tap tap tap roll   tap tap tap-tap (rest).

On December 2nd, we sang the Memorial Mass for President Kennedy at Brown University. The place was packed and people were still a mess but we got through the Mass and we, along with the rest of the country, got through the time, scarred but still on our feet, never the same but not without hope. He had given us enough to last for a good while.

We sang another six concerts during the first half of December, including our second annual we-pay-our-dues performance at Holy Name Grammar School and then on December 18th, we got into the cars and drove to the City Squire Hotel in New York City where we would stay for the next five nights.

The bell captain was struck momentarily speechless when he spotted Walter. Obviously, no one had told him that we were back for a return engagement. He had been standing near the front desk, leaning on one elbow and casually talking to someone behind the counter when we came through the revolving doors, and now suddenly he looked as if the counter was the only thing holding him up. Walter often had that effect on people.

We checked in, parked the station wagons in the underground garage and went to bed early that night. The next day would be a long one. In the morning we were all going to get on a plane together and fly to Cleveland for our second appearance on the *Mike Douglas Show*.

What planning it took to coordinate ten children on these trips. We had an eight A.M. flight leaving from Newark Airport. Catching the flight on time meant rising at five A.M., dressing for the TV show and leaving the hotel without forgetting anything, then taking those crazy-driving, stop-and-start-nauseating, car-honking yellow New York taxicabs from the city to the airport before the morning rush hour slowed traffic to a crawl and finally, planning it all so that we arrived an hour before the plane was to take off.

None of us had ever flown before and some were reluctant to board. It was snowing lightly but blowing pretty hard. I stood outside the plane in my kneesocks and green cape, one gloved hand holding down my pillbox hat while the wind whipped around my knees. "Fly the Friendly Skies!" it said on my ticket. I studied the gathering clouds, inspected the outside of the plane, and wished dearly that I knew more about weather patterns, particularly the density of certain cloud formations and the exact temperature at which ice forms. It was incredible to me that we were going to fly off the ground and then up in this thing. Someone standing next to me said, "At least we'll all die together." What a marvelous comfort.

We all lined up on the portable stairs leading to the door of the plane and waved like starlets for the movie camera. Then we walked in and found our seats. Dad looked green; his shiny eyes and weak smile tried to encourage and failed miserably. We all knew he was terrified. Riding on air currents was obviously not his thing and now he sat belted in with a taut grin.

Snow was falling harder in Cleveland. The plane bounced lightly two times and then roared down the runway. Color was beginning to return to Dad's cheeks and all of us were happy to put our feet on solid ground again.

Mike Douglas gave us another warm welcome and soon he and Dad, along with the other production people, worked out what we would be doing on the show. Mike said he'd introduce us and we'd sing "The First Noel." Then he'd interview Dad and Mum about the tour we had just finished, talk about what was in the works and maybe ask us how we celebrate Christmas. Then, to wrap it up, Mike asked Dad if he could sing a Christmas carol with us. This was great. Mike held the microphone up to his mouth and crooned the melody an octave below the sopranos like Bing Crosby with the boys choir in *Going My Way*. The applause sign lit up again at the end of it, and I still wondered why they thought it was necessary.

We weren't alone on the show. We were joined by Joe E. Brown, a box-office star in the 1930s and a very kind man who, after losing his son in WW II, directed his comic energies and much of his time to entertaining the troops in the USO. He could also open his mouth wider than anyone I ever saw. Besides Joe E. Brown, Shari Lewis and her puppets, Lamb Chop and Charlie Horse, were on the show. I had often watched her TV show and was very excited to meet her and very surprised and disappointed when I did. People are not always what they seem. Maybe she was having a bad day, but I thought that for someone who didn't like children she sure had picked a strange profession.

Joe E. Brown, on the other hand, couldn't get enough of Walt and Pete. The plan was that he'd read, "'Twas the Night Before Christmas" to them on the show. They sat on either side of him and while the TV people adjusted the lights, Joe E. Brown put a hand around Peter's neck and pulled him in closer. That's the kind of guy he was. Walt, on the other side, was busy pawing at the large broadcast microphone stationed on a floor stand between him and Joe E. Brown. He did this a couple of times and then quickly and surreptitiously pulled the microphone stand closer to himself. That's the kind of kid *he* was.

"'Twas the Night Before Christmas" went off without a hitch. Walt and Pete actually sat still through most of it. We watched Shari Lewis from afar, sang our bit with Mike Douglas, who was as warm as ever and told us we'd be hearing from him again, and then flew back to New York that night.

We were not vacationing, we were in New York to sing. Our final performance of 1963 would be on the Ed Sullivan Show and we were flying high. Forget the airplane. Our feet were hardly touching the ground.

There was a one o'clock rehearsal set for the next day at Showcase Studios at 950 Fifth Avenue up on the second floor. This was the first of three days of afternoon rehearsals before the taping in front of a "live" audience on the evening of December 22nd. We were scheduled to sing "Silent Night" and the Bach "Alleluia from Motet VI" and we were going to have a real orchestra backing us up. Far out. Ray Block and his orchestra could easily whip up a nice accompaniment for "Silent Night" but the Bach "Alleluia" was something else. It was one of the most difficult songs we sang and ad libbing the orchestral parts for Bach's intricate winding melodies was out of the question.

Enter the not-quite-graduated-from-Boston-College guy, my dad. While we went sight-seeing, he stayed in his hotel room and, without benefit of piano (or any other instrument), wrote out the orchestral parts for the Bach "Alleluia."

Dad was one of those people who could look at whole groups of notes on two staves and actually hear the sounds they made in his head. He didn't have to hum each line of notes or figure it out on a piano. He could hear whole groups of harmonies without playing them. One day I watched him as he stared at a sheet of complicated music. Finally, I went over to him and said, "Can you *hear* that?"

"Yeah."

"*How* can you hear that?"

"I know what each note sounds like." I looked into his eyes to see if he was kidding. Yeah, okay . . . I thought and just walked away.

On the second day of rehearsal, he passed out the parts he'd written, and then Ray Block lifted his baton and Dad grinned at us and raised his hands. One of them counted one-two-three and then everybody began playing and singing like crazy. Big sound all around us. Grinning violinists. They didn't get to play this longhaired music too often on *The Ed Sullivan Show*, and they were getting into it. Some of the instruments were playing my 2nd alto part as I sang it, but I couldn't figure out which ones. Everything was moving so fast that I had all I could do to hold on to my part. Then the music stopped and another sound began. Tapping.

We were still sort of dazed by the size of the sound that had just ended and now we watched as the orchestra members began to tap their violins with bows or pluck their strings. Popping sounds, like the whole room was an open bottle of champagne, the low rumble of the bass fiddles, the high trilling of the wind instruments and the tapping. Ray Block used his baton to tap his music stand.

We were thoroughly bewildered by this activity. Mother and every one of us kids were at a complete loss. Had we done something wrong? It didn't look that way. They were all smiling at us. We looked over at Dad and he was beaming. No. He looked like God could call him home at any time now and that'd be just fine with him. He was laughing. We still didn't get it. "They're complimenting you!" he explained over the din. "Oh!" we smiled back at them.

The rehearsal process was exciting, particularly when we worked with the orchestra, but it also involved a lot of waiting. We didn't see a whole lot of Ed Sullivan. We met him, of course, and he was very cordial, but it seemed that his son-in-law, Bob Precht, was mostly running the show. It was he who sent white orchid corsages to the City Squire for Mum and the five of us girls. It wasn't necessary. We were thrilled to be there, but it was a nice touch.

The Ed Sullivan Show was organized, but it was loose, too. Ed Sullivan was a former newspaperman who went after fresh talent the same way he had gone after fresh news. If someone made a recent hit on Broadway or somebody else with a hot new album was in town, sometimes they'd get a call and Ed would fit them in someplace in the show. Also, Ed might get a call from an agent telling him that their big name client was in town and would be out in the audience and would Ed mention that so-and-so was here and they'd stand up and take a bow.

If there were a few people out in the audience, this took time out of the scheduled program and some other performer could get bumped. Ed would promise them another appearance or two. He made deals and changed the lineup depending upon what was happening and who was in town. Consequently, the names that appeared in the *TV Guide*, which had a lead time of about six weeks, were not necessarily those who appeared on a given Sunday night.

Then there were some performers who couldn't be there and had pre-recorded their segments. For instance, on the December 22 show, George Kirby had taped his stand-up comedy act earlier and the tape was played during the show.

Most of the performers, however, were there in Studio 50 that night. Tessie O'Shea and her gang appeared live, straight out of the English music halls, all fish-net legs high-kicking and mouths open to sing and dance to "London Is A Bit of All Right." Frank Ifield from Australia was there to sing "Waltzing Matilda," and Buster Keaton was undeniably present for his act. Especially memorable was the last bit where he spilled milk onto a sandwich sitting in his lap, looked out at the audience with that deadpan expression under the crushed hat, and then proceeded to pick up the sandwich and literally wring it dry. "Oh my God...." Dad said, as he watched all the milk spill onto one of the chalk circles on the stage floor. We were going out there next and there wasn't time to wipe it up. One of us would be standing in milk. Buster was there all right.

That night, George Abbott, one of the big Broadway directors, was out in the audience and he stood up and took a bow. That night, the sponsors for the show were Lipton Tea, Anacin, Pillsbury and Kent cigarettes. That night, we performed with an orchestra. That night, we all drank a glass of champagne back at the City Squire, clinked our glasses together and toasted each other. That night, I looked out the hotel window at the night lights below and felt like I owned the place.

Burke Family Singers meet SONGS *and* CREDO, *first tour, 1963*

CHAPTER 21

Ambassadors
of Good Will

ADOLESCENCE. IT'S DIFFICULT TO describe how I looked
at twelve. I was going through that peculiar time in life when
one's body parts stretch at unequal rates. In this my solo race to
adulthood, it was legs, feet and hands that neared the finish line
while breasts dawdled back by the starting gate. I was no longer
cute. I looked awful in my Holy Name uniform. Wrinkled, un-
kempt, sprouting and embarrassed. I was in the sixth grade and
stretching mercilessly. No matter what I did, I looked thrown
together. Mother took the hem down on my uniform skirt and

tried to tell me that everything would catch up eventually and I'd be beautiful. I wasn't so sure.

I was slamming into things. I seemed to be unable to calculate distances with this new body. Cut and bruised, I peered around corners, looking out for sharp objects, knowing that at any moment I would get in my own way. It was around this time that Mother, with every good intention, decided that what I needed above all else was a good strong pair of sturdy shoes. She must have been talking to her Aunt Sarah.

My great aunt, Sarah Josephine Devine, after whom I was named, was a maiden aunt who had devoted herself to taking her niece, Anne Devine, to the opera, the ballet, the Pops and the Boston Symphony Orchestra. Besides being a devotee of the arts, she was a New England telephone supervisor for years, and perhaps it was this line of work that had convinced her that one could skimp on any part of a wardrobe, but not on shoes. Never on shoes.

For years Aunt Sarah had periodically solicited Mother for foot sizes so that she could supply us with good shoes. Mother would lift us up to stand on top of the kitchen table in Peace Dale and giggle with us as she traced our ticklish, squirming feet in pen on cardboard. She'd cut along the tracing, write the name of the owner and mail the cut-outs to Aunt Sarah, who then stuck them into shoes for the right fit. Before long, a package arrived from Boston.

In the early days of 1964, things were different. We could now afford to buy our own good shoes and now Mother was following Aunt Sarah's advice with a vengeance. She took me to the Lad and Lassie shoe store on Hope Street. She'd seen a pair in the window and had fallen in love. These were "sensible" shoes and they were going to be all mine—no matter what.

I hated the Lad and Lassie shoe store. It was for matrons and frumps. Mother kept driving. In we went. Mother pointed. The salesman smiled and held one out for me to see. I stared in horror. Couldn't everyone see that my legs were two long thin sticks and that there was enough leather here to saddle a pony? These shoes would last forever. They were big heavy brown leather oxfords, flaps and all. I hated them on sight and seeing them on my feet was truly hideous. Mother was smiling. Why? Couldn't she see what I saw? They looked like gunboats and I would spend the next three years dragging and scraping them over every sidewalk I could find.

The one consolation in all this was that I was now able to look down on Walter—the only thing growing on him were his feet. Misery loves company and I surely was miserable, so I tried to include Walt as much as possible.

Mum looked down at my feet.

"Why aren't you wearing your new shoes, deah?"

"I forgot to pack them." I put on my most innocent look. Judging from the look I got, she was having none of it. It was March and we were on our way to Canada for our second tour. It wasn't a long tour—only about two weeks, but it would be an important one. There was a man in one of those Canadian audiences who could effectively keep Steve out of Vietnam.

We sang in Windsor and Toronto, Ontario, and then went north to Montreal and Trois-Rivieres in Quebec. It was in the main ballroom of the Sheraton Mount Royal Hotel in Montreal that we sang for and later met Jerome T. Gaspard, the

Consul General of the United States. The concert was sponsored by Marionapolis College and Mrs. Pierre, the chairwoman, was expecting 200 people. Nine hundred showed up and the poor lady was in a dither, especially when everyone stayed for the sherry reception afterwards. People often wanted to visit with us and ask questions. The Consul General was no exception, and when he came over to Dad and Mum, he warmly shook their hands and said, "You are excellent Ambassadors for the United States!"

My father looked at him for a moment and then asked, "Would you be willing to put that in writing?"

Monsieur Gaspard said, "Well...sure, I can put it in writing."

Dad was thinking ahead. It was 1964 and Steve was due to graduate from Providence College in about a year. The draft board wasn't interested that he was in a family singing group. For them, life was simple. His student deferment would be up soon and his body was A-1, so when he graduated from Providence College, he would go to Nam or he would go to jail.

As it turned out, that letter would be very useful. At a hearing of the Westerly draft board a year later, Steve was given a national security deferment because Dad could prove that we were useful assets to the country as a singing group and he could show that Stephen, as the bass section, was indispensable to the existence of the Burke Family Singers. That's how we were able to keep Steve with us and away from Vietnam.

We didn't want him to go. I didn't want him to go mostly because he was my oldest brother and I didn't want him to go anywhere. I also didn't want the Singers to break up. But there was something else—something that felt "sneaky" about this thing in Vietnam.

In 1964 the war was just beginning to really escalate. The Gulf of Tonkin incident and the U.S. bombing of North Vietnam that followed it were just a few months away. There was talk of Eisenhower's domino theory and Truman's broad containment policy that committed the U.S. to stopping any Communist advances anywhere in the free world—but even at twelve, I wondered, how could we stop the rise of communism every place in the world? I also wondered why we needed to send 16,000 military advisors over there. Couldn't a hundred advisors go over there, split up and give the South Vietnamese people advice?

This war wasn't like World War II. My mother's brother, my Uncle Red, died in St. Lo on the first day of the siege of Normandy. I never met him and I'm sorry I didn't get that chance but I never wondered why he went to France. After watching documentaries about Hitler and listening to Mother talk about the war, it was clear that Hitler had to be stopped. Vietnam was not clear at all. We didn't know what it was about. They weren't even calling it a war.

An official-looking letter on foreign service stationery arrived about two months after we returned from Canada. It said:

> May 27, 1964
> The Burke Family Singers are ambassadors of
> good will for the United States. I was present on

March 4 of this year when they sang a concert at
Marionapolis College here in Montreal.

By their personality and their singing ability they
won the enthusiastic acclaim of their audience.
They performed with humor and virtuosity.

I am very proud that the United States has produced such a gifted group.

Jerome T. Gaspard
Consul General of the
United States of America

There it was—Steve's ticket out.

Not everybody in the family felt the way I did about that
war. We were just as split as the country was about it. A few
years later, both John and Jim would fight in Vietnam: John in
1967 with the 3rd Battalion, 26th Marines, and Jimmy in 1970
with the Army, 1st Cavalry Division, 7th Cavalry Regiment.

When John got back, he let his hair grow out, wore an
orange-and-yellow dashiki that said "Nirvana" all over it and
hung out on the corner of Elgin and Hope Streets in Providence for over a year. I didn't recognize him for a while there.
He says he doesn't remember much about that time. "You
know what they say, Sare—if you remember the '60s, you
weren't really there."

Jimmy was about halfway through his tour of the bush in
Vietnam when he developed a bad toothache and was sent to
the rear area in Quan Loi to get it pulled. By that time he had
been in a few good firefights, so when he saw a big re-up sign
that promised a month's leave effective immediately if you

signed up for another hitch, he looked long and hard at it. He thought if he re-enlisted: 1) Chances were good that Walter wouldn't have to go to Nam. (At that time you couldn't have two brothers in combat at the same time.) It was 1970 and by the time he'd have finished his second stint, maybe the war would be winding down and Walt wouldn't have to go; 2) Maybe if he re-upped, he'd be able to pick a job and if he could do that, something like clerk/typist sounded real nice; and 3) If he re-enlisted, he could go *home* for a month and he could do it right now.

He wrote a letter to Mum and Dad explaining what he was going to do and why (a letter Mother kept, of course) and assured them that no, he hadn't lost his mind. Soon after the letter arrived, he came home for his leave.

Ten days into it while fishing at Waterman Lake in Greenville, Jimmy became seriously ill. It turned out that at least two mosquitoes back in Nam had swapped some of their malaria virus for some of his blood and now he had two of the worst reoccurring strains; vivax and, they discovered a few weeks later, falciparum. Chills, fever, anemia, vomiting and diarrhea. He spent three and a half months at the Newport Naval Hospital, got down to skin and bones and nearly died.

As it turned out, Walt's lottery number was 101 and he never got drafted. Jimmy never went back to Nam. He finished out his time in Indiantown Gap, Pennsylvania. John made it to Woodstock—and doesn't remember much about that, either. And I went to the anti-war demonstrations at Brown University and later on "inherited" John's orange and yellow dashiki.

*   *   *

But in 1964 Monsieur Gaspard's letter held off the draft board and Steve was allowed to sing and drive CREDO some more. I, for one, was very happy to study the back of his neck as we moved over the miles. As we left Montreal and headed for Trois Rivieres, there were fewer and fewer signs in English. I wondered how we were going to be able to communicate, but Dad was fearless with his college French. In Trois Rivieres we performed on a French television program and on French radio and on both occasions, Dad made all the introductions and announcements in French.

He only blew it once. We were all sitting in a French restaurant and Dad decided he wanted a cup of coffee. He flagged down the waitress and she came over.

"Sanka cafe, s'il vous plait," he said.

The waitress looked confused.

"Cinq cafe, monsieur?" she asked.

"Oui, Sanka cafe," Dad said and smiled confidently up at her.

"Oui, monsieur," she sighed and off she went.

She came back holding a tray with five cups of coffee on it and set them all down in front of Dad. His mouth dropped open.

"Cinq cafe, monsieur," she said and walked away.

We were falling out of our seats. Mother thought it was so funny that she wrote it up for Reader's Digest and they published it in their Canadian magazine.

We got home from the Canadian tour on March 10th and had a short breather before singing concerts on March 14th,

15th, 16th and 17th in various places in Massachusetts. Because they were on or around Saint Patrick's Day, we sang more Irish songs than usual. The girls wore white chiffon knee-length dresses with full skirts and Kelly green chiffon sashes that hung from one shoulder, tucked in at the waist and then flowed down to the hem. We looked very Irish. This was easy. We *were* very Irish. And this St. Patrick's Day we were planning a little surprise.

For the past year when we weren't traveling, Gemma, Annie and I took Irish step dancing lessons. I picked up a few of the steps but when I was told to stand erect, move nothing from the waist up and stare straight ahead when I danced, I often had trouble keeping my balance. I needed to see what my feet were doing, to visually direct them. If I stared straight ahead and left my feet to their own devices, God only knew what they'd come up with. It was clear that I was not ready to perform as a dancer. This did not get me off the hook, however. Jigs could and should be played on flutes, my father said. "I'm not ready!" I cried. "Sure you are," he said and passed sheet music to me.

It was a jig called "The Old Clay Pipe." I worked my tail off and tried to figure out where I was going to be able to breathe, how I would play all the notes that fast while keeping a steady rhythm and not faint. This was not a violin I was playing; I had to breathe in order to produce sound and that is a very big difference between me and a fiddle player. Someone who plays a mouth instrument could drop dead before they get enough air. Fiddle players have it easy. So do piano players.

I was explaining all this to my father. I was leading up to

the "Maybe we could take it a little slower" question. "No," he said, "They won't be able to dance to it if it's too slow." Then he took the metronome off the top of the piano, set it to a medium tempo and said, "When you can play it with no mistakes, set it a little faster. Keep doing that until you can play it this fast" and then he pointed way, *way* down on the dial and left the room. Our theory session was over.

And so it was just Annie and Gemma who got out there and step danced a jig on St. Patrick's Day for the Catholic Women's Club in Weymouth, Massachusetts. Dad played "The Old Clay Pipe" on the piano. I played the flute—softly. Coughed once. Got lost, then came in again on the next section while Gem and Annie danced. They were doing pretty well, too—until Gemma's shoe came off. It wasn't a shoe, really, and that was the problem. They wore strapless gold slippers with pointed toes. Unfortunately, strapless slippers are not the ideal shoe for the high kicking which is part of Irish step dancing.

Halfway through the dance, Gem kicked out and off came the slipper. I'm sure the moment was not one of the high points in her life, but to her credit, she kept on dancing until the jig was over.

I was standing over at the piano next to Dad and I could see the shoe fly. I also saw the line of family standing behind the dancers—just standing there watching. When that shoe flew, the stakes on keeping a straight face shot up considerably. I saw the frozen smiles and the slightly bug-eyed, concentrated stares focused dead ahead. Standing in that performance line was often like being in a pressure cooker. One look at another family member and it would have been all over—we'd be rolling in the aisles. We all got through it, but it was the first and the last step dancing performance by the Burke girls. It was not, however, the last time I had to blow all the fast jig notes, stealing breath where I could to catch the relentless rhythms of my piano-playing father.

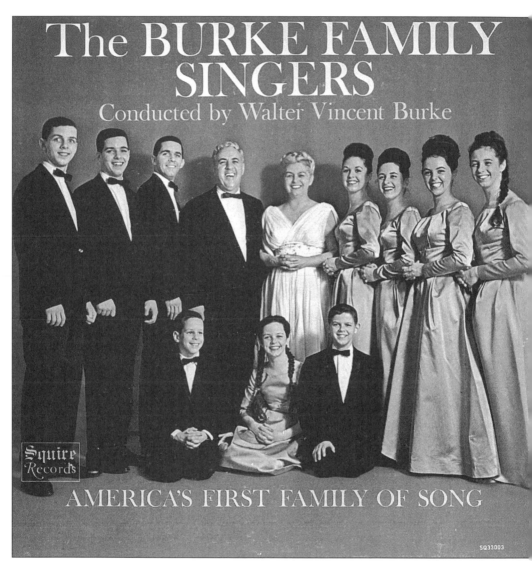

The BURKE FAMILY
SINGERS

Conducted by Walter Vincent Burke

Squire
Records

AMERICA'S FIRST FAMILY OF SONG

SQ33003

March 1964

CHAPTER 22

America's First
Family of Song

AFTER OUR ST. PATRICK'S Day performance, we went back to school for another two weeks and then took off again for a month. It was Monday, March 30, 1964, and this time we were setting out on our first full Southern tour.

Before we headed south of the Mason-Dixon line, we were going to New York City to record our first album. We drove to the City Squire and pulled the cars into the underground parking lot where they would stay until Friday.

The bell captain recognized us immediately. He spotted

Walter and smiled weakly. Walt looked pretty much the same. His feet continued to grow but that was all. Mother wondered about his slow development, too. Around the end of the tour, she made this note: "April 24th—Today is Walter's birthday. He is a terrible teenager now and so short it's hard to believe."

But you had to believe him because there he was, standing just inside the revolving doors, grinning expectantly, ready to see what he could get into, ready to take on anybody. The bell captain sighed and then walked over to help with our bags.

We went to Fine Studios and recorded sixteen songs over the next four days. It was hard work. We sang each song once through first so that the technicians could set levels and then tried to totally tune in and get it right the first time they recorded. This did not happen often and some of the songs had many "takes" before Dad felt they were worth listening to on playback. After a while, it was hard to hear what sounded right and what was wrong, and there were points when I wanted to scratch my scalp real hard or step on Peter's foot, bend Annie's arm back or give Walt a karate chop to the back of the neck.

It was dry in there; hot, tense and sweaty. We had to concentrate for hours at a time. And sometimes we sang a song beautifully but there was a problem on the technical end and Fred Christie, the engineer, said we needed to do it over and I'd think to myself, "Oh man! We'll never be able to do it like that again!" But we did it again and over the next four days, Dad got to know when it was time to quit for the day by reading our fried little faces.

The album was recorded on Squire Records, a new record label that we shared with Joan Baez and a few others. It was titled *The Burke Family Singers* and under the full-sized laughing picture of all of us were the words, *America's First Family of Song*. The boys wore tuxedoes, the girls blue-and-yellow satin gowns and most of us had to take our shoes off so we wouldn't scuff or rip the deep red paper that was used as the background. It was a great picture—except that Annie's toes are showing under her gown.

The album came out at the end of June. The Jordan Marsh Company took out a good-sized ad in the *Boston Sunday Herald* with a picture of the album cover and told everybody they were selling it for $2.77 in mono and $3.67 for a stereo record. Ruth Tripp wrote a review in the *Providence Journal* and called the record a "worthwhile release." And though she felt "America the Beautiful is one of the most effective songs, the Irish folk music unusually graceful and valid," she thought "Mr. Burke's arrangement of the Brahms Lullaby is slightly ornate and to a purist, the introduction of harmonies other than those of Brahms is not welcome." Actually, I liked that arrangement of Brahms Lullaby. We always sang it at the very end of a concert—after sometimes four encores. Dad introduced it as the song that began in the Burke family as a solo, and then he'd ask the audience to sing it with us. And they did, usually in full voice. They made a sea of sound out there in the dark, all warmed up now and easy and ready to sing. They soared on the melody while we sang those close harmonies under them, people in the front rows smiling as they sang the sweet lullaby, tucking each other in and then off home to bed. It *is* possible to hug a thousand people good night.

*   *   *

We left New York and set off on our third tour. Dad and Steve drove, Florrie navigated, Mum took notes and Gemma was the accounting department, tallying every single receipt: food, motel, gas, snacks and sundries—right down to a seven-cent doughnut. She didn't mess around. Even on that first tour when we drove away from an apple stand, abandoning her at a nearby gas station, she came out of the ladies' room looking for the cherry cider receipts. Dad counted on her to gather and itemize figures for the tax man and Gem took care of business.

When she wasn't tallying receipts, she was an active participant in the heady diversions of the CREDO crowd. This particular morning she was coming up with "Which twin has the Toni?" It was another CREDO word game. The point was to either name or sing out every advertising blurb you could think of and Mother and Gem were going back and forth in a verbal tennis match:

"Which twin has the Toni?"

"Good to the last drop—Maxwell House"

"Children cry for it—Castoria"

"Wouldn't you rather drive a Buick?"

"Ajax, the foaming cleanser" (Annie chimed in with that one.)

"99/100% pure—Ivory" (That was Steve.)

"I'd sooner Lipton"

"Take tea and see"

"Babies are our only business—Gerbers"

On it went. I nearly blew a gasket trying to come up with a slogan, but I just wasn't quick enough. Anyway, who could think with all those words flying around the car?

This was our first Southern tour but it could have been

called our "Tennessee tour," because we went back and forth over the Great Smoky Mountains singing concerts in Milligan, Gallatin, Harriman, Morristown, Fayetteville, Cookeville and McMinneville. With so many concerts in the same state, we didn't have long distances to drive. This meant less push and more time for sightseeing.

Outside of McMinnville we saw a sign that read. "MARTIN FARM—TENNESSEE WALKING HORSES." Dad decided to turn onto the dirt farm road and Steve followed. We met the trainer and the owners of a beautiful three-year-old Walker named G's Merry Boy. Dad, who never arrived empty-handed, blew a note on his trusty pitchpipe and we sang "Dixie." The three of them were grinning from ear to ear by the end of it. Then the trainer said, "Would you like to see what this horse can do?"

"We sure would!"

I never saw a horse move the way that one did. His head bobbed up and down and his two front legs moved in a high-stepping strut while the back two followed in a different step. The trainer never allowed the horse to break into a run but controlled him until G's Merry Boy hit a new stride: a speed that was more than a trot, maybe less than a canter and mostly like gliding. He sailed over the pasture with incredible power and grace. What a thing it was to see—and I got to stand behind the fence and watch instead of sitting in a Holy Name classroom.

We took a trip down into the Tuckaleechee Caverns in Townsend, Tennessee, 450 feet under a mountain and saw stalactites and stalagmites. It was eerie and old and beautiful, and it sure beat looking at the picture in my Physical Science book.

Our next stop was the birthplace of Davy Crockett in Limestone, Tennessee. I don't know what happened in that gift shop, but we went crazy buying souvenirs. Gem and Marty bought tall, patched, black-felt hillbilly hats, I picked out an Indian drum and Walt and Pete talked Mother into buying them raccoon hats. Walt pushed for a corncob pipe, too, and got it.

While everyone modeled their accessories, Jimmy grabbed his rod and reel and his tackle box and was casting out into the stream behind Davy Crockett's log cabin. Jimmy never missed an opportunity to fish, no matter how little time he had. He developed his own "catch and release" program before it became fashionable. There was neither the time nor the facilities to cook what he caught, so he let the fish go.

Jim was a great fisherman, but he had a sick mind. As we in CREDO pulled alongside SONGS, we saw him sitting in the back seat with a large orange lure hooked to the left side of his lower lip. His head tilted to one side, mouth hung open and unblinking eyes stared straight ahead. Jim would do almost anything for a laugh.

. . . a '60s fashion statement

CHAPTER 23

"I'm a Mormon, Too!"

THERE WAS NO CLOWNING around during our visit to Andrew Jackson's home, "The Hermitage," near Nashville. We toured the mansion, the Cotton Patch, Uncle Alfred's Cabin and the surrounding cabins for two hours. We read the placards, studied the furniture and the utensils in the roped-off rooms and learned a little about how people lived in the early the 1800s: people with a lot of money and people with none.

We stood in the front rooms and sang "Dixie" and "America the Beautiful" for a busload of touring high school students and though we'd sung those songs many times before, it felt different singing them here. There was so much history in these rooms—and as we sang, we couldn't help but be aware of new history being made in the present civil rights struggle happening around the country.

Besides the sightseeing, we were singing a concert tour and that was going quite well, too. The first thing we had to get over was auditoriums full of people standing up for "Dixie" like it was their national anthem. They stood at every concert we sang in the South. The first time it happened we were taken totally by surprise. Dad played about twelve notes of introduction on the piano and then Steve began singing his solo, "I wish I was in the land of cotton, old times there are not forgotten..." He got as far as "I wish" and suddenly, we heard the sound of more than fifteen hundred people getting up from their seats. We thought they were leaving and Dad turned around, but Steve kept on singing, so the rest of us joined him on the chorus. I'm sure we looked as surprised as we felt.

That was one powerful song. When we sang "Dixie" at George & Dave's Restaurant in Gallatin, Tennessee, Dave tore up the bill and it was after we sang "Dixie" in Rock City, Georgia, that a very dignified old white lady slowly approached us.

She was wearing an elegant, broad-brimmed straw hat and walked with the help of a silver-headed cane. Everything about her was unhurried. She came to a stop in front of Mum and Dad, leaned forward with both hands on the cane in front of her and looked directly at them as she drawled, "Well...I can't tell you how good it does this old Southern heart of mine—to hear you *damn* Yankees singin' 'Dixie.'" We all laughed, but we knew she meant it.

It was a different world down South. One morning I ordered eggs for breakfast. I was about to tell the waitress how I wanted them, but as soon as she heard me say "eggs," she ran a whole bunch of words together, tossed them my way and then looked at me expectantly. It was clear that she was waiting for a response, but I had no idea what she'd said. I stared at her for a moment while I mentally played back the sounds she had just made trying to decipher a meaning. "I'm sorry. Would you mind saying that again?" I asked.

"Scatidsmuthidacovid" is what I heard for the second time. But I had no idea what it meant. Again, I asked her to repeat herself. After the third time, I could see she was getting impatient. Finally I said, "What does that mean?"

She broke the words up. I imitated her. We began to communicate. The first word was "scattered," which meant "Would you like scrambled eggs?" The second word was "smothered," which meant "Want those eggs smothered in onions?" The third word was "and/or" and the fourth word was "covered," which meant "How about having those eggs with melted cheese on top?"

Now I understood! I told her I wanted my eggs sunnyside up and on toast. She squinted at me, wrote something on her little green pad and called over to the cook, "Eyebahlson-points!" Oatmeal. I should have ordered oatmeal.

The expressions were unique and colorful below the Mason-Dixon line and so were the attitudes. There was no doubt that these Southern states were united with each other, but it wasn't clear just how united they wanted to be with their northern neighbors and this question of allegiance came out in their dry-as-dust humor. For instance, there was the time when we returned to the motel after our trip to the Tuckaleechee Caverns and found Steve, who had asked to stay behind to study, talking with the motel owners. They liked him so much, they said, that "he's the first Yank they'd run for Vice President."

We had come to the South during a time of intense civil rights struggle and so we saw some of the worst and the best of people. Their world was changing and they were scared and some were angry. After a hundred years, they were again being invaded by the North as busloads of volunteers traveled South to help with voter registration. They were friendly and defensive and so we sought out not the differences but the similarities between us.

We wanted to connect with people, black and white. That's why we kept singing "Dixie" and "America the Beautiful" and the medley of Negro spirituals ("Go Tell It On The Mountain," "Mary Had A Baby" and "Behold That Star") at every concert. We sang them together because we wanted to bring people together—people of different attitudes, religions, colors and cultures. We knew it was working when a smiling ten-year-old girl approached my mother during an after-concert reception in Gallatin, Tennessee, and whispered up to her confidentially, "I'm a Mormon, too!"

I wouldn't say we were a very political family. We were down there to sing concerts and we mostly concentrated on what we were there to do. There was one time, though, that my father made a very clear stand.

I don't remember what town it was but we were in one of

those small Ma-and-Pa type restaurants. I know it was in a town where we were going to sing that night because there were posters of us in the restaurant. The proprietor spotted the capes and recognized us at once. He seemed thrilled that we were going to have lunch at his place and was all smiles as he bustled us into booths and gave us menus. While we were looking at them, my father noticed a black man approach the counter and sit down. I noticed him, too. The owner went over to him and spoke softly. The black man seemed upset and got up to leave. The owner looked nervous when he saw Dad watching.

Dad got up and walked over to the counter. He wasn't speaking in a loud voice but I heard him ask, "Is something wrong over here? Is there a problem?" By now the owner was looking extremely tense and the black guy was watching Dad.

"Mr. Burke, I've told him that we don't serve coloreds here."

Dad looked him in the eye and said calmly, "You don't? Well ... if he's not good enough to eat here, I don't think we're good enough to eat here either." And with that he called over to all of us, twelve prospective meals and a little something the guy could talk about over coffee tomorrow morning, "C'mon, kids. We're leaving." We all got up and left.

But that was unusual. It was uncommon for us to witness such overt racism. People were nervous and careful about what they said. If we noticed racism at all, it was of the more subtle variety—like the reporting of the Academy Awards.

We didn't have a concert that night so the five of us girls holed up in our motel room to watch the Academy Awards on TV and did what most Americans were doing: ogling the stars, voting on dresses, commenting on hairdos, makeup and people's weight, and hoping to catch someone in outrageous behavior. We were thrilled to see Sidney Poitier walk to the podium to receive his award. We thought he was gorgeous. He had won the Oscar for Best Actor for his role in *Lilies of the Field*. We never would have known it if we hadn't seen it, though.

In the car the next morning, we listened to the news on a Knoxville radio station. There was no mention of Sidney Poitier. The reporter announced that the movie *Tom Jones* had received the award for Best Picture and that Patricia Neal won Best Actress for her role in *Hud*. Then they went on to other news. We stared stupidly at the radio and then at each other. That was the end of the announcement. No Best Actor.

There was one other incident that stands out in my mind during that first Southern tour. That's because it was the only time that they all drove off and left *me* behind at a gas station—about halfway down Lookout Mountain in Chattanooga, Tennessee.

We had just come from a tourist attraction called Rock City at the top of Lookout Mountain and I admit I was still somewhat dazed from the experience. The others in CREDO must have been in the same shape because they didn't notice my absence for quite some time. Anyone who has driven up that particular mountain needs no further explanation. But for those who haven't made the trek, forwarned is forearmed.

Rock City was truly a tourist event. We began to see the first painted signs for Rock City on barns and billboards about five hundred miles away and we kept on seeing them. We saw so many SEE ROCK CITY signs that we, like everyone else, figured that it must *really* be something to see. Rock City was a monument to the power of advertising.

After a long, punishing climb up the mountain, twisting around hairpin turns and often driving almost straight up in a vertical line, we pulled the two over-heated station wagons into the parking lot where they joined many other wheezing and clicking vehicles. Locking the doors behind us, we eagerly set off to see this fabulous city.

We entered the city and stopped, momentarily stunned by the sound of at least four melodies going on at once and the sight of hundreds of small bearded figurines. There were statues of dwarfs everywhere: dwarfs mining in a sparkling cave of calcite and druse crystals; dwarf wives and children playing by small waterfalls. There was the "Dwarf Grist Mill" and a big room called "The Hall of the Mountain King" where dwarfs in red and green pointed hats were gathered in large numbers to drink from casks of beer and toast each other to Bavarian music.

In the "Fairyland Caverns" there were miniature scenes taken from "Goldilocks and the Three Bears," "Cinderella" and "Snow White and the Seven Dwarfs," each and every scene set to its own canned fairy tale music. There was also the "Gnome's Overpass" featuring a fishpond with a small rock bridge—and that was just inside.

Outside were narrow rock pathways with small rock walls built on either side to keep all the tourists on the same track. We weren't alone. Many others had followed the SEE ROCK CITY signs.

The path hugged the side of the mountain and as it curved, we saw live deer fenced in below us. There was a swinging bridge that took the weary traveler to Lover's Leap. Once there, you could jump (which, at that point, was probably a real temptation for many of the tourists) or you could look out over seven states: Alabama, Georgia, Tennessee, Kentucky, Virginia, North Carolina and South Carolina.

That's what they claimed. Of course, we didn't know *where* each state was, really. The day was clear, but nothing was marked. As I looked out over the horizon, I was hoping to see border signs or maybe little colored flags waving gaily along the edge of each state. I studied the vista slowly. There *was* something out there... way out... far below in the distance. It was a sign. Squinting, I could just make it out. SEE ROCK CITY.

As we headed down Lookout Mountain, Steve checked the fuel gauge and signaled Dad that CREDO needed gas. Both cars pulled into a station about halfway down. Business was booming. The cars that weren't at the pumps were resting. I had to use the bathroom so I walked around to the other side of the building.

I was met with three doors. One read LADIES, another read GENTLEMEN and the third read COLORED.

Being the know-it-all twelve-year-old that I was, I didn't hesitate and chose Door Number Three. When I came out, the gas station attendant was waiting for me.

He yelled, "Can't you read?"

I assured him that I could.

"You must be from the North," he sneered.

"I am," I shot back, "and I think this is disgusting!" I gave him a few more pieces of my mind and was preparing to make a righteous exit into the arms of my big supportive family when

I noticed that the cars were gone. I moved to the edge of the road and began to reassess the situation. The attendant was very angry and I was very much alone. It was a full half-hour before those two station wagons returned and found an unrepentant but rather subdued little girl waiting for them on the curb.

We sang our last concert of the tour on a Monday night in Sylacauga, Alabama, and the next morning headed north toward home. By early Thursday afternoon, we had reached the Washington D.C. area and Dad asked us if we wanted to stop at Arlington National Cemetery to visit President Kennedy's grave. We did. It was five months after his assassination and the middle of a workday, so we thought we'd have the place to ourselves. We were wrong. We were just a small part of a very long quiet line filing past the roped-off grave and the eternal flame. An eternal flame. I couldn't grasp the permanence of the word. I watched it that April of 1964 and wondered how long it would really burn.

We had two more concerts that month: one at John Hancock Hall in Boston and the last one of the season on April 30th at a college in Chicopee, Massachusetts. It was Annie's fourteenth birthday and we surprised her by singing for her at the beginning of the second half of the concert. Four parts crooned "Happy Birthday, dear Annie" and "How old are you now?" and she stood there looking out, and then to one side and the other and then down at her feet, grinning the whole time.

Dad's hand on Pete—family room, 1962

New York World's Fair—Bell Telephone Pavillion, August 1964

CHAPTER 24

Just Regular Kids

WE TOOK THE SUMMER off. This meant that although we still had weekly rehearsals, we didn't have any concerts so we could turn up the flame under the saucepan labeled "just regular kids," let it boil over a little if we wanted to, while the kettle of singers whistled softly on the back burner. For instance, I now had time to fashion my own version of a corncob pipe. I had been coveting Walter's prize from the Davy Crockett birthplace gift shop for a good couple of weeks, and after offering to trade just about everything but my body parts, I finally realized that the only way I was going to own a pipe was to make one myself. Materials were not too much of a problem. We didn't have any cornfields in my neighborhood but we *did* have horse chestnut trees.

First, I carved a small bowl in just the right-sized chestnut. Size was important. Before I cut into it, I tested it, letting it rest on my bent middle finger while curving my index finger and thumb around it to see if it had just the right feel. After carving another small hole into its side, I inserted a hollow twig from a strange large bush that grew on the far corner of our backyard.

I loved that bush. The branches grew up from the root and stalks and then draped over the sides of it leaving a great hiding space inside. I often sat inside this bush to think undisturbed and to observe others unseen. Actually, three could fit under that bush without being discovered and there were times when Walt, Peter and I held council under those leaves. Sometimes Dolores "Tay" Taylor and I met there to discuss what was on our twelve-year-old minds. It was a great place. I don't know what kind of bush it was, but it was the only kind I knew that had hollow branches—just perfect for drawing in pipe smoke.

Unfortunately, there was no pipe tobacco available. There were, however, plenty of cigarette butts on the sidewalk and for a while there, I kept the streets clean.

One late afternoon that bush looked like it was about to catch fire. Smoke poured out through the top of it. If Mother had looked out the kitchen window while she was preparing supper, she would've either called the fire department or run down there, kicked off her shoes and fallen to her knees waiting for God to speak. It's a good thing she didn't look out the window and run down to the burning bush because "God" was coughing quite a bit at that point. By the time I was called in for supper, I was looking pretty green and feeling not at all hungry. As soon as I sat down, Annie said, "God! It smells like smoke in here!" and though Mother's watchful gaze rested on me, she said nothing. When I mumbled that I didn't feel well and asked to be excused early from the table, she just nodded. I made it to the third-floor bathroom where I clung to the toilet bowl and vowed to give up pipes forever.

On August 24th we were back at it. After a local appearance on the *Jay Kroll TV Show* in the afternoon, we drove to North Conway, New Hampshire for an outdoor evening concert at the Skimobile. It was a cool night with a full moon and a mountain backdrop. The microphones were good and easily carried our voices out to the large crowd sitting under the stars on a patchwork of blankets.

Two days later we drove to the City Squire in New York City and spent probably the busiest six days of our singing career. None of us (Walt, included) could get into too much trouble at the hotel because there just wasn't the time. We posed for pictures until our smiles hurt. We gave interviews, recorded a Christmas album on the Squire label, auditioned for Radio City Music Hall and, at the request of the State Department, gave a concert in the United States Pavilion at the World's Fair in New York.

Dad was having the time of his life. Since Peace Dale days he had used the same yellow legal-sized pads. Back then, it was to organize household chores, list errands or record the names of doctors and money owed. Now he was writing out concert programs and schedules of a very different kind. Mother, thinking that these particular yellow sheets might be interesting to look at later on, pulled them out from under one of the six piles of sheet music on top of Dad's piano and stuck them in a file cabinet. Good ole Mum.

6 Days in New York City

Wed. Aug. 26, 1964

12 noon–3 P.M.   Interview with Sidney Fields, syndicated columnist of the N. Y. Daily News. *1½ hrs. with photographers.*

4–5:30 P.M.   Interview with Clementine Paddleford, the syndicated Home Economics editor of N.Y. Herald Tribune *and* This Week *magazine. An hour with photographers.*

7–9 P.M.   Rehearsal

Thurs. Aug. 27

12:30 P.M.   Dinner guests of the Americana Hotel Mgr. More photogs. in main dining room.

2 P.M.–3 P.M.   Public relations appt. on 5th floor patio for N.Y. Herald Tribune. *More pictures.*

6–11:30 P.M.   Recording session at Fine Studios for Squire Records. Exhausting and very successful.

Fri. Aug. 28

11:30 A.M.–12:30 P.M.   Luncheon appt. with Fr. Wal-

ter Abbott of America magazine at City Squire
Hotel.

2 P.M.–3 P.M. Audition at Radio City Music Hall
with the producer, Russell Markert, the conductor, Raymond Paige, the director, Mr. Leonidoff,
etc. They want us for Radio City Music Hall appearances.

3:30 P.M. Interview with Frank Bowers of Earl Wilson's staff (Earl Wilson—Traveler Broadway
Columnist)

4–5 P.M. Radio interview with Barbara Gold at Station WNCN-FM radio.

5:30–5:45 P.M. Audition at Fine Studio for Columbia
Concert Artists Assoc.

5:45–11:30 P.M. Second recording session.

Sat. Aug. 29

12 noon–7 P.M. Work on Copyrights and Credits for
the record album (by Dad) in hotel room.

7:30 P.M. Whole family except Dad are guests of the
Music Director of Radio City Music Hall,
Raymond Paige. He took them all through the
tremendous building and showed the maze of elevators, lighting, etc., etc.

Sun. Aug. 30

9–9:45 A.M. Mass at St. Patrick's Cathedral.

11–12:30 P.M. (at World's Fair) Gave concert in color
television at the R.C.A. Pavilion.

*1–2 P.M.   Were guests of the Public Relations Dept. of
    the Bell Telephone System at their unusual booth
    (shaped like a huge egg), many photogs. Children
    made call to grandparents in Boston.*

*4–5 P.M.   Full concert at the United States Pavilion
    at the invitation of the State Dept.*

Mon. Aug. 31

*9 A.M.–12:30 P.M.   Dad works at Squire Records on
    program and liner notes & art work for cover.*

2 P.M.   Leave for home.

We had a lot to think about on that four-hour ride home, especially Dad. He was thinking about his kids living in a New York hotel for a six-week stint while they sang four shows a day, five days a week at Radio City Music Hall. What would that kind of exposure to New York City do to the kids? And what about school? Commercially speaking, he'd be crazy not to take the offer. The publicity would be incredible—but was this the right direction to go? Would they ask us to sing popular music? Maybe we should continue to focus on the college tours, singing for schools and art series. As long as we were getting TV exposure on some shows like *Mike Douglas*, we'd stay in the public eye and be able to get bookings for concert tours.

And as he thought about television exposure, his attention shifted to another piece of news and settled there. Bob Allen from the National Council of Catholic Men (the group who had sponsored our first national television appearance on *Look Up and Live*) had shown up at the recording studio on Thursday night and asked if we'd like to appear on a Christmas Eve nationwide broadcast with Maria von Trapp at the family lodge in Stowe, Vermont. And they want to call the show *The Sound of Christmas*. Geez. Singing with the Trapps. Now *there* was a piece of news! He didn't have to think long about that offer. He had listened to and admired the Trapp family sound for years and was delighted with the idea of us singing with some of them.

Cruising up Route 95 toward Providence, he mentally scanned the events of the past few days. What a marathon. Sidney Fields had written a great column in the *Daily News*. And Earl Wilson had done a nice article, too. And what about those people from Columbia Artists who heard us Friday night at the studio? Five men and one woman. They seemed to like us, but we'll see what they tell Buck.

His thoughts drifted, lighting on images that stayed for a moment and then moved on. Representing the United States, the kids fooling around at the RCA Pavilion... "See yourself on color television"... images of the girls in blue and green brocaded dresses and their hair in buns or braids, young Walter carrying a bag of tuxedoes over his shoulder and mangling them. He's going to turn into a monkey if he keeps making that face. Short thoughts and fleeting pictures came and went inside his tired, happy head as he rode up the freeway toward Providence.

The decision about Radio City Music Hall was a pivotal one (if not *the* pivotal one) in our singing career and I think Dad was aware of its significance even then. I think he consciously chose not to get us involved with big fame. He was afraid of its demands and the interference it would cause in our individual lives. He was afraid of the wolves, the moral danger in an arena that size. We were his and Mother's charge and they decided not to risk us.

Dad said no to Russell Markert and Raymond Paige at Radio City and not long after, Buck called and said that the group from Columbia Artists had decided not to take us on for tours. There was so much going on at the time that we didn't think a lot about either decision. We had tours ahead of us: another Midwest tour booked in October, a second Southern tour in the spring of 1965 and a far west/Canadian tour for that autumn. The Christmas album would soon be coming out, we had the Trapp special coming up and a local Christmas TV Special. Jack Paar had invited us to appear on his Easter show and Mike Douglas wanted us for a third show. We were pretty busy—and someplace in the middle of all that, we were supposed to be good students.

The students in the family now were Steve and the youngest six of us—John, Jim, Annie, Walt, me and Pete. Marty, Florrie and Gemma had graduated from high school and were working at Rhode Island Hospital, Fireman's Mutual Insurance Company and Hospital Trust Bank, respectively. The people they worked for seemed to be very understanding about giving them time off from work. I'm not sure why, but these employers seemed to work around the girls' schedules.

Steve was beginning his senior year at Providence College and looking at the University of Connecticut's School of Social Work in Hartford for graduate studies in psychiatric social work. He was quiet in nature and inclined to be analytical. God knows he had enough test subjects all around him. One day he said to Mother, "I think I've got this family figured out. You, Sarah and I run at 33 1/3 RPM. Dad, Florrie and John run at 78 RPM and the rest of the family at 45!" I don't know. I would've included Marty and maybe Walt with the 78s. In fact, that whole SONGS car was strung pretty tight, if you ask me.

Then there were the rest of us traveling students. Me and my buddy, Dramamine, were doing very nicely together. My love for stories, coupled with my desire to get away from everyone else in the family as often as possible, turned me into quite an avid reader. "I vant to be alone!" I moaned with Greta Garbo. At home in the wintertime, I sat on the couch in the den with the fire blazing, curled up with a good book and was transported for hours at a time. At the beginning of summer, I was happy to take on the twelve-to-twenty-book reading list that the Holy Name nuns provided. On tour, I took half a Dramamine a day, which meant I could read in the car. I was set. The other kids weren't doing so hot.

For one thing, they got sick in the car when they tried to read, and for another thing, they mostly didn't try to read. They weren't inclined. They excelled in some subjects, but in general, I think they saw school as something they had to get through. They had other interests, like talking, baking or drawing, dancing, playing Scrabble, football, basketball, or developing relationships with the opposite sex.

Jim was full of extra-curricular activities. The family survived his chemistry set phase relatively unscathed. There was one minor explosion followed by a real nasty smell that emanated from his third-floor bedroom and eventually floated to every part of the house. I believe he was working with sulphur at the time.

Then there was his priest phase, when he turned his bureau into an altar and said Mass using a scarf for a stole and Sunbeam bread, smashed down flat and cut into little circles, for hosts. Walt and Pete were the two altar boys and I was the congregation.

One afternoon Mum heard four voices singing antiphonal responses in sloppy Latin high above her. She came up to the third floor to investigate and found Jim piously officiating in dress pants, shoes and covered from shoulder to calf in a surplice-type bed sheet and scarf. Mother explained that as much as she *loved* the idea of us playing "Mass," maybe it would be better if we saved it for when the real priest said it over at Holy Name. She was probably afraid of what new rituals we'd develop on that altar.

And there was always fishing. Late at night, Jim and Walt and sometimes Pete would sneak out to the backyard with flashlights to gather nightcrawlers for the next fishing expedition. One Friday night after a particularly successful campaign, they put a pickle jar full of the fat, slimy worms into the fridge and though they remembered to put holes in the jar lid, they forgot to screw it on. The next morning when Mum opened the refrigerator, she found at least forty nightcrawlers doing what they do best—crawling and leaving a slime trail all over the walls, the food, the grills, everything. Mother laughed about it ... later.

Between the extra-curricular activities, the disrupting travel and the fact that the School Sisters of Notre Dame did not give marks away, the young Burkes' school record was not fabulous. It was not horrible but it was not fabulous.

School started up again and for September and most of October, we were back in class. I enjoyed school but when it came time to leave for our second Midwest tour, no one had to pry me away from my desk and chair. I took advance work with me and mailed back postcards, book reports, travelogues and other assignments.

We had logged 23,000 miles on the tours so far and we were ready for more. The appeal of getting out of school and seeing more of the country together had not diminished with experience. If anything, it was stronger. This was the time of our lives and we knew it. Well, I knew it. I can't speak for Peter and the others but as I looked around, I knew then that my life was very different from the life of every other 6th grader in my class at Holy Name.

I mention Peter in particular because, though he may not have been fully cognizant of the far-reaching repercussions of this time in his life, he was, in fact, having his own profound thoughts around this time...and Mother was right there with pad in hand.

We had been traveling west for three days and had stopped at Edison's birthplace in Milan, Ohio. After the visit and a nice lunch at the Milan Inn, we got on the road again. Steve was chewing on a toothpick while he drove and Mother was writing something about Edison in one of her little pads when Pete said, "I hope I'm the first to die." Steve glanced over at Mum. Suddenly, there was silence in the car.

"Why, Pete?" Mum asked.

"I don't want to go to anyone's funeral," he said. Steve looked down at him, grinned and came back with, "Well, I don't want to go to *yours!*" Pete thought about that for a moment, then said, "Well, you can suck wind, Steve!" We had to laugh. From the back seat we could barely see the top of his head in the front. Every once in while we got a glimpse into Pete's brain and it was always ... well ... *different* in there.

The next morning we checked out of the Tou Rest Motel in Peru, Illinois, without making our beds (another touring perk) and headed for the motel restaurant, a twelve-seat establishment that went from no-one-home to full house pretty quick. Steve perused the menu, ordered ground hog & eggs with juice and black coffee and headed to the bathroom. Unfortunately, his coffee arrived at the table before he did.

John slid the cup and saucer over to the condiments at the end of the booth and rubbed his hands together. Let's see now. What would Steve like in his coffee? John became a blur of activity. In less than a minute he had concocted a real waker-upper. Salt, lots of pepper, sugar and a little ketchup, A.1. and Tabasco for taste, were all blending nicely in the dark steaming liquid by the time Steve got back to the table.

Steve never had a clue. Not with Jim, John and Florrie sitting in that booth. Not until he spit the coffee back in the cup and all over the table. It wasn't so much that his mouth was contorted and his tongue was trembling and just hangin' out there. We expected that. It was the stupid "Wha-happened?" look on his face and the little frown of confusion that just cracked us up.

We sang our first concert at Graceland College in Lamoni, Iowa. The program was followed by four encores and at least three curtain calls. Time and practice were now players that had joined us in our musical huddle, beefing up the ranks. We were growing into our voices, singing stronger and surer and developing our musical ears as we listened for blend and pitch.

All of us were pretty tired and, after having cheeseburgers and milk at the reception, we fell into bed. The next morning at seven A.M. we discovered that Jim, Walt and Pete had left with the fishing poles. We were ready to leave an hour later and still they hadn't come back. Dad was not pleased and gave Mum "the eye." No words were spoken, but they were having a conversation about the fact that she had prevailed upon him in the matter of taking the fishing poles along in the first place.

We loaded the station wagons that morning and found messages written on the dust of our car windows: "You're great" "We love you" "Come again" and "We crave you the most." We decided that this last message did not come from a music aficionado. Whoever wrote that one was definitely interested in somebody wearing a crew cut.

Jim, Walt and Pete came strolling into the motel just as we were driving out to look for them. Mother wrote: "3 boys return—caught two fish & hell from Dad."

We left Iowa, sang a concert in Mayville, North Dakota, then headed south, stopping for a while in a Minnesota border town called Breckenridge. We sat and waited while 140 railroad cars of the Great Northern line passed by. The low moan of the whistle and the heavy rhythmic click of all that weight passing over the tracks was mesmerizing. Car after car just kept on coming. I hardly ever heard trains in Providence and I never imagined anything so long as this train. I loved how it stopped us. Nothing to do but watch it roll past.

We drove south through Nebraska and down to Kansas for concerts in Newton and McPherson. We were still traveling straight south through Oklahoma toward a concert in George-town, Texas, when we heard the radio announcer report a duel in Wichita. Two men in The Morocco Club shoot each other, one twenty-six-year-old took five bullets and the other, a twenty-year-old, was hit with three bullets and pronounced dead on arrival. It sounded like an old western movie. Two cowboys filling each other with lead. It sounded ridiculous but there it was. The next news item was stranger still. A 15-year-old Wichita Indian boy killed a coyote within city limits, breaking the law, because, he said, the coyote was chasing his cat.

We kept our eyes open, looking out for Colt .45s and wild animals. What we saw as we got into southern Oklahoma were more and more ten-gallon hats, pointy-toed cowboy boots and our first cactus. We stopped at a Buffalo Ranch in Afton, Ok-lahoma, and ate our first (and only) buffalo burgers. (Not even Dramamine could save me an hour later when I moaned, "Steve, stop the car.")

We drove on into Texas and stayed that night at the Ramada Inn in Fort Worth. Jim wanted a ten-gallon hat real bad, so we stopped at a cowboy shop and he came swaggering out of that place wearing a hat that was so high it was difficult to turn his head in the car.

Gemma bought a nifty pair of cowgirl boots and just as we drove over the line into Texas, she took them out of the box and put them on. She was "going native" and this was just her style. Years later, Gemma's ability to acclimate herself to different cultures and surroundings would serve her well as a military wife. While stationed in Naples, she learned to speak Italian, gesture in Italian, cook Italian, drive Italian and basically become Italian. I saw her twice in Italy and if I hadn't known she was one-hundred percent Irish, I would've *sworn* she was Italian.

While living in Hawaii, she took hula and Tahitian dancing lessons, learned to sing some traditional Hawaiian chants and understood the rudiments of that language. When in Maine, she's a Mainer and south of the Mason-Dixon line, her style is definitely Southern. Gemma was and is a chameleon and because I have difficulty adjusting to just about everything, it's a trait I heartily admire. Back in November of 1964 she was simply celebrating Texas. She still had her boots on when we pulled into the Parkway Motel in Georgetown.

It was around two on a hot afternoon. Dad walked in to the motel office to see about the price of an overnight stay. Though we were supposed to stay in the cars while Dad negotiated with the motel owners, John just couldn't resist the urge to play Texas State Trooper.

He came out of SONGS wearing Jim's ten-gallon hat and a pair of sunglasses and chewing on a toothpick. Strutting slowly and officiously over to Steve's open window, he took the hat off, rubbed his hair back with one easy motion, leaned his elbow on the open window, spit on the ground and said, "I'm sorry, suh, but you busted the speed limit back there and I'm afraid I'm gonna hafta tuck it to yuh." With our laughter following him, he sauntered back to SONGS and slipped into the backseat just before Dad came back out.

After singing at Southwestern University, we headed north toward Dallas and got there at lunchtime. We ate at a cafeteria called Gaston's and then took a very sobering ride down Elm Street past the Texas Book Depository. It was not quite a year since the assassination of President Kennedy and I wasn't quite ready to like Dallas.

The next few days we drove north to sing concerts in Fayette, Iowa and Menonomie, Wisconsin, and then headed home to catch our breath before the start of the Christmas season.

1954—What a difference 10 years can make . . .

Burkes with Johannes, Rosemarie, and Maria von Trapp—Trapp Lodge, 1964

CHAPTER 25

"The Burkes Meet
The Trapps"

ONE OF THE FIRST things Mother did after every tour was answer correspondence and write thank-you letters. "Thank you for sending the forgotten tie." "Thank you for sending your record and music. We regret that it is not the kind of music that we sing." "Thanks for the great article in *America* magazine." "Thank you for the Mennonite Hymnal and the wonderful visit. As promised, we are sending our recordings to you." "Sorry, the boys can't come to your wild game dinner ... but I was interested to read of your weaving. For some time now I've thought about buying a loom. What do you use, Doctor? A small company in Providence makes what looks like a very efficient loom from aluminum. We have never done any weaving but thought it would be an interesting family project..."

Weaving! As if we didn't have enough of a family project! My favorite letter was the last of nine in a row. She began with "Dear Mr. Flynn..." and by the last paragraph, she wrote: "Thank you again, Mr. Lynch..." I hope she made up her mind before she sent it.

A week after arriving home from the Midwest, the letters were finished, Thanksgiving dinner was leftovers and the Christmas fruitcakes were made and stored. Mum and her female helpers were about to start in on the Christmas cookies and the Christmas card list, which had grown in proportion to our singing career.

This was a far cry from Peace Dale days, when warm thoughts were hurriedly written, often in pencil, on various inexpensive cards and sent only to relatives and very close friends. Now the cards were all the same and chosen in advance. Five hundred arrived from the printers with "Best Wishes for a Happy and Holy Holiday Season—The Burke Family Singers." Mother, Marty, Florrie and Gemma wrote notes in each of them. They were beautiful. They were elegant. Not a spot of Gerber's fruit or baby formula on any one of them.

Our Christmas album had just come out. It was titled, "The Burke Family Singers Caroling at Christmas" and featured an angle shot of all of us in a xylophone line, from tallest to shortest with Mum and Dad bringing up the rear. The camera caught me in a wide grin and I know why. They had just placed my older brother Walter behind me. The record reviews were very favorable and, apart from the copies Mother kept sending away as gifts, sales were good.

The deadlines for the usual Christmas preparations were pushed up this year because of the CBS special with the Trapps. We had to be at the Trapp lodge in Stowe, Vermont, for a four-day shoot on December 21st. Before that, we had to do all the shopping, cards, baking, catch up with school, take exams and tape another local Christmas television special.

Ready for Christmas or not, we took off for the Trapp lodge in Stowe, Vermont on the afternoon of the 20th. As usual, Dad wanted to get us settled in before everyone else arrived and the place got crazy. Smart idea. It had snowed about seven or eight inches overnight and when we woke up, we were glad that we didn't have to travel.

The snow didn't seem to affect the TV people. Early in the morning on the 21st, the CBS trucks pulled in with their crews. We watched them from the windows as they stepped out into a snowy wonderland. Many looked glad to be out of New York City. They jumped out grinning, lugging all kinds of gear, giving orders to each other, setting up lights and sound equipment, taping down wires. I never saw anything like it. When those trucks pulled in and they started to unload I felt like I was on the movie set of *Christmas in Connecticut* or *Holiday Inn*. Honestly, I was half-waiting for Bing Crosby to jump down from one of them, carrying a pipe and humming to himself. The whole thing felt like magic, like anything could happen.

We knew some of these guys. They were the same ones who worked on the *Look Up and Live* show. And they knew us. They remembered Jim impersonating Walter Brennan and Steve's jokes, Buck's magic tricks and John doing the funky chicken and they greeted us warmly. They were psyched. The Baroness and the Burkes at Christmastime. That lodge was a happenin' place to be.

It was also a beautiful place to be. From the ceilings to the floors, there was wood everywhere—knotty pine, oak and maple. Fine antiques filled every room, some with elegant figures carved in relief, along with sturdy old comfortable couches and stuffed chairs, tapestries, Oriental rugs and lots of plants brought in for the winter, some in hangers and many more lined up in pots along the windows.

On one wall above a long table in the dining room was a very large oil portrait of the Captain, Baron Georg von Trapp, standing at the bow of a ship, looking thoughtfully out to sea or eyeing my strudel, I wasn't sure which. One thing was for sure. Anyone sitting in that dining room wasn't likely to forget about the Baron for long.

The same could be said for the Baroness. The half-hour television special, sponsored by CBS News and the National Council of Catholic Men, was going to be called *The Sound of Christmas,* and the idea was that the Burkes were going to go Christmas caroling at the Baroness's house and then come in for a visit. The producers offered a script to the Baroness but she would have none of it. She wanted to ad lib and, as the papers put it, to have "an informal atmosphere in which she could show the Burkes around the Alpine-style guest lodge—just as though CBS cameras weren't set up for the occasion." From the very beginning, it was quite clear who was running the show and who was used to running the show.

"Ya, unt now ve go!" declared the Baroness and off everybody went.

Walter Burke and Maria von Trapp working together was really something to watch. The power and personal charisma of each of their personalities made their meetings interesting, to say the least. And then there was Anne Devine. Holy Smokes! Sometimes you could just about feel the electricity in the air.

Dad waltzed very smoothly with Maria. He understood that we were on her turf and she'd do it her way and that was just fine with him. He was sincerely thrilled to be there because he had great respect for the Trapp family sound. He knew that for years they were not recognized for their achievement in this country. He understood that the romantic story and the simple, easy-to-sing music that made up the soundtrack for *The Sound of Music* did not reflect the professional caliber of their sound or the real truth of their story. They were a brilliant musical ensemble, not a cute family singing just for the fun of it. Neither were we, for that matter, and singing with them fulfilled one of my father's dreams.

It wasn't long before we were all singing around the Trapps' large kitchen table. Maria sang in the alto section with Gemma on one side and me on the other. Johannes, who was about Gemma's age, was a bass and sang between Dad and Steve. Rosemarie, older than Steve and the only other Trapp child home at the time, would sing with us later.

Dad directed with one hand and he looked like he died and

went to heaven. He couldn't keep the grin off his face and at the end of it, Steve let out a whoop and spontaneously leaned over Johannes to thump Dad on the hand (in a sort of a pre-high five gesture), which made even the shy Johannes chuckle in delight.

Singing together was a wonderful idea. We didn't really know these people. Both Trapp children were very shy and reserved and Maria was polite but tentative. Dad rightly guessed that the best and quickest way for us to warm up to each other was to sing together. Both families knew from years of experience, the power music had to warm and communicate and when he suggested that we all sing "Stiller Nacht" around the table, he knew exactly what he was doing.

For the Trapps it was clearly as comfortable as putting on a warm pair of thick woolen socks. We could see the recognition on their faces as they listened while they sang, like they were hearing from an old friend. And of course, we Burkes thought the combo was pretty fabulous and grinned shamelessly as we flexed our musical muscles.

I do not want to leave the impression that this time in Stowe was all fun and games. Far from it. Once the initial excitement and singing encounters were over, we got down to more serious work. Some of the rehearsals were pretty grueling during that four-day taping session. Dad was nervous and when Dad got nervous, *we* got nervous. He wanted this to go right real bad. He wanted us to sing better than we ever had before and his tension was contagious. I think the waltzing also wore him down a bit. He wasn't used to following.

One night the wreath in the chapel caught on fire while we were all there having an Advent service. Steve and John grabbed it and threw it out of the window. Into the dark and down it fell, still burning after it hit the snow. I watched it and had new thoughts about all the wood in that lodge. Though I was saddened, I was not very surprised to hear that it burned down some years later.

One morning after another snowfall, we had a wild snowball fight with the CBS cameramen and technicians. Grown men, including Buck Spurr and producers Chalmers (Chum) Dale and Joe Chromyn, were dodging around our parked cars and their trucks, packing them tight, lobbing them, then ducking and laughing like crazy. When we started to tape again, our color was great, but hair and makeup needed a little work.

Fresh snow seemed to be a constant at the lodge and so was great food. The dishes were a little tough to pronounce, but they were scrumptious. In one day we had Viennese Backhuehner, Schnitzel Holstein, Gurkensalat, Kaiserschmarrn, Zwetschkenknoedel, Mozartkugeln and Pischinger Torte. (That's roast chicken, veal cutlet, cucumber salad, Emperor's omelet, prune dumplings, chocolate pastry and a chocolate/hazelnut torte).

One night Rosemarie taught me how to spin wool. I had noticed the spinning wheel over in a corner of one of the main rooms and thought it was just another antique until I went closer and saw that it actually had wool on it. I asked Rosemarie if she knew how to spin and would she teach me. She took the time and I was delighted.

While we were spinning, some of the others were on their way to Stowe. It had been a very tense day and Steve, Johannes, Marty, Florrie, Gemma and John decided to get out and let off a little steam. They walked from the lodge down into the town of Stowe to see a movie called *The Pink Panther* that had just come out. Out in the countryside, Johannes taught them a simple yodel and before long, they heard their own "Hed-deet-tee, hed-deet-tee, hed-deet-tee-oh-ho-deet-tee, oh-ho-deet-tee's" bouncing off the hills back to them. They got to the movie in time and before long, Inspector Clouseau had them howling. Peter Sellers was a very funny guy, but I think he was particularly funny that night because they needed a good laugh.

The Sound of Christmas aired around the country on Christmas Eve in 1964. The opening shots showed the family standing outside the lodge in heavy red coats or green capes with red sweater hoods. We held white tapered candles and caroled for the Baroness while she stood by the open glass double doors of the chalet listening and smiling. She wore a dirndl and in the living room behind her, stood a tall, fat, beautiful Christmas tree decorated with round sugar and gingerbread cookies, red ribbons, silver icicles and wrapped candies.

As the show progressed, the Baroness talked about some Austrian Christmas traditions and the origin of "Stille Nacht" or "Silent Night." We sang maybe ten songs in all. The Trapps joined us for the last two and the whole thing was over way too soon.

We watched it on the East Coast from eleven-thirty to midnight on Christmas Eve. It was a good show and a lot of people were up watching it, thanks to the press. The *Boston Globe* had some fun. "The Burkes Meet the Trapps" was their headline.

Sounded like the Clantons meet Wyatt Earp and Doc Holliday. As usual, the newspapers had been very good to us.

"Yuletide Warmth By the Burke Family Singers," "The Family Sound" and "Christmastime is Burke Family Time" were some of the other headlines.

It was a wonderful time of year and the year had been a particularly good one. Buck sent a copy of Dorothy Kilgallen's "Voice of Broadway" Christmas article from the *New York Journal-American* that year. It was titled, "It's the Time for Merry Rhyme" and there, right in the middle of her long list of celebrities, was us!

> ... *Merry Christmas, lads and lasses*
> *Guys and dolls and boys and girls,*
> *Tony Curtis, A. Onassis,*
> *Tony Quinn, the Milton Berles,*
> *Susan Snaper, Eric Berry,*
> *Dana Wynter, C.P. Snow,*
> *Boris Karloff, who's the very*
> *Sweetest-tempered ghoul I know,*
> *Arlene Francis, Nancy Kelly,*
> *Annie Bancroft and her groom,*
> *Ringo-Starr of stage, screen, telly,*
> *And of operating room!*
> *Merry Christmas, big and little,*
> *Rich and poor and young and old,*
> *Jeanie Bach and Y.A. Tittle,*
> *Philip Silvers, Ernest Gold,*
> *Every blithe Burke Family Singer,*

Florence Henderson, Jane White,
Tammy Grimes, the highest swinger
In "High Spirits" every night,
Greta Garbo, still so icily
Nixing pix at any price,
Barbra Streisand, so precis-i-ly
Spicily right as Fanny Brice . . . .

and on it went.

It was a good year and a wonderful Christmas. I stared at the tree, mesmerized by the blinking Christmas lights and the warmth of the fireplace crackling behind me and thought "Don't forget this. Don't forget any of it."

On The Mike Douglas Show—*January 1965*

CHAPTER 26

Montgomery

THE MARRIAGE YEARS WERE coming. I could feel them blowing in, like the cold advance winds warning an early autumn. They were coming and there was nothing I could do to stop them. The strangers would come—the new sisters and brothers. Already they were showing up on our doorstep, meeting the parents, staying for Sunday dinner, kissing under the mistletoe and still kissing after we took it down. I hid under the dining room table with Pete and watched. Sometimes Walt joined us, and if the couple got too sappy we'd start to giggle until we were found and chased out.

Sheila was the first. She was Steve's all-Irish girlfriend: pretty, petite, soft-spoken with long dark hair and blue eyes that sparkled, especially when she looked at Steve. I tried not to treat her like she had rabies but it was difficult. I was in no mood to lose my oldest brother. I didn't care if she was a walking saint, she wasn't passing muster with me. And right on her heels came Denis for Marty and Vin for Florrie, all of them kissing in the front foyer and mooning over each other. I could see that a change was coming eventually but I chose to ignore it and the newcomers for as long as I could.

One way we could leave the sweethearts behind was by getting in the Chevrolet station wagons and taking to the road. Dad had just traded in our old maroon cars for a brand-new blue set so we were ready to go. Like the others, they had "Burke Family Singers" printed on all four front doors. Florrie and Gemma had made lightweight maroon capes that spring and had just finished a third set of capes and pillbox hats in blue wool to match the cars.

Our first destination in the new cars was KYW-TV in Cleveland, Ohio. It was January 20th, 1965. New year, old gig. Mike Douglas had asked us back, and we appeared this time with Sylvia Sydney, Hermione Gingold and Rip Taylor.

Sylvia Sydney kept to herself but Hermione Gingold sure stood out. She was dressed in an Early American sort of outfit and was there to give a needlepoint demonstration. I have no idea why. I had known her only as an actress in such great old movies as *Bell, Book and Candle, Gigi, Around the World in Eighty Days, Pickwick Papers* and *The Music Man,* where I laughed to see her raise her arms over her head and stick one foot out behind her while uttering, *"One Grecian urn"* in that very deep, rich dramatic voice of hers.

She often played dotty old English ladies, and now that I met her I could see why. She was a delightful woman in a zany sort of way. She seemed very concerned about catching cold. She'd be chatting pleasantly and chain-smoking until she felt a cool breeze, then she'd pull her shawl tight around her and call out authoritatively, *"Close the doors!"* or *"Keep the draft out!"* and then she'd pick right up where she'd left off.

Rip Taylor was simply out of his mind. After joking around with my brothers, he suddenly began an impromptu solo performance. With his back to us, he put his arms around himself in a tight embrace, moving his neck and hands as if "making out" and raised one foot up behind him in sheer ecstasy. I didn't know what to make of him. My brothers thought he was hysterical.

And Mike Douglas was his same old warm self. He didn't seem to fit the typical showbiz personality profile. He was relaxed and open, he smiled easily, and he wasn't self-involved. We always enjoyed being on his show and this one was no exception, but this time Mother was eager to get back home. We had company coming.

It was my mother's mother, "Maggie Jiggs," the milkman's daughter, coming to Doyle Avenue for the weekend. She had recently returned from Switzerland where she had been living with my uncle Jim Devine, who was U.S. Minister to the Geneva Conference. My mother couldn't wait to see her.

When Mum and Dad brought her home from the train station, I could see she was frail.

My older brothers made a hammock of their strong arms and she sat with her arms around their shoulders while they carried her up the wide wooden stairs to the front door of the house. Grammy Devine laughed and was amazed at the place and couldn't believe how big the boys were that carried her. Gemma gave Gram her bedroom and Mother and the girls got her nicely tucked in.

Gram was so weak that Mother called Dr. Karas on Sunday afternoon and asked if he wouldn't mind coming over to take a look at her. He came, examined her and told Dad and Mum that she had widespread cancer and had only a short time to live.

She must have known. On Sunday night while Marty was walking her to the bathroom, she said, "If it's God's will, I think I'd like to die here." The next day, she couldn't get out of bed.

We coddled her and we prayed with her and we loved her, and it was very easy to do because she was a dear lady. My three oldest sisters were dating Providence College guys at the time and before they went out on their dates, they asked the guys if they wouldn't mind praying the rosary "with my Gram." That was fine with the boys and Grammy couldn't keep the grin off her face as she lay there and said the rosary with all those big, handsome, sweet-smelling young faces kneeling around her bed.

For the first week she was fragile but not entirely bed-ridden. I think my brothers enjoyed carrying her and having her beam up at them, the big lugs. Gram attended our re-hearsals down the hall in the Family Room. We were getting ready for another tour. No one sat in on our rehearsals but there she was, making up for lost time, smiling and crocheting. Gemma had shown her a new stitch and she was using it to start a new afghan. Not a wasted moment. Now I saw where Mother got it. That fruit fell straight down off the tree.

Grammy didn't seem to be in any pain. When it was time, young Father Coleman came over from Holy Name to give her the Eucharist and the last rites. Mum met him at the front door with the candles and the holy water and he followed her upstairs. We were all lined up along the stairs leading to Gram's room and we sang "Ave Verum Corpus" in parts. It was so beautiful, this sung prayer, that poor Father Coleman had tears rolling down his cheeks and he wasn't alone.

After two weeks, Grammy Devine slipped into a coma. The older ones kept a constant vigil by her side. She lived a holy life serving others and she died a holy peaceful death. Margaret Elizabeth Roche Devine died on February 3, 1965, considerate to the very last. She was buried on a Saturday and we were scheduled to leave for a concert in Pennsylvania on Monday.

On March 13th, we left school to take to the road again. I enjoyed this style of schooling. I was never there long enough to get bored, there were always stories to tell when I got back and I'll be honest, it felt great to be an exception to the rule. The School Sisters of Notre Dame continued to assist by preparing assignments for us to take in advance. If we had a four-week tour, they'd give us two or three weeks' work in advance and when we got home, we'd make up the rest. Though playing catch-up with assignments when I got back could be grueling, I discovered that the freedom was well worth it.

This was our fifth tour and our second trip to the South.

The first audience to stand for "Dixie" on this tour was the crowd at Campbell College, a Baptist school in Buies Creek, North Carolina. It was our third concert of the tour and from then on, every audience got on their feet for that song. Looking out at those smiling, determined faces, I felt like I was in a foreign country.

It was a crazy time to be down South—tensions were so high. We drove through Dunn, North Carolina, and saw Confederate flags everywhere. We didn't know what was going on. It looked like the South was rising again. Turns out they were celebrating their centenary and had scheduled a mock Civil War battle for the next day followed by a memorial service at the local cemetery—but we didn't find that out until later.

In Silver City, North Carolina, we passed our first road gang. Ten men, wearing those black-and-white striped outfits I thought were only worn in the movies, worked by the side of the road. They were shackled to each other with leg irons, and a guard with shiny shoes, immaculate clothes, mirrored sunglasses and a toothpick hanging out of his mouth, carried a rifle and quietly watched them. We would see many work gangs and they were always either all-white or all-black.

The car radio gave a clear indication of the atmosphere we were driving into at that time. One man on WBOK in Birmingham, Alabama reported "Two niggers assaulted. One shot his friend's daughter in Philadelphia suppertime last night." There was no other comment. And then, about an hour away from Birmingham we heard on the radio that three bombs had been found there, one in a black Catholic church. The report said, "All are live and they are attempting to disarm them."

We skirted Birmingham and headed east to Gadsden and the Holiday Host Motel/Restaurant. We had met the owners, Mr. and Mrs. Donaldson and Mr. and Mrs. Worthington on our earlier tour to the South and these four had shown us just what was meant by "Southern hospitality." Our second visit was no different.

We got to the Holiday Host around three-thirty in the afternoon and the Donaldsons and Worthingtons came running with open arms. We couldn't have picked a better time to come. They were opening a new room in the restaurant called "The Plantation Room," and a radio program from WGAD had just begun. The announcer was urging people to visit the new room, have a buffet dinner, and listen to entertainer Judy Short, "Miss Alabama, 1964" play the marimba.

First thing I spotted was the pie slices that covered a whole table. They had key lime and pecan, pumpkin, chocolate creme, lemon meringue and apple pie. I had my eye on one big piece of pecan pie with whipped cream, and I kept my eye on it while we sang "Shenandoah," "Hospodi Pomiluii," "Skip to m'Lou," "America the Beautiful" and "Dixie" (twice) on the radio. It was the best pecan pie I ever had.

Though we were having a fine time in Gadsden, it was hard not to think about those bombs in Birmingham. What a strange experience. At Gadsden, life went on as usual and everyone seemed to blissfully ignore Birmingham, Selma and Montgomery. Maybe if they ignored it, it would go away.

It was hard to figure. The contrasts were so jarring. There was the warmth of Southern hospitality on the one hand and then on the other, there were the signs of hatred around us—

like the sign on the office door of the "Heart of Perry" Motel in Perry, Georgia, that asked, "WHAT ABOUT MY RIGHTS?" And the sign on the marquee of the only movie theatre in that same town that read, "COMMITTEE OF 1000—PRIVATE," which successfully kept the blacks out of the theatre.

We sang a concert in Perry, Georgia, and Dad spoke on stage about us eating collards and rutabagas for the first time and the audience laughed—but it was a different laugh—more like laughing *at* us. At intermisson, Dad asked a stagehand why they laughed and he said, "That's the colored people's diet. White people don't eat that food." We thought we were trying out Southern cooking. I ate it and thought it tasted great. Why would anyone *not* want to eat something that tasted good?

After the concert that night, we went to a nearby diner for a sandwich. There was no one in there except for the owners and one older man who sat on a bar stool by the counter. Steve went over and sat next to him and I followed and sat down next to Steve. They began to talk about the trouble going on and the man shook his head and said:

"I can't understand all the hatred. I work in a prison and I look after a work crew and I's good to my niggers. I don't beat 'em . . . . There was one time . . . I was drivin' the truck with another guard and there was thirteen niggers on the back of the truck. Now I know all my boys and when I felt that truck lighten up, I knew it was ole Joe. I knew he'd run me—and I knew where he was gonna go. He was goin' into town to get drunk. So I stopped the truck and I said, 'Git off, boys. Line up now and count off, boys' and they counted off one to twelve and I said, 'How many we got?'

'We got thirteen, boss.'

'They was coverin' for 'im.'" He chuckled. "So we went back to town and shore 'nough, there he was ... and we didn't beat 'im. We just brought 'im back ..." Then he looked at Steve with a know-what-I-mean? look. This story was a demonstration of how good he was to "his niggers." No wonder he couldn't understand the hate. In his mind, a black man wasn't equal enough to hate.

The tension in the South at that time felt so real you could almost physically touch it. At a motel office in Dothan, Alabama, we were having a pleasant conversation with the owner when the phone rang. He picked it up, greeted the caller, said "Ayuh" a couple of times, and then said, "I see you got some nigger doin's up there ..." In one moment, the atmosphere could suddenly change.

The next day we arrived in Andalusia. It was a beautiful drive. The azaleas, camellias and dogwood were in bloom and there were many stands of pine along the road. Andalusia was full of gracious homes with gorgeous landscaping. We checked into the Gables Motor Hotel, got some lunch and then went back to our room to rest before the concert. We turned the TV on and watched the climax of the march on Montgomery.

That night we sang to a large audience. Mother wrote: "They are very responsive. This audience is different from the others—they seem filled with emotion. When Walter mentions the beauties of the state they applaud with great relief. Everyone stood for 'Dixie' with alacrity and an almost fierceness. We are told afterwards that a march is planned here in ten days. 'I hope we won't make all the American papers' was spoken in fearful tones. God help them and us. The man in charge of the concert was a Presbyterian minister and all of us liked him very much. When we return to motel we find 12 sandwiches and 2½ gallons of milk waiting."

In the morning Dad made some phone calls. It was the day after the march from Selma and we were scheduled to sing in Montgomery that night. He called our contact there to see if all was well. He found out that the concert had not been cancelled and the 2,000-seat hall was sold out. Next, he called to make reservations at the Coliseum Motel, the place suggested on our itinerary. The owner apologized and said that his place was full of state troopers but he'd call a friend of his who owned the Continental Motel, a few blocks from City Hall in downtown Montgomery. He called Dad back and told him that there were three rooms being held for us.

Our apprehension really began with that phone call. The motel was full of state troopers?! What was going *on* over there? What were we driving into? The weather was no help. We drove the 50 or 60 miles to Montgomery in a driving rain on a two-lane highway and listened to the radio blat out cancellations for everything in Montgomery except our concert. The next advisory was a tornado warning for the area.

Our new Chevrolet seemed to have a leak over the driver's windshield. Steve was having a tough enough time trying to see the road without having to take a bath, too. He tucked a rag under the visor and kept the defroster on. I don't know how we were fogging up the windows. No one spoke the whole way.

With great relief, we pulled into the Continental Motel and immediately saw what they meant by all the state troopers. There were identical gray cars everywhere you looked. There were eighteen in our motel alone. It was still raining heavily so we got sandwiches to go and retreated to the privacy of our rooms for an afternoon nap before the concert.

You might think we'd feel safe with all those state troopers around but actually, their presence seemed to raise the tension level. The troopers weren't staying alone. They had brought their wives and children with them. We figured they had to be pretty scared to do that. When we asked, we were told that they were "concerned about retaliation." Were they making some sort of last stand? And what were *we* doing in the middle of all this?

Florrie struck up a conversation with one of the troopers before we left for the concert and naturally, they began to talk about what was going on in Montgomery and about Mrs. Viola Liuzzo, who had been killed the day before while ferrying black voters from Montgomery back to Selma after the march. Four Klansmen had pulled alongside her Buick on Route 80 and shot her in the head, and this trooper said to Florrie, "What's a white woman doin' in a car with all them niggers anyway?"

When we first heard about the shooting, Gemma had said, "Dad, Isn't Route 80 the road we're taking?"

The curtain opened at Lanier High Auditorium in Montgomery that night and, instead of a full 2000-seat house, we looked out on a scattered crowd of about 400 people. Dad asked them if they wouldn't mind moving up close to the front near us so we could sing to them. "We'll just make believe you're in our living room," he said and they all moved up. Dad was a wreck. He covered it well but we knew it. It was a very warm, very intense concert. This crowd did not stand for "Dixie," but they did give "America the Beautiful" a standing ovation. After the concert a woman walked up to Mum and thanked us for coming. Then she said, "Oh, what must you think of us? We aren't *all* like this!" and she started to cry. And Mum put her arms around the woman and said, "I know, deah," and let her cry.

(A footnote on the murder of Mrs. Violet Liuzzo...The four Klansmen were brought to trial in criminal court and acquitted. Later, an FBI informant helped convict three of the four in 1966 for violating Mrs. Liuzzo's civil rights—not for murdering her, but for violating her civil rights.)

The family room/rehearsal room, 1965

CHAPTER 27

"Look, Mum! They're All Marked Sunkist!"

WE DROVE OUT OF Montgomery on a sunny Saturday morning. Once we were out of the city, we opened the car windows
in CREDO and breathed deeply again. Mother told us that a
seventy-five-year old man named Myers came up to Dad last
night after the concert and said, "I never felt closer to heaven as
I did when listening to y'all! I have some friends in town here
and I was wonderin'... how would y'all like to have a tour of
our beautiful State House and maybe sing a song or two for
Governor Wallace?" She said that Dad had declined gracefully

explaining that our schedule was very tight. Mother, (clearly not a George Wallace fan) looked over at Steve and said, "Sing for Governor Wallace?! I'd rather choke!"

Our next concert was in Florida and we couldn't get there fast enough. It wasn't long before we saw our first orange groves. Rows and rows of green trees with little orange balls spread out over the hilly terrain as far as we could see. Dad pulled over to the side of the road and Steve followed.

Jim was one of the first ones out of the car. He ran down a hill to the trees, examined one orange and then another and suddenly called over to Mother, "Look, Mum! They're all marked SUNKIST!"

"Really?" said Mother, and hurried toward Jimmy to take a look. In a moment, everyone was laughing. We couldn't believe she fell for it. She must've been pretty strung out in Alabama.

The Sunkist incident wasn't the first time this sort of thing had happened. Mother was often open to suggestion. Was she just gullible? Maybe so. But I think there was more to it than that. Underneath her trustfulness lay a simple fact. Mother believed in miracles. For her, life was full of possibilities. Anything could happen. The boys in the family seemed to know this about her and there were times when she'd be halfway down the street before she realized she'd been taken for a ride.

Luckily, she was able to laugh at herself and now joined in the laughter around her. We all needed a good laugh and again, it was Jimmy who provided it. That seemed to be his role. Between giving "Crying Loon" interviews, doing impersonations and all kinds of slapstick comedy, he would have us laughing ourselves sick. He was very loose with his body and with his facial muscles, in particular. He was a contortionist, really, and when things got tense, as they often did, it was Jimmy who stepped in and turned the situation around completely—loving us back into laughter.

Our stomachs were sore by the time we got back into the cars. The laughter had only encouraged Jim, who went right into an imitation of Mother running down the hill—only he added a birdlike step to the run. He looked like an ostrich with leg spasms, racing down at full tilt, arms waving wildly and yelling in a high falsetto, "*Really*, Jimmy? *Whee*-ah? *Whee*-ah?"

We hadn't gotten too far into Florida when a fast-moving Cadillac convertible zoomed past both CREDO and SONGS. A middle-aged Floridian flew by with the wind in her hair and the gas pedal to the floor, her pink scarf whipping away from the back of her neck like a banner on a large medieval tent. She wore wide sunglasses, thick gold loop earrings and a defiant set about her jaw that made me wonder if she was newly divorced. The velocity did nothing for her looks. Gravity and age had already loosened the flesh around her face and now centrifugal force caused her jowls to pull a little toward the back seat.

She was alone. There was no one to advise her when it suddenly began to rain. The sky burst open as it does in semitropical places like Florida, and the water poured down. Twelve pairs of eyes watched from the other lane. Jimmy got the movie camera out and began to film. Would she pull over to put up the top? Would she at least slow down? Nope. She had hit the button on her automatic roof and now the canvas slowly started to rise. We could hear the whine of the small motor as it struggled to lift against the powerful wind.

Slack-jawed, we watched her in the passing lane while Dad and then Steve veered to the right, hugging the shoulder of the road. She was taking quite a beating. We marveled at her perseverance. The canvas top was now straight up in the air but could not push forward against the wind. Then we heard a ripping sound and that seemed to give her pause. We quickly passed her car, craning our necks in amazement. The left side of the convertible top was in shreds. Rain coursed off her face and the pink scarf clung to her neck like some small half-drowned animal. She released the button or it broke, I don't know which, but the top fell back against the back seat and she hit the pedal again, quickly picking up enough speed to pass us once more. So. This was Florida.

We continued traveling south, past forests of palm trees and truckloads of grapefruit and sang concerts in Sanford and Fort Pierce, Miami and Avon Park.

We toured a Seminole Indian village with a big Seminole named Jimmy Tiger and saw live alligators in pits and a woman hanging wet laundry on a line. It looked like a display in an art gallery: long billowy skirts decorated in zig-zag designs and hand-sewn shirts in just about every color imaginable. The women wore strings of black beads around their necks; some wore so many that it looked like they had difficulty moving their necks. They did not speak English and were very shy so we sang "Ave Maris Stella" and "The Spinning Top" for them and they warmed right up. Jimmy Tiger interpreted their answers to our questions and our answers to their questions.

"Are you all one family?"

"Yes."

"Why do you wear so many layers of beads around your necks?"

"For every good deed a woman does, she adds a set of beads."

"But you wear so many! How will you be able to move your neck?"

"At a certain age, we begin to take a strand off for every good deed."

"Oh!"

Before we left, Jimmy Tiger told us that if we wanted to take a ride through the Everglades, there were airboats just up the road from the village. These boats were also run by the Seminoles, and as we pulled in I wondered what they fed these guys.

The two men who took us out were massive. I mean really big. They were mahogany-skinned and silent. Rounded black sunglasses covered their eyes from view. They wore their hair long and stood like statues in the rear of these powerful wind machines. I was hoping they'd say something, crack a smile or at least move a facial muscle before I stepped into their boat and they took me into Alligator Alley—but no such luck. We split into two groups of six with Mum in one group and Dad in another and gingerly stepped into the boats. Tweedledum and Tweedledee turned on the big fans in the back and off we went.

I kept half an eye on them and the only thing I saw move was their hair and their arms on the rudder.

How exciting to skim over the water at high speed and how terrifying it was to cut through tall grasses and lily pads and not be able to see what was up ahead. This was very different than being on a motorboat in the ocean. There was no view of the horizon. We could have hit a rock or an alligator and flipped the boat over and I, for one, was just as happy to get off that boat.

After our last Florida concert, we went to Sunday Mass at Our Lady of Grace Church in Avon Park. The place was jammed with old people. The priest, Father Gregoire, sounded just like Bela Lugosi and some of us laughed all through Mass.

We had lunch in Ocala and arrived back in Montgomery Sunday night, covering 510 miles that day. We weren't real thrilled to be driving back into the civil rights tension, but we had a concert the next night in Livingston, Alabama. Between Montgomery and Selma on Route 80, we passed a huge billboard that showed a picture of Martin Luther King standing alongside others in some sort of assembly. The caption above it read, "MARTIN LUTHER KING AT COMMUNIST TRAINING SCHOOL."

We were welcomed into the city of Selma by the Selma National Bank. Their billboard read, "SELMA NATIONAL BANK WELCOMES YOU TO SELMA—*THE CITY WITH 100% HUMAN INTEREST!*" Judging from the number of reporters and cameramen milling around the courthouse, I'd say there was a whole bunch of human interest in that town. We stopped at the post office to mail letters and saw a long line of blacks waiting to register to vote outside the courthouse. Many television cameras and newsmen were taking pictures but there was no commotion. It could have been a theatre line for *Mary Poppins*.

At one point Walt waved at a black man driving a one-horse buckboard. He snapped his neck around and did a double take. He looked so surprised. He didn't wave back.

On the road from Selma to Livingston we saw a long, angular older black woman in a bandanna striding down the road with the use of a cane. We slowed up and Mother smiled and waved to her. Stephen chuckled a moment later. He had been looking into his rearview mirror and had watched the woman spit meaningfully on the road after we passed. Mother may have waved warmly to show her support but this woman was obviously not interested in any white good wishes. Her animosity saddened us, but we couldn't blame her.

On Monday, April 5th, we sang our last concert of the tour to a very enthusiastic crowd at Livingston State College. When the show was over, we sang a few encores and took more curtain calls than ever before. Finally, we let them clap until they got tired out. It was a nice way to end an emotion-packed tour. We were tired, but before we could go home, we had to go to New York City to tape the *Jack Paar Easter Show* on NBC.

We appeared with Bob Newhart, Charlton Heston and Morris L. West. Bob Newhart was just as he seemed: warm, funny and unpretentious. Charlton Heston was performing a dramatic reading from his role as Michaelangelo in *The Agony and the Ecstasy*, a 1965 movie on the painter's life. Offstage, Mr. Heston kept to himself.

The other guest on the show, author Morris L. West, had

gained national popularity with his 1963 bestseller (and subsequent movie) *The Shoes of the Fisherman* and was on the show to talk about his newly-released novel, *The Ambassador*.

Jack Paar, the host of the show, was a pioneer of late-night talk shows and a very high-strung man. Steve asked one of the staff if Paar was always this nervous and was told, "He's like this before every show."

We taped a few songs including "Were You There?" and "Tu Es Petrus" for the *Easter Show* to be aired at ten P.M. on Friday, April 16th, and then headed home to New England.

After a tour, we usually made one last stop before returning to Doyle Avenue and that stop was Grammy and Grampa Burke's house at 63 Ridgemont Street in Brighton, Massachusetts. Like soldiers returning home victorious from the wars, we overran that modest house and told our new stories. Grammy and Aunts Maerose and Alice fed us the first home-cooked dinner we'd had in a month, usually boiled ham or corned beef, and we'd sing for them. Father Joe Leo would usually come over and sometimes my father's brothers or his sister, my Aunt Florence, would show up. One time my great Aunt Sarah (the telephone operator) from my mother's side of the family was there, too. These gatherings were wild and warm and impromptu. As far as entertainment went, we got as good as we gave.

Dad's side of the family always reminded me of race horses: bred too close and just a little crazy. Our singing was only a part of the show that seemed to proceed non-stop from the minute we walked in until the moment we walked back out to the cars. That piano seat never got cold as one Burke after another took a turn on it. Though none of us kids took up piano, everybody in Dad's family could play and we heard quite a variety of music from Grampa's classical to Grammy singing "Rueben and Rachael" and something else with a refrain that went "Birds were twittering Tra-la-la! Gaily twittering Tra-la-la!"

After dinner, somebody would move the table to one side, roll up the Oriental rug and Aunt Maerose would tap dance or do modern jazz routines to show tunes played by Aunt Florence and sung by Aunt Alice. One time, my sister Annie and Aunt Maerose were step-shuffle-ball-changing their way across the floor. Annie had quickly learned the new routine while I stumbled along behind, skinny and bow-legged with full grown size 8½ feet. Unable to shuffle with my right leg, I missed the "change" and ended up going stage left like a crab. My older sisters thought that was real funny.

And there was joke telling, an Irish art form that seemed to be dominated by the men. The women were too busy laughing which, of course, only encouraged the boys further as they took turns in rapid fire to outdo one another. Father Joe Leo Flynn was holding his own nicely. He was the retreat director at the Passionist Monastery and he'd heard a million stories. His timing was quite good. And then Uncle Fran would take the floor. Like the rest of the family, he had such a good musical ear that he easily used accents and once he did a whole routine holding an imaginary phone in one hand and conducting a one-sided conversation using a thick German accent. He did this while trying to untangle the phone cord which, of course, wasn't there and then he'd move around the room looking for a pad to write on and trip over the non-existent wire, talking all the while. We were doubled-up laughing.

When it was time to leave, they always came outside to the cars to see us off. Right up to the last good-bye, Aunts Alice and Maerose stood leaning against the front porch railing on this, the last house on a dead-end street, watching while we got ourselves organized, and then waving with my grandparents until we took the turn and drove out of sight.

Annie, Pete, Jim

Gemma, Sarah Jo, Jim, Mum

CHAPTER 28

The Pubonic Plague

Spring of 1965. Mrs. Halton could be seen raking the leaves out of her flowerbeds, the two Gilbane sisters began to venture back and forth from their massive houses, Mum took us girls over to Ann & Hope to buy Easter outfits and hats and the three youngest Burkes, along with their friends, started to tear up the neighborhood on our bikes.

Soon I would be thirteen, a terrible teenager my Mother called it. Years later, my sister Gemma would coin the phrase "pubonic plague" to describe the onset of puberty that ushered in her children's teenage years.

I was just at the edge of it—wild and reckless—flying down the long Doyle Avenue hill toward Blackstone Boulevard and Swan Point Cemetery, a 200-acre city with narrow paved streets and everywhere tombstones, statues and stone vaults. The city of the dead. It fascinated me.

When the really warm weather came, I hit the tennis courts, particularly the backboard at Moses Brown, a private boys school. From morning to dusk, I spent many summer days alone with that backboard, hitting a tennis ball against it over and over again, working out the rebellion, the energy and the confusion of my adolescence by placing that tennis ball under submission. This was a problem I could solve and eventually I did. I could pinpoint just where I wanted the ball to contact the board: an inch or two over the "net," a white horizontal line painted against the green board.

Eventually, I became a "lefty" with a mean backhand. I loved the precision of the game but I quickly learned, after unleashing that directed power on a couple of potential boyfriends, that they didn't appreciate my skill. When the ball came at them, flying hard, low and fast, barely skimming over the net, sometimes they couldn't hit it at all and the mixed look of admiration and disapproval convinced me that the tennis court was not the best place to bring a date. Only with my brother Walt could I be mercilessly competitive.

And when the heat really set in, there was always the beach. On the weekends, Florrie or Gem would drive a bunch of us down to the Narragansett/Galilee area where we'd join the rest of the state of Rhode Island.

The two most popular state beaches were Scarborough

Beach in Narragansett, the beach preferred by young adults looking for other young adults and those who wanted more vigorous surf, and Sand Hill Cove, the family beach, also known as the baby beach, where there was little or no surf.

We had one carload and two age groups. When the older ones wanted to check out the action over at Scarborough, they'd drop the younger set off at Sand Hill and then drive over to join up with the other big kids. At thirteen, I had had it with the squealing and bawling children and was chomping at the bit to get into Scarborough, but I could forget about it for at least another two years.

I had to be content with catching crabs, snails and eels by the rocks; building drip-sand castles with moats, walking along the beach, feeding clam cakes to the seagulls, lathering on the Johnson's baby oil to bake in the sun for as long as I could stand to lie still, which wasn't long at all, playing in the water until my skin pruned up, listening to the jukebox music on the boardwalk and illegally tunneling under it to look for dropped coins, and smelling the mouth-watering aroma, unique to the beach, of French fries with white vinegar coming from the concession stand.

When I finally did make it to Scarborough, I was amazed to discover how different two beaches can be. The jukebox thumped away on a much larger boardwalk while hundreds of teens and twenty to twenty-five-year-olds loitered and posed in very sophisticated swimming attire. You could almost see the estrogen and testosterone smogging up the air as they leaned against anything they could find; the railing, the building, each other.

Many more bodies stretched out on nearly every square inch of the beach in a patchwork quilt of blankets. There were few children at this beach and people here didn't take kindly to anyone running past blankets and kicking up sand. The beach was packed but few came to swim. Slick with Coppertone and Hawaiian Tropic, they came to worship the sun and the power of their own youth. And they were powerful. I felt like a very small fish in a large sea, content to watch from a distance.

The summer of 1965 ran its course of watermelon days and fresh corn cookout nights, but before it came to a close, Steve, Marty, Florrie and/or Gemma had gotten an idea. Dad and Mum's 25th wedding anniversary was coming up on September 16th and they decided that we should give them a big surprise party to celebrate.

The three girls had full-time jobs, but to do it right, they'd need a lot more money, so they put together a plan that would keep them very busy for the rest of the summer. They took on extra hours at work and did some babysitting, but the most backbreaking job they signed up for was apple picking over at Steere's Apple Farm in Greenville, Rhode Island. Marty actually had to climb trees and it nearly killed her. I don't know why no one asked me. I was very good at climbing trees. The rest of us helped out as best we could. The older boys caddied and mowed lawns and Annie and I must have done something to make money. I was thirteen after all and not totally useless.

Right up to the morning of their anniversary, Mum and Dad never suspected a thing. They might have wondered what was up when we kicked the two of them out of the house for the day and told them not to come back until six—but that couldn't be helped. We had to clean the place, cook, pick people up from the airport, buy a whole lot of food and drink, stop at Hope Street Bakery for the wedding cake and rolls, McCarron's Florists to buy flowers and do a million other things.

We invited the Peace Dale parents who made up the Big Five—the Laffeys, the Fagans, the Ladds and the Warners. Dad and Mum's brothers and sisters all showed up, some flying in from the Washington, D.C. area. We planned to have them renew their vows so before long, Father Joe Leo and Father Joe Murphy arrived to help set things up and to get in the way. We hired Joe Conte, first violinist with the Rhode Island Philharmonic Orchestra and a good friend of my father's, to come with his string quartet and play classical music.

The street was quiet when they pulled up to the curb. We had asked people to park a few blocks away so there'd be no last-minute slip-ups and, thankfully, everyone had arrived on time—including Dad and Mum, who walked through the front door and were greeted by more than a hundred people yelling "Surprise!" and throwing confetti. Gem and Marty presented them with leis and kissed them on both cheeks. They looked completely stunned and when the string quartet began to play, it was too much for Dad. Mum was already a mess and squealing and hugging her sisters whom she didn't often get to see.

It was a wonderful night. So many dear people came, Boston relatives and Peace Dale and Providence friends. It was strange to see these people from different worlds all together in one place. Following the custom of 25th anniversaries, many guests came bearing silver and it was all lovely but the best gift, by far, was the one that sent Mum and Dad on a search throughout the house.

There were clues on this treasure hunt. These notes sent them from room to room through all three floors with the whole entourage of curious loved ones following. The opener read: "The first place you go is into the den—you'll find the next note to help you and then—follow each paper as best you can—and you'll find a great gift from your special ten." Dad or Mum read each clue and moans or laughter followed. The final clue led them back to their starting place.

An envelope was tucked under the seat cushion of one of the high-backed stuffed chairs in the front room. In it was a letter of invitation from Aer Lingus informing them that two seats had been reserved for them by their children. The flight would leave from Logan Airport in Boston, arrive at Shannon Airport in Ireland and then return to Boston in two weeks. Well, they read that out loud. That is, they read it as best they could—and then they just sat there for a moment looking around at their kids while we grinned at them. Then came the hugging and the whooping.

1954 was the last time the two of them had gotten away together. They had gone to Canada for a week and had dropped us off, two by two, to friends' houses. Now we kids were the ones sending them off. It seemed right.

I looked around that night. It was clear that this family was beginning to expand. Steve was never too far from Sheila. Denis and Marty were joined at the hip and Florrie and Vin were almost as bad. Gemma had a boyfriend in attendance but nothing serious. The three oldest wouldn't be home for too much longer and I, for one, was not thrilled by this turn of events.

The party went until the wee hours and then some, and quite a few of the guests didn't leave. When I came downstairs the next morning, I was surprised to find strange bodies sleeping on the den couch, on the orange rug by the fireplace, on the cushions beneath the bay window, on various spots on the carpeted floors of the front rooms. It looked like an adult pajama party. I noticed all the boyfriends stayed. There they lay, bow ties half-off, bartender arm cuffs still on, chins in varying stages of stubble, mouths open, softly snoring. It wasn't a pretty sight.

Top row: Mum, Peter, Sarah Jo, Walt, Annie, Jim, Dad
Bottom row: Gemma, John, Florrie, Steve, Marty

CHAPTER 29

Rock Hounds

ABOUT A MONTH LATER, we left for our sixth tour. This time we headed toward the Northwest, zig-zagging across Canada and the northern United States all the way to Vancouver Island in British Columbia, and then traveling back from coast to coast, across the length of our country.

It wasn't long before Walter was getting "the squeeze" in the backseat of SONGS. Some things didn't change. As long as Walt remained short and obnoxious, he could count on getting free doses of John-'n-Jim's Slenderizin' Treatment.

We drove 610 miles that first day and checked in to the -

Bee-Jay Motel in Mentor, Ohio. The next morning a priest at Sunday Mass recognized us and told us that Maria von Trapp was in town to give a lecture. We'd run into her a few weeks later at the Mormon Tabernacle in Salt Lake City, Utah. From the beginning all the way through to the end of our career, it seemed that, in one way or another, our paths continued to crisscross with the Trapps.

The movie version of *The Sound of Music*, with Julie Andrews playing the role of "Maria," had just come out that March and was already a smash hit across the country. The success of the movie put the Baroness back into the celebrity spotlight. By now, millions of Americans had watched the image of her, swinging her guitar case while singing on a sunny mountainside. This renewed interest and name recognition could have easily increased her tour bookings. And I'm sure that the singing family idea that had captivated America didn't hurt us, either. For us, the timing was perfect. We were out there doing it.

Our first concert was in Fort William, Ontario, 423 miles into Canada. To get there, we had to drive part way around Lake Superior on a new road that had been built only five years earlier. Before that, it was just wilderness. We had never seen Lake Superior, and what a beautiful ride it was. Green, clean water with whitecaps, waves that hit the rocks in the coves and no view of land on the horizon. It almost looked like the ocean, but there was no salt smell.

We stopped for gas and Mum and Steve got to talking with the Dutchman who owned the place. They were talking about the lake and he said, "Superior is the most treacherous of the Great Lakes. It's so bad that commercial fishing is discouraged because so many men have been lost. The Lake never gives up their bodies. They are never found." Well, that gave me something to think about as I stared out at the water and the miles rolled away under us on the only road around the lake.

The Lake was deadly but it was so beautiful. Mother was enthralled. Staring out the window of CREDO, she exclaimed, "There's pink! And jet black! Look at that green!"

In the last few months there had been a noticeable change in Mother, a shift in interest. I don't know when it happened exactly. I'm not sure if it was her first good look at the red clay dirt down South that piqued her curiosity and started the whole thing or if it was the experience of seeing man's inhumanity to man on the last tour that drove her to study inanimate objects, but whatever it was, by the time we began this sixth tour, she had become a dyed-in-the-wool, I-got-bit-bad rock hound.

Her tour notes took on a decidedly mineral and crystalline slant. Suddenly she was writing about taconite, agates, stone quarries, quartz, iron ore, fossils and Thomsonite. During this period, which lasted a few years, Mother kept her head down a lot. She was either looking at the ground or at the walls of blasted rock along the road, mesmerized by the strata of sedimentary rock, layer upon age-old layer exposed for her to study. "Ooo, isn't that interesting!" she cried or "Would you look at that!" Mum now had a new and endlessly intriguing object of interest—and it was everywhere.

Eventually, she stopped into a rock shop and bought a little "rock hammer" for herself. Kept it in the glove compartment along with her notepad. She was ready to take a sample at a moment's notice.

This geology craze was infectious. Soon Steve had to have his own hammer. Gemma was bitten next, and eventually we were all looking down when we walked.

There was no way of knowing for sure what exactly set this madness off, but it was surely with us now—and the two main instigators sat right in front of me, in the front seat of CREDO.

After singing in Fort William, Ontario, we headed toward the U.S. border. We were on our way to Duluth, Minnesota, when a rock shop in Grand Marais caught Mum's eye. We stopped in and an old arthritic rock hound named Oliver Anderson gave us twelve Thompsonites, stones found only in Grand Marais. We sang three songs for him. He was so surprised his eyebrows went up and the smile took up his whole face.

Next door to a restaurant in Beaver Bay was an Agate Shop, where Mum and Steve hung out until one of us had to go in and tell them their breakfast was on the table. Before we left Beaver Bay, all of us sang for the Agate Shop owners, Mr. and Mrs. Lind, who then handed us a big bag of rock candy and an agate for each of us.

With more and more rock gifts and specimens now being tucked away into CREDO's body, I began to wonder how much heavier the car would become by the end of this tour. How low to the ground would the muffler get and what about the added stress on the tires? There was no point in talking to the two up in the front seat. These days, Mum and Steve's eyes often took on a glazed-over, faraway look as they gazed out at the passing landscape. I didn't know how reliable they were anymore, so I kept my misgivings to myself.

It helped to get them away from the Lake Superior shoreline and back into the mainland—fewer stones.

We drove through Minnesota, South Dakota, and then on into Big Springs, Nebraska, for our concert that night and were amazed to find that the population was only 507. Where they came from I don't know, but 1,200 people showed up that night, a lot of them standing in the back and along the sides of the auditorium. They were friendly farm people who served up home-cooked cakes and pies at the reception that followed.

I watched Annie head for the chocolate cake. Chocolate was Annie's middle name. She was the reigning Scrabble and Fudge Queen, fifteen years old and going through puberty her own way—with lots of chocolate. Almost every afternoon for at least two summers, Annie walked three doors down Doyle Avenue to Lee Cohen's house with a full pan of fudge for their routine two-games-a-day of Scrabble. Neither one of them gained weight, but they both complained constantly of zits. They never felt bad enough to quit the fudge, however. Grinning, I now watched her pleased face as she polished off the last bite.

We slept that night in Julesburg, Colorado, just ten miles from Big Springs, and when we stepped outside the next morning, we knew we were in cattle country. The odor was rich! For 200 miles we saw nothing but cattle and by noontime, we had reached Hot Springs, South Dakota—just in time to have the worst meal of the tour at a place called the Stake House. This was one of those Ma-and-Pa places that actually made you think nice thoughts about the food in restaurant chains. As we got up from the table, Annie said, "I can't wait for supper."

Wind Cave National Park was just north of The Stake House in Hot Springs, which was good because all of us needed a little fresh air and some time to digest. A park ranger took us 200 feet down in an elevator, deep into the earth. Mother wasn't herself for a while after that.

Later that day, we drove into the Black Hills National Forest and as the shadows lengthened, we hurried to see Mount Rushmore before it got dark. We made it up the steep, winding road and arrived at the viewing area as the sun began to set. I don't think there could have been a better time to see it.

There was no one there. No park ranger. No cars. Not a soul there but us. Steve and Dad shut the car motors off and then there was complete silence. We got out of the cars and just stood there looking at this incredibly large monument carved out of the rock face. Presidents Washington, Jefferson, Lincoln and Roosevelt. Nobody said anything. We just stood there. It felt holy, a moment not to be forgotten, like God had cleared the place out so that we'd have this special gift without distractions.

For three years now we had been traveling across this beautiful country and in those years, President Kennedy had been shot, the Vietnam war continued to escalate amid increasing student protest and the Civil Rights Movement was in full swing. There was so much going on in the country. So much struggle. And here were four who had played such a major role in the shaping of it. Dad broke the silence. He said, "America the Beautiful" and then blew a note on the pitch pipe he always carried in his pocket.

We sang it to the hills and to those giant faces across the valley. We prayed it and the prayer moved us. As the silence replaced the last echo of sound and the sun set, we stood there a few moments longer and then quietly got into the cars. Not a word was spoken—and for my family, that's saying something!

It was dark when we carefully headed back down the sharp, pig's-tail turns of this mountain-sized Black Hill toward Rapid City and a night's sleep. We entered Rapid City from the heights and it looked like a fairyland of lights.

As we were finishing the meal at the Town n' Country Motel/Restaurant, the owner, who had obviously taken a shine to my brother Walt, invited him to a little wager. Well, it was more like a dare.

He said, "If you can eat *all* of a banana split that I'll make just for you, you won't have to pay for it."

Dad looked at the guy and then grinned over to Walt. Giving Walt a dare was always a safe bet. He would definitely take it, whether he had seen the banana split beforehand or not. "Okay," challenged Walt, "bring it on." Walt *lived* for moments like these.

About ten minutes later, they carried it out. It was the second monument we had seen that day. This thing was enormous. I gasped, thinking not even Walter could finish anything as big as that. It took a while and he wasn't lookin' too good by the end, but he did it.

Pete lights the Advent wreath candle

CHAPTER 30

A Close Call

OUR NEXT CONCERT WAS up in Weyburn in the Saskatchewan province of Canada. Musically, the Weyburn concert was
the best one we had ever sung. Dad said that the pitch on the
first half was flawless, and he never lied about pitch. We had
been singing for a few years now and our voices were becoming
mature. Practice, repetition and an increasing sensitivity to the
voices around us continued to enhance the unique vocal blend
that was already there. There were different shadings to the
voices and some were naturally stronger than others but the
"blood-blend" was a built-in feature of family singing.

Our next concert was scheduled for the following night in Yorkton, Saskatchewan, 200 miles away and it was another success. We ate very little before a concert so we were usually ravenous after we sang. At Yorkton, instead of the usual after-concert reception with desserts or little sandwiches and soft drinks, a large dinner table was set for us and we sat down to and thoroughly enjoyed a salmon meatloaf meal while we visited with many people. Mother wrote down some of their comments:

"You brought back many memories of days in England when my father would gather me and my four brothers around the organ at home."

"Even if one was deaf, one would have enjoyed every minute of your concert."

"We saw the Don Cossacks last week and enjoyed you far more."

"Our little Zoria wanted to cut her long braids until tonight—now she'll keep them."

Little Zoria must have been checking out the alto section. My two braids hung below my waist. In fact, they were long enough to make fairly good whips—especially when wet. Of course, you needed to be close to your target, but that was easy when we all were confined to the car. Pete, up in the front seat, never even saw it coming. Annie, who sat on my right, had hair almost as long as mine. If her hair was braided, she could hold her own in a whipwar. Like two male elk locking horns in a fight for supremacy, we'd lean our heads in close together and whip each other mercilessly. I grinned when I heard about the little girl. That's good. You keep your braids, Zoria.

Judging from the comments and the number of encores audiences asked for, the singing on this tour was going just fine. The scheduling, however, was a different story. We arrived in Prince Albert, Saskatchewan, to sing a concert we thought was set for eight P.M. and discovered, once we got into town and Dad made the contact call, that the people at the Orpheum Theatre planned to have us sing at three P.M. Luckily, we had arrived early enough to attend.

As Dad checked the itinerary more closely for the where and when of the next concert and mapped it, figuring the mileage, he realized that Mr. Zuckerman, who booked this tour for the Overture Concert Series, was asking us to drive 833 miles in a day and a half and then sing a concert that night in Victoria, British Columbia. Dad called Buck Spurr in Boston and said, "What is this guy thinking about? It's too far. We can't possibly do that!" Buck called Zuckerman and then called us back to say it would be cancelled. We were now getting twelve to fifteen hundred dollars per concert and it was a shame to have to cancel because of poor planning, but we had no choice.

The Orpheum Theatre in Prince Albert was packed that afternoon and poor Mrs. Fayerman, the woman in charge, said her "phone was ringing off the hook all morning with people wanting single tickets for the performance," but she "had to refuse because it wasn't fair to those who bought season tickets..." and on and on she went.

Mrs. Fayerman was one of those few, gifted individuals who could breathe and speak simultaneously. There were no pauses in her speech. The sound was not unlike a bagpipe drone, and I found myself watching her stomach for any movement and, seeing none, tried to breathe for her. I finally moved away from her after I heard myself sighing.

She had done a fine job organizing this event. Every seat was full at the Orpheum Theatre: full of Ukrainians, Eskimos and Cree Indians. We did four encores and then "God Save the Queen" at the end of it and they all sang with us.

The next morning we leisurely headed to our next concert in Camrose, Alberta, stopping for lunch in Lloydminster near the border of Saskatchewan and Alberta. We had ordered and were waiting for the food when we heard group laughter coming from another room.

"What's going on over there?" Dad asked the waitress.

"Oh, it's a Rotary meeting."

"A group of nice people," my father thinks. Of course his next thought is "Why don't we sing for them?"

Just because I haven't mentioned that pitch pipe recently— that doesn't mean he wasn't still carrying and using it. We sang "Hospodi Pomilui" and *The Sound of Music* medley for the Rotary crowd. Afterward, one of the Rotarians got to talking with Mother and she asked about a well-known rock collection in Lloydminster, and this guy just happened to personally know the owners of said collection and he says, "Sure, I can take you up there."

So we go over there, look at the rocks and sing "Wondrous Love" for a Mr. and Mrs. Delp. Then Mrs. Delp says, "Gee, wouldn't it be great if they could hear you sing at a school nearby. It's only about a mile away." So we get in the cars and sing again at this school for children with Down's Syndrome. By the time we got out of there, it was almost suppertime—

which meant going into another restaurant. It was amazing the trouble you could get into with a pitch pipe.

We finally got on the road again and as we approached our destination, Mother wrote:

> *60 miles out of Camrose, Alberta*
> *Town of Killem—Entrance says:*
> DRIVE CAREFULLY
> WE LOVE OUR CHILDREN
> KILLEM
> *As you leave town:*
> THANK YOU

I looked this one up on the map and saw that the name of the town was spelled "Killam." Someone had a sense of humor back in 1965. Question is, was it the townspeople or Mother?

The concert in Camrose took place in a gymnasium-type auditorium with great acoustics. We sang to an enthusiastic, full house and were told later that some drove more than 100 miles to be there. And they wanted to stay. The end of the concert was becoming an Irish farewell. We did five encores. If we sang any more, we'd have had to call it "the third half" of the concert.

The next morning we drove into Calgary and the Canadian Rockies. It was one hair-raising trip, driving on hard-packed snow with an ice surface. Like driving on a pond. That was the downside of touring Canada in November: the weather could get bad. The next day, we in CREDO would find out exactly how dangerous bad weather could be.

To get to our next two concerts on Vancouver Island, we

had to cross the Rockies. We got our first sight of them just past Calgary. They were huge and a bit frightening—not like the Smokies in the South or the White or Green mountains of New England. We drove on the Trans-Canada Highway and entered Banff National Park. Suddenly there were snow-covered mountains on all sides of us.

We ascended gradually, up into the mist until we were in a foggy, winter wonderland. We saw three moose in a glade in the middle of a ponderosa pine forest. At a turn in the road we were stopped by a herd of sturdy, thick-limbed mountain goats that took their sweet time moving out of the way. We saw caribou and not long after, we slowed for a wolf that watched us for a moment, then loped back into the woods.

That night we stayed at the brand new Golden Rim Motor Inn, above the town of Golden, British Columbia. After spending the day in the car, we all enjoyed the swimming pool and sauna, the pool tables and shuffleboard.

Every once in a while, we'd find a place like this on tour, a place that made us feel pretty fabulous. Laying on the hot boards of the sauna after a cool swim, I wondered how everyone was getting along back at Holy Name. Who was sweating at the blackboard trying to diagram sentences for subject, predicate, pronouns, adverbs, adjectives? I could feel the grin on my face. All the dreaded math classes I was skipping made me giggle. I didn't miss any of it: the uniform, the saddle shoes, the cliques, the predictable schedule, the tension of being called on when you didn't have the right answer.

I swear some of those nuns had radar. They knew just when to call on you. It was uncanny. You could sit there, mentally answering every single question correctly all during class except the one that began with, "Sarah, . . . ?" They waited in silence while you desperately cast your thoughts out into the dark, hoping to grab it somehow before their eyes burned a hole through your forehead. Tonight, that tension seemed so very far away. I lay there grinning and sweating in the dry heat, alone with my thoughts.

The morning was rainy and overcast as we drove through Glacier National Park, heading toward Rogers Pass. It was dangerous and beautiful country. The road was clear and wet and we continued to climb. I saw a slide area full of fallen ponderosa pine, like a giant's game of pick up sticks. Where the mountains rose above us and avalanches were likely, there were snow sheds, cement coverings over the road. We went through many as we approached Rogers Pass.

A few months after we drove through Rogers Pass, there was a recall on the 1965 Chevrolet station wagons. The problem with the '65 model was that it was built without a slush guard under the accelerator. The travelers in CREDO were about to find out just how important a slush guard could be.

As the cars continued to climb, the soft rain turned into a light snow. Visibility was getting tough and the drivers needed a break so we stopped for coffee and donuts at the Northlander Motel at the beginning of the pass. There was a sign here warning motorists not to drive the pass without chains or ground-grips on their tires. Both cars had snow tires, so after the coffee break, we continued driving up the mountain.

It was afternoon but the snowfall turned the sky dark and it seemed like early evening. Steve drove cautiously and the snow tires gripped the snowy road nicely, taking us all the way to the top. It was the trip down the other side that was terrifying.

As we traveled up the mountain, with Steve's foot holding down the gas pedal, slush began to gather underneath the car. It gathered and froze the linkage from the accelerator to the engine. When Steve went to brake on the downhill side, nothing happened. Well, that's not exactly right. Something was definitely happening. We were accelerating. I was dozing and woke up suddenly to the panicked sound of Mother's voice saying, "Jesus, Mary and Joseph! Jesus, Mary and Joseph!" over and over again. The car had gone into a skid and was heading right for the precipice. It slammed against the guardrail. I could see a lake far, far below us and I thought, "This is it. We're going to die."

Then Steve's head was gone from sight. He had one hand on the wheel and with the other, was manually pulling up the gas pedal while feathering the brake. For much more time than I liked, we tangoed with the edge of that drop. Finally Steve got the car under control and as soon as he could, he pulled over and we all practiced breathing again.

Dad drove on, unaware of what had happened. His car wasn't affected, perhaps because it was the lead car and there was no vehicle in front of his creating slush. He was not in the dark for long, though. When we pulled over behind him to get gas in Revelstoke, he got an earful!

The snow turned back to rain in the lower altitude and gradually the sky cleared somewhat, making me wonder if the incident at Rogers Pass had really happened at all. It seemed like a different day entirely. We drove by beautiful rivers and lakes with signs announcing the presence of sockeye salmon and near Kamloops, we passed our first hop farm.

We traveled 503 miles that day and finally entered Vancouver in the dark. After the kind of day we'd had, going up and down all those curvy mountain roads and particularly after the near-death experience, those of us in CREDO saw the city lights and felt like we were entering the city of Oz.

We took a ferry to sing our next concerts in Port Alberni and Courtenay on Vancouver Island and then drove south for a final concert in Nampa, Idaho where we had the most enthusiastic audience of the tour. The motel owner went and with tears in her eyes said to Mum, "I don't know who is more blessed—the children or you and your husband!" Blessed is how we felt, too. Blessed and sort of dumbfounded—being able to sing together like this and getting to see the country. Six encores and they were still clapping like crazy. Dad just stood there laughing and had us take one more bow while he signaled to the stagehand to close the curtain.

We meet Maria von Trapp again

CHAPTER 31

Singing for the Choir

ON WEDNESDAY, NOVEMBER 17TH, Mother consulted her map. It told her that Nampa was about twenty miles from Boise and from Boise to Boston was 2,776 miles. We were a long way from home. The drive would have been a straight shot across the country but Dad had one detour in mind. We weren't that far from Salt Lake City and it was one of his dreams to hear the Mormon Tabernacle Choir sing live—in the Tabernacle. He'd been listening to their records for years and we were so close. So, instead of straight east, we headed south to Utah.

Leaving Boise we saw a huge sign, "THIS ROAD FOR WOMEN ONLY—MEN TAKE DETOUR—UNLESS ACCOMPANIED BY PARENT OR GUARDIAN" Mother said, "Now what can *that* mean?" A moment later another big sign warned, "METHODISTS WATCH OUT FOR MORMON CRICKETS" What was going on here? Was it some local humor? There was more. Next, the signmakers invited us to "WRITE TO YOUR PEN PALS—THE PAROLE BOARD" and another read, "REPORT SMOKE SIGNALS TO WESTERN UNION." Somebody was having fun. These weren't cheap, makeshift signs, either. They were put up to stay awhile, which made them all the more strange. Here came another: "ELKS, MOOSE, LIONS & EAGLES—PAY YOUR DUES," then "LONELY HEARTS CLUB PICNIC AREA" and finally, "THIS ROAD UNDER CONSTRUCTION—SINCE 1857." What a bunch of nuts. For travelers with the number of miles we had to go, however, these signs were a delightful distraction.

Actually, they brought back memories of all the little, red Burma-Shave signs that we saw on our first Midwest tour in 1963. Burma-Shave always had us snickering. We'd recite each sign in the series that made up a verse. For example, there was this series of five: "SHE KISSED / THE HAIRBRUSH BY MISTAKE / SHE THOUGHT IT WAS / HER HUSBAND JAKE." And another: "MY JOB IS / KEEPING FACES CLEAN / AND NOBODY KNOWS DE STUBBLE / I'VE SEEN."

They had thousands of them. In fact, they had more than 35,000 individual signs planted all over the country. The first signs were put up in Minnesota way back in the fall of 1925 to advertise Burma-Shave, the first brushless shaving cream produced in this country. In February 1963, after thirty-eight years of providing roadside entertainment for the country's travelers, the Burma-Vita Company was bought out by Phillip Morris, Inc. Phillip Morris decided that the costs of road sign upkeep and the yearly rents for land use paid to farmers all over the country (up to $200,000 by the 1960s) were too high and that it was time to move to more standard advertising vehicles, like radio, television and newspapers.*

We were lucky enough to catch the last sight of these clever signs in October 1963. By 1964, they would be gone. Before then, however, this Burma-Shave verse was certainly true: "IF YOU / DON'T KNOW / WHOSE SIGNS / THESE ARE / YOU CAN'T HAVE / DRIVEN VERY FAR / BURMA-SHAVE."

We stayed that night in Burley, Idaho, and by noon the next day, we were in Ogden, Utah, having a buffet lunch at the Holiday Inn. The restaurant manager recognized us from *The Ed Sullivan Show*. Naturally, Dad thought that was reason enough to sing for her while we waited for the chef to bring out more roast beef. Some of us had full plates of hot food at the time. Ah well. No matter. The lady was so thrilled that she decided to surprise Florrie with a birthday cake. Pete looked at me, wide-eyed. How did she know it was Florrie's birthday? What a coincidence!

---

* *The Verse by the Side of the Road: The Story of the Burma-Shave Signs and Jingles* by Frank Rowsome, Jr. The Stephen Greene Press, 1965, Lexington, Massachusetts

We set off again, stopped into a rock shop where Mum got specimens of snake-skin agate and veriquoise, both native to Utah, and were told that five miles beyond the shop was a blanket of garnet. Of course, we stopped to get some. We arrived in Salt Lake City at three forty-five, went right to the Tabernacle grounds, and were told that the last guided tour for the day would begin in a few minutes. We were also told that Maria von Trapp was lecturing at the Assembly Hall at eight that evening.

We took the tour with a Mr. Fongler and when we came to the Rehearsal Hall, he gave that incredible demonstration of the acoustics. He took us to the farthest end of the hall, left us there while he walked all the way back to the podium on the main platform, quietly asked us to listen and then dropped a common pin on the podium. We could clearly hear it. One look at Dad and we knew he wanted to sing here in the worst way! He asked and Mr. Fongler said, "Sure!"

Once we sang, it was Mr. Fongler's turn to get excited. He asked us if we'd mind waiting while he made a phone call. He was back in no time flat and said that he'd been talking to Richard Condie, the conductor of the Tabernacle Choir. Did we know that the Tabernacle Choir rehearses on Thursday nights?

"Tonight?" my father asked.

"Yes," Mr. Fongler replied, "and Mr. Condie also said that if you'd like to, he and the choir would love to hear you sing tonight."

If we'd like to? Dad and the rest of us made a beeline out of there and booked a place to stay. We got cleaned up, changed, hurried out for a hamburger and were back at the Tabernacle in time for the choir's vocal warm-up.

They stood on multilevel platforms like the bleachers for an audience in a basketball game. Only they weren't watching the excitement down below. This audience *was* the show. Three hundred and eighty-six voices sang out to the accompaniment of a monster pipe organ. What a sound. Before long, the director began working with the altos. Gemma and I grinned at each other and then looked again at the sea of altos on stage. In our little ensemble, when the music required a first and second alto part, she was the "first alto section" and I was the "second alto section." Now we listened to all those deep, powerful women's voices. This was incredible. I could have set up a lemonade stand in the middle of all those altos and no one would have noticed!

At around quarter after nine, Maria von Trapp arrived with some people who had attended her eight o'clock lecture at Assembly Hall. She spoke to the choir for a few minutes, spoke to Marty and Florrie and then waved to the rest of us. After she left, we were asked to sing.

Walking onto this stage to sing was unlike any other experience we'd had and we were nervous. For one thing, we were singing for 386 professional choral singers. For another, instead of looking down, we were looking *up* at this formidable audience and finally, if these acoustics could carry the sound of a pin dropping, they could carry every little mistake that we made just as well.

We sang "Tu es Petrus" and "Il Bianco e Dolce Cigno" and their applause was enthusiastic. Dad was beaming.

For the final song, he decided we'd sing "Hospodi Pomilui," (Russian for "Lord Have Mercy" sung 75 times at top speed.) How would that tongue-twister sound in this space? From the moment we started to sing it, we noticed the choir members grinning and looking at one another. Something was going on. The applause was thunderous at the end of it and Mr. Condie explained that the choir had tried to sing "Hospodi Pomilui" right here in the Tabernacle and they couldn't do it. Not with these acoustics. There were too many of them and the sound kept bouncing all around the hall. The sections were too far apart and couldn't hear to hold their parts. Gem and I looked at each other again, feeling like David to their Goliath.

The next morning we toured Brigham Young's home, sang for the twenty or so women who worked there and left with many warm farewells. It was raining but we prevailed upon Dad to stop at the Great Salt Lake, about fifteen miles out of town. Jim and Walt took off their shoes and socks and waded in with an empty jug to get a sample of the stuff so we could all taste it. Being Ocean State kids, we had all swallowed our share of salt water and were sure this Salt Lake wouldn't taste too different. Were we wrong! It was amazingly salty and so were Walt and Jim's feet. They were dry now but the salt had turned them a corpse-white. This, of course, pleased them no end.

Now it was time for the trek home. In Wyoming I noticed how long a ride it was between towns—towns like Medicine Bow, Laramie and Cheyenne—and thought how good they must have looked after a horse ride over these plains.

Horses might have been safer. As we neared Cheyenne, SONGS left front tire had a blowout. One big bang and the thing was in shreds. There was the screech of brakes—Dad's, then Steve's. Nobody breathed while SONGS swerved. Dad got the car under control and finally pulled it over to the side of the road. He had a handkerchief out and was mopping his very white face as he stood by the car. Mother squeezed his arm and told him how wonderful he was while three of the boys quickly changed the tire. We stopped for lunch in Cheyenne. Dad bought a new tire and had the wheels aligned and we were on our way again.

That night we stayed at the Capri Motel in North Platte, Nebraska. We'd stayed here before and they fixed up the same rooms for us. Twenty dollars for all three. You couldn't beat it.

The next morning was Monday, November 21st, and here we were in western Nebraska, but that didn't stop people in both cars from talking about making it home in time for Thanksgiving. By the end of that day we had reached Des Moines, Iowa. Late on the 22nd we pulled into Bailey's Motel in Howe, Indiana, and from Howe, Indiana, on Wednesday, the 23rd, we drove 875 miles and arrived at Doyle Avenue at quarter to three Thanksgiving morning. We'd been gone a month, driven 9,224 miles and as I slowly climbed up the stairs and slid under the covers, nothing felt as good as my own bed.

Bob Kennedy Contact Show—WBZ-TV, Boston, 1967

With Perry Como at the Americana Hotel, NYC, 1966

CHAPTER 32

Breakfast at the Biltmore

WE APPEARED ON TELEVISION at seven o'clock Thanksgiving night. It was not a live performance. We had taped the half-hour special for WPRI-TV before we left for the tour and now, as we sat or lay on the floor in the family room, overstuffed and half-dead, we watched the TV feeling very grateful to whomever had invented videotape.

The sweethearts—Sheila, Denis and Vin—were grateful, too. They had arrived at Doyle Avenue well before noon. The phone line had been jumpin' first thing Thanksgiving morning. When the oldest three finally got off the phone, they all had that same dreamy-eyed look on their faces, like sailboats set adrift on a blowy afternoon.

Clearly, Florrie had lost her moorings. She was standing by the kitchen counter rolling out dough for an apple pie, but she was not in the room. Only her hands were there, hands that had made hundreds of pies and knew what to do. The rest of her functioned in a support capacity only. Her brain was gone. I know. I was peeling potatoes by the sink.

Marty was in no better shape. Her Denis was one of those real romantic types. He would prove it again in February by sneaking into our backyard in the middle of the night and sticking two long poles into the ground. Attached to the poles was a proclamation. On a Queen-size white sheet he had painted a red Cupid holding a bow, a heart shot through with Cupid's arrow and the words, "Happy Valentine's Day, Darling—I Love You, Denis" slopped in bold red paint. Dad nicked himself shaving when he spotted it from the bathroom window the next morning. He woke Marty and Florrie, and I woke to the sound of laughter and sighing females. Honestly! This morning Marty was vacuuming the wall-to-wall carpeting in the dining room. She could have been out sucking up the grass in the backyard with that machine and I don't think she would have known the difference.

Steve should have been exhausted after driving 875 miles in one day, but as I passed the open bathroom door, there he was, lathering on the shaving cream and humming the bass line to "Quittez Pasteurs." Full of energy. Grinning into the mirror. Soon he'd leave to pick up Sheila, now his fiancée, and bring her over. I noticed it took them way too long to get back. "Errands," Steve said.

And they were still hangin' around at seven P.M., adding three more to the body count in the family room. Looking around, I knew (and so did everyone else in the room) that the family we watched singing on TV wouldn't be doing it for too much longer.

In December 1965 we sang for the Holiday Festival at the Albee Theatre in downtown Providence. It was a strange thing. We had performed all over the country but, apart from local Christmas TV specials and an hour of daytime caroling at the Main Office of Industrial National Bank, we hadn't sung a public concert in Providence in more than three years. Now here it was December 21st, the middle of the holiday rush and we were singing one for the home crowd. It felt great.

The relatives and the friends, teachers and classmates, the neighbors and co-workers, the sweethearts and their families, they all showed up. Hundreds of students from South Kingstown High were bused in and their tickets paid for by Kenyon's Department Store in Wakefield. It was crazy. All those familiar faces looking at us. It felt wonderful to sing for this audience.

Two weeks before Christmas Dad handed out red Christmas money envelopes to each of us. This was a fabulous new custom and quite a change from the Peace Dale shopping lists. Now we had money to buy each other presents. I looked inside my envelope and figured that one big present for the family was better than eleven small, cheap presents. Besides, I didn't know when I'd come into this kind of money again—so I decided to blow it all on a miniature pool table.

I put it together, wrapped a big red bow around it and stood it in the middle of the front foyer on Christmas Eve. Walt and Pete and I loved it. The others? Well, Jim and John played a game but they were used to regular-size pool tables and were soon bored. The older girls gave the table, and then me, "the eye." "What?! I thought everybody liked pool!" I reasoned. They weren't buying it.

1966 started off nice and easy. In January the younger set caught up on schoolwork, friendships and snowball fights; the older girls returned to their respective jobs and Steve went back to Providence College. I was now in the eighth grade and enjoying my last year at Holy Name Grammar School. I had been caught kissing Teddy Clements in the cloak room. I had sweated through horrible math tests and had laughed hysterically with Dolores Taylor behind Sister Winifred's back while she gave Tommy Maguire hell for something the three of us had pulled. Eighth grade was whizzing by.

We got out of school again on February 15th in order to sing in the Imperial Ballroom at the Americana Hotel in New York City. The Catholic Youth Organization (CYO) Club of Champions was honoring Perry Como with a Gold Medal for his work in CYO and we were the guest artists for the event along with Peter Lind Hayes and Mary Healy, a husband-and-wife musical team. Perry Como was just what he appeared to be—a very mellow, soft-spoken, gentle man.

In April, we packed the cars for a week-long tour to Ohio and Pennsylvania. Before we got on the road, we went to Mass over at Holy Name, and then Dad and Mum decided that it would be nice to have breakfast at the Biltmore Hotel in downtown Providence before we took off. They knew that this would probably be our last tour together and the Biltmore seemed a good place to start. Although no one came right out and said anything, the significance of this unusual side trip did not escape any of us.

It was quiet inside on a Sunday morning. We had been around a little since we sang here for the Catholic Women's Club in 1960. Actually, I don't think we had been in the hotel since then. It was still a very elegant place.

Mum's opening tour notes were typical of her attitude and her indomitable spirit. She wrote: "The Burke Family Singers on the move! Our last tour together unless God wills otherwise. Everyone is light-hearted and eager! It is a beautiful day and God is in His Heaven!"

Not everyone was light-hearted. I don't think Dad was and I know I wasn't. But there was nothing to do about it. Life goes on, kids get married and move away. Mum and Dad had decided years ago that they would not hold the Singers together any longer than was natural. But it was tough.

As usual, Mother's buoyant personality played the necessary counterpoint to Dad's more pessimistic nature. She wrote about the colorful Hex signs on the barns in Pennsylvania Dutch country, about eating shoofly pie (that's pie with a molasses and brown sugar filling) and scrapple (that's a mush of ground pork and cornmeal, set in a mold, sliced and fried).

We stayed in Krumsville Sunday night and in Dillsburg on Monday night after singing a concert at Messiah College in nearby Grantham, Pennsylvania. Tuesday was overcast and Mother wrote that "everyone in car rather quiet today. We drive through small part of West Virginia—the outskirts of Wheeling. This is coal mining country and very dismal looking. Steve said he wouldn't give a can of Alpo for the whole city of Wheeling. It is raining—which doesn't help much. It's so depressing that we've decided we don't want to even fly over it."

We drove into the huge city of Cincinnati, into the soapy air coming from the Proctor & Gamble Company. Our next concert was at the College of Mount St. Joseph-on-the-Ohio on the other side of the city's loop near the Kentucky line.

Before the concert, a Franciscan named Brother William approached us with four loaves of homemade bread and invited us to the Mt. Alverni School for Delinquent Boys the next day. He wrote his phone number on Walter's cast and then went to join the audience. (Walter had broken his arm while ice-skating. He would turn fifteen in four days—if he lived that long.)

Henry S. Humphreys, a critic for the *Cincinnati Inquirer*, was sitting in the audience that night and wrote a review that came out the following morning. Dad was so thrilled by it that he knocked on the girls' motel room door in his bare feet to read it to us and then he ran to the boys' room to read it to them.

April 21, 1966—
BURKE FAMILY ENTHRALLS
   If Walter Vincent Burke and Anne Burke are proud of their good-looking, carolling sons and daughters (five boys, five girls and all very good-

looking), I am sure that America is equally proud of the Burke Family as a manifestation of New World family artistry which is no mere imitation of the Trapp Family Singers, but a superb choral group dependent on nothing more than the inspiring direction of a pater-familias plus God-given voices and musicianship.

Ranging in age from 24 (Stephen, soon to be inducted into the US Marine Corps) to Peter (11), the Burke Family Singers sang with a very special dolcezza, Wednesday night, at the College of Mount St. Joseph; for their destiny is the destiny of all family groups—sooner or later marriage and individual careers break up the "charmed circle." But a rose is no less precious because it has not the durability of a stone in the field. And if musical notes could be transformed into roses, the Burke Family would be one big bouquet of American Beauties.

Intonation, expression, phrasing, enunciation—you name it, Walter Vincent and Anne and their fine children have all these vocal assets...

...and on it went. Dad was delighted. The timing couldn't have been better and I think the article was a great comfort to him.

Mr. Humphreys got his lines crossed about Steve, though. It was not Steve, but John who'd heard from Uncle Sam.

Back in March, a letter was delivered to the Prudential Center in Boston just about thirty minutes before we were to sing a concert. It was addressed to John and began with "Greetings from Uncle Sam!" Somehow the draft board had gotten a copy of our itinerary. The timing couldn't have been worse. Everyone was crying and the manager for the event said to Buck, "How is this family supposed to go out there and sing tonight?"

But we walked on stage and formed our choral line. Mother and Steve, who stood on either side of John, seemed to lean in a little closer to him that night. I don't believe it was our spunkiest concert, but we got through it.

When John showed up at the draft board, they gave him and others the option of enlisting in some other branch of the service besides the Army if they had a preference. John preferred the Marines and in September 1966 he joined hundreds of others at Parris Island to begin training. Actually, he left the day after Steve's wedding.

Steve had graduated from Providence College in May 1965. In September he would begin graduate studies at the University of Connecticut's School of Social Work. He decided to take a full load of night courses that summer. He knew that the longer he stayed in school, the better his chances were of staying out of the military.

1966 was quite a year. John left. Steve married Sheila and moved to Connecticut in September. Then in November, Marty and Florrie had a double wedding.

What a day that was. Dad had his brother Fran play the opening procession music while he took Marty down the aisle. Then he went to the back of the church to escort Florrie to the altar and from there he headed to the organ to direct the choir and play the new Mass he had written for his two oldest girls. It was a family affair. All the boys were groomsmen and Gemma, Annie and I were bridesmaids.

I remember wondering how it was possible that I could be so happy and so miserable at the same time. These two were more than big sisters. They were mothers to me. They had brought me up and now, as they got into the limousines with their new husbands, they looked so happy to be going away. The young adult in me understood, but the child felt utterly deserted. Marty stayed in town so I didn't lose her entirely, but Florrie would move to Shaker Heights, Ohio.

With Steve in Connecticut and Florrie in Ohio, it became next to impossible to plan concerts, never mind rehearsal time. Add to that the fact that the offspring were as fertile as their parents and the situation was further complicated. Sheila, Steve's wife, was already pregnant at the November double wedding and both Marty and Florrie would conceive on their honeymoons. We would continue singing until 1970 but the concerts would be few and far between.

John wouldn't be with us during Christmas of 1966 and we missed him and his voice. Walter's 15-year-old voice was beginning to drop down to tenor range, which filled in the musical hole somewhat while leaving Florrie, Marty, Annie and Pete to sing the soprano section. Steve drove in and Florrie flew home a month after her wedding to sing another Christmas Special at WPRI-TV studios in Providence.

We had begun taping these half-hour Christmas Specials, sponsored by Industrial National Bank, back in 1964 and would continue doing them through 1969, making a total of six shows. The contract each year was for a TV Special plus an hour of Christmas caroling at the Main Office of Industrial National Bank in downtown Providence. By 1970, we couldn't all get together early enough to do a studio taping so we simply caroled at the bank.

In December of 1967, we got a surprise. We had been asked to appear on the *Bob Kennedy Contact Show*, a morning talk/variety show on WBZ-TV in Boston.

As the name of the show inferred, Bob Kennedy was in the business of contacting people and he usually did this by using the phone on the little table near his chair.

We sang "We Wish You a Merry Christmas" and "O Come All Ye Faithful." Then we all sat down, the girls in one row and the boys on a platform behind us. Mum and Dad sat next to Bob and gabbed a little and then the telephone rang. We were expecting that. Dad's copy of the program format said there'd be a "Santa phone call bit." What we didn't expect was that Bob would ask Mother to answer the phone.

It was John calling from Okinawa. We hadn't seen him in a year and we knew he was headed for Vietnam soon. Mother heard his voice, said "Hi, darling" and choked up, passed the phone to Dad, then got herself together and signaled that she wanted the phone back. We all leaned toward Mum, trying to figure what John was saying by how she responded to him. It was only a three-minute phone call but for that brief time, we were all connected again.

In 1968, with John still away, we sang a concert at the Belcourt Castle, one of the famous millionaire mansions on the twelve-mile Ocean drive in Newport, Rhode Island. After the performance, a formal picture was taken of us in front of the fireplace. Two of the boys stood on each side of Mum and Dad and the five girls sat on a long wooden bench to make the front row. Pete was the tallest. Walt was now taller than Jim, Dad and Steve. His pituitary gland had finally kicked in. And for the first time, it wasn't easy to pick out the youngest girl.

Before Mother framed this picture, she put in a small picture of Lance Corporal John in his Marine dress blues and his medals. It was a profile shot so it seems as though he's looking over at us and it clearly answers the question "Why do women sigh over a man in uniform?"

John came home from the service in 1969 and then Jimmy got his draft notice from the Army. Jim came home after training at Fort Dix (and before going to Nam) in time to hear us sing at the Industrial National Bank at Christmastime. He looked pretty slick in his Army uniform. Jim joined us for a few songs, then Dad kicked him off the stage and told him we had something for him.

It was a song we had just learned called "Hurry Home for Christmas" and it was one schmaltzy tune. Incredibly, Dad had finally broken down and allowed us to sing something easy, something popular, with tight harmonies and sappy lyrics. We were so ecstatic about doing this Andrews Sisters-type music that we just leaned all over that song. We were making up for lost time, grinning down at him and rocking back and forth to the rhythm. Jimmy couldn't believe it. It was shocking enough that Dad had actually taught us a song like this, but then seeing that we had learned it as a surprise for him, well, Mister Squared-Away-Shiny-Shoes did his best not to choke up and failed miserably.

We sang at the Governor's Inaugural Ball in 1969, at a Retreat Convention and on other occasions during those last couple of years but only one other performance stands out in my mind—and that was when we sang for the dedication of the new Bishop McVinney Auditorium in Providence.

Alexander Peloquin, the organist for the Cathedral of Saints Peter and Paul, was there to direct his professional choir, The Peloquin Chorale. Alex and my father had had a friendly rivalry going for years. Both men were church organists for large parishes and very capable, creative musicians. Both loved their loud, powerful pipe organs and were inclined to be dramatic in their personalities and in their music. They were quick to compliment each other on the latest achievement and were just as quick to compete.

Alex never married and devoted himself to church music and his chorale. Dad's life was entirely different and I think he sometimes envied Alex's freedom from distractions. This would be the first time their two choral groups would be performing in the same concert and we knew that Dad was eager for us to make a good showing.

Alex strode in to the auditorium smiling, head high, music in hand and black cape flowing out behind him. My father greeted him and congratulated him on the new Mass he had written. Gracious as always, Alex acknowledged the compliment and then said, "But Walter, look what *you've* created!" and with that he let his arm sweep over all of us standing there. Dad just laughed. You had to appreciate that kind of flair.

The Peloquin Chorale was very fine. They sang with a polish and control that proved that this was no typical church choir that does the best it can with the parish talent. These were professional singers who came from all over the state to audition for the privilege of singing with this group—and it showed. Their music was beautiful.

Then it was our turn. We were a little jittery and Dad smiled confidently at us, softly blew a note on his pitch pipe and raised his hands to direct. I don't know how else to put this—we were fabulous.

There were no more boy sopranos in the family. Florrie, Marty and Annie sang the high part. Walt was a tenor and now Peter stood next to Steve and sang in the bass section. Dad jumped back and forth from bass to tenor. This shift from mostly high voices to a real balance between high and low gave us a different sound. Suddenly there was a strong bottom, a base that grounded the music. All the voices were mature.

The last song before intermission was "Il Bianco e Dolce Cigno." We bowed to the applause and walked offstage. Dad stopped us once we'd gotten past the curtain. He had tears in his eyes and he said to us, "I want you to know that for the first time—you sang Il Bianco in perfect pitch from start to finish." Finally, and maybe only once, he'd gotten to hear that song as he'd imagined it could be.

During the second half of the concert, Dad took us all by

surprise. We were about to sing "The Irish Girl" and were expecting him to introduce it the same way he had done countless times before. Instead, he said, "I'd like to take this opportunity to say something about my wife, Anne. For years now I have jokingly referred to her as 'the producer of our show,' but she is so much more than that. She has always been the heart of this family."

Then he took a folded piece of paper out of his tuxedo jacket and said, "I'd like to read this passage from Proverbs 31. It describes my wife Anne, better than I ever could."

> *When one finds a worthy wife,*
> *her value is far beyond pearls.*
> *Her husband, entrusting his heart to her,*
> *has an unfailing prize.*
> *She brings him good, and not evil,*
> *all the days of her life....*
> *She rises while it is still night,*
> *and distributes food to her household.*
> *She is clothed with strength and dignity,*
> *and she laughs at the days to come.*
> *She opens her mouth in wisdom,*
> *and on her tongue is kindly counsel....*
> *Her children rise up and praise her;*
> *her husband, too, extols her:*
> *"Many are the women of proven worth,*
> *but you have excelled them all."*

Charm is deceptive and beauty fleeting;
the woman who fears the LORD is
to be praised.
Give her a reward of her labors,
and let her works praise her
at the city gates.

We were trying to hold it together. It didn't help that he choked on the last three lines. There was silence and then the place went crazy. Dad walked over and hugged Mum right there on stage. The rest of that concert was a blur.

Dad with Blessed Sacrament Boys Choir—Providence, RI

CHAPTER 33

One Last Song

AFTER CAROLING AT THE Industrial National Bank in December of 1970, our family blended back into society. We had been an unusually interdependent unit—working, playing and traveling together—and now we had to make our way in the world as individuals. Some of us got married, some of us got divorced. Many of us took jobs in the public service sector: in nursing, social work, the fire department, postal service, working with troubled youth, delivering food for the city, cooking for the elderly. We have a choir director and a few cantors. None of us is rich. Most of us are happy.

We've had our disagreements. Like the parents who bore us, every one of us has a strong opinion on just about everything and though we get angry with one another, we don't stay angry. The love that binds us is strong. I am amazed to see how different we are becoming as we get older and I notice that we are learning to avoid certain hot-button topics. Mother is still mothering and grandmothering and great-grandmothering. Keeps her busy.

When the Burke Family Singers ended in 1970, I think a part of Dad died with it. In December of 1972, the *Providence Sunday Journal* did a big spread with pictures about what the Burke family was doing now. When asked about the breakup of the Singers, Dad was quoted as saying, "I felt a terrible sense of loss, like something breaking..." He was still organist and choirmaster at Blessed Sacrament Church, and he had formed a new choir called the Word of God Singers, which kept him occupied and gave him great comfort—but it was not the same kind of musical ensemble. It wasn't his kids.

At 6:30 A.M. on January 18th, 1977, Dad was doing what he had done every morning for the last twenty-three years. He was getting ready to go play Mass over at Blessed Sacrament. But on this morning, when he bent over to tie his shoelaces, his heart burst and he sighed and died. It was that sudden.

At the time I lived in an apartment upstairs from Marty's family. She woke me up and said, "Dad's had a heart attack. Do you want to come to the hospital with me to see him?" Not understanding, I told her I had to go to work. She said, "Sarah, I'm going to see him for the last time. Do you want to come?"

She and I went to the emergency room and he was in one of the curtained-off rooms. There was a sheet over him. Marty uncovered his face and kept stroking his forehead and his hair. I lifted the sheet where his hand was. I remember wanting to see his hand, to touch the fingers that played the music while they were still warm.

The next four days were really something. No one that close to me had ever died before and it felt like the bottom had dropped out. The grief was numbing. I was in a daze. Probably all of us were. We hung out together at my parents' apartment. The beautiful house on Doyle Avenue had been given up a few years earlier—too few bodies and too big a mortgage. Now my parents lived in the first floor apartment of a triple-decker owned by Steve and Sheila, whose family occupied the two upper floors.

Marty and Denis' house was next door and my apartment was on their third floor so there were plenty of places to go, but we all seemed to gravitate to Mum's apartment, laughing, crying, talking and singing together in between the wake sessions. Actually, we sang a lot. It was a comfort.

The wake lasted for three days in order to give everyone time to fly in—one of whom was my sister Gemma, who was living in Hawaii with her Marine husband.

I couldn't believe how many people showed up during that time. At the wake, the line was out the door, down the street and around the block. People I didn't know came and took the hands of each one of us as we stood by the casket in a long family line from oldest to youngest. Many of them had their heads down as they whispered to each of us, "Sorry for your troubles."

Sorry for your troubles? I'd never heard that before and now I was hearing it for hours on end. Evidently, this was the standard wake expression, but what did it mean?

The funeral home happened to be one block away from Mum's apartment so we walked back and forth. Back at Mum's, Jim approached John with his head down, took his hands and said, "Sorry for your troubles." Of course John started to laugh and before long, a lot of us were doing it off and on during that surreal four-day period until it got to be very funny. You'd ask for a knife to put mayonnaise on your sandwich, somebody'd pass it to you reverently with a "Sorry for you troubles." Laughing about strange wake customs kept our minds off Dad for a little while.

Gemma arrived from Hawaii on the second day of the wake. She walked in with her husband, Norman, while we were standing in the line by the casket. She wore a beautiful lei around her neck and as she approached the coffin, she took it off and put it around Dad's neck. I felt so bad for her. She looked crushed. She hadn't seen Dad in over two years.

Grief made us all a little crazy and we knew it, so we were particularly gentle with one another. We all mourned in our own way. I wanted to keen on tin whistle at some point during the funeral Mass and the others said I could—so I did. Someone suggested that we sing "The Minstrel Boy," an a capella, Irish patriot song, around the casket near the end of the Mass. Dad loved this song and had written an arrangement of it for four parts. Jimmy wanted to direct us and it was decided the night before that if any one of us was in too bad a shape or didn't want to sing, they only had to nod their head "No" and we wouldn't do it.

There were thirty-five priests and three bishops on the altar to concelebrate my father's funeral Mass. The Word of God Singers sang the Mass that Dad had recently written and Uncle Fran played the organ. The homily was given by our old friend, Father Joe Leo Flynn. The church was packed and everyone sang. It was a celebration of Dad's life and his homecoming.

After Communion Steve turned to look at each one of us and we all looked back at him. Then we got up out of the pews and stood around the casket. Jim blew a note softly on Dad's pitch pipe and we sang:

> *The minstrel boy to the war has gone,*
> *In the ranks of death you'll find him;*
> *His father's sword he hath girded on,*
> *And his wild harp slung behind him:*
> *"Land of song," cried the warrior bard,*
> *"Though all the world betrays thee,*
> *One sword at least thy right shall guard,*
> *One faithful harp shall praise thee."*
>
> *The minstrel fell but the foeman's chain*
> *Could not bring that proud soul under,*
> *The harp he lov'd ne'er spoke again,*
> *For he tore it's chords asunder;*
> *And said, "No chains shall sully thee,*

Thou soul of love and bravery!
Thy songs were made for the pure and free,
They shall never sound in slavery."

One last song for him. There was absolute silence. I cannot explain the power, the control and the love that poured out of us during that song. We sat down and the bishops gave the final blessing. Then the thirty-five priests walked down the aisle and one stopped at every third or fourth pew, making an honor guard for the casket, and then us, to pass through. It was lovely of them.

We got into the black limousines and rode for an hour. A long, long line of cars followed us as we headed back to Peace Dale, back to our roots to bury Dad at Saint Francis Cemetery near his old friend and first pastor, Father Greenan.

Mum meets the Pope

Epilogue

December 1998

I've been coming home to put up Mum's Christmas tree for years now. Come to think of it, since 1978 I've flown or bused in to Providence, to the strongest "home" of my heart, where that old lady is. She never remarried after Dad's death, though she was only sixty-one at the time. Said she'd never find anyone who could measure up to Walter so there was no use looking.

And she gets zanier by the year. Still keeps a notebook going at all times. You never know when a thought's going to come up that needs remembering. She still keeps materials for projects tucked away. She's eighty-three. I keep telling her the time is now. I think she now has sixteen full scrapbooks filled with all kinds of odds and ends, newspaper articles, cards, programs, wine labels from special events, pictures, cartoons, prayers. The list goes on.

Oh, yes. And she has something else. She keeps her own pine box casket in the living room. It's fit to size and comes complete with three rope handles on either side. Her son-in-law made it for her. Making a casket for your mother-in-law. She thinks that's very funny.

Chuckling, she said to me the other day, "Have you ever noticed how people who have never been here before take a step back when they spot the casket? Watch, it happens every time!" It was true. She'd forgotten but I happened to be there when she brought the mailman in for a tour. He sauntered in with the mail and a friendly smile. Though he'd never been inside, he knew her well from her packages. Mother lived in Italy with my sister Gemma for more than a year and before she left had decided to ship home most of the southern part of that country.

The mailman, standing surprisingly erect, was now looking with interest at the pictures hanging on the wall near the front entrance. There was one of the family laughing with Jimmy Durante, another with Perry Como and a full compliment of us posing with various clergy—from priest friends to Cardinal Cushing right on up to a photo of her and Pope John Paul. I looked at that one again and noticed for the first time that they looked like twins.

Mother was all in white just like the Pope. They both had snow-white hair and as the picture showed them leaning forward to greet each other, each with a warm smile and hands extended, they looked like mirror images of each other. The only difference was that the cross Mother wore was larger.

I was about to comment on this but the mailman had all ready turned to see more of the house. He didn't get very far. He glanced down and suddenly, his eyes widened and he looked at my Mother. She said, "Oh, that's my coffin . . . " Sure enough, he stepped back. Mother flashed me a look and then smiled demurely at the man. He said, "Oh, really . . . " and smiled uncertainly, looking to me for some sort of assistance, but he was on his own. I was trying unsuccessfully to keep the smirk off my face and said nothing. Mother, not missing a beat, continued chatting while she showed him what had been in a lot of the packages he'd been lugging. He left charmed, though a little dazed. "Well, what d'ya think of him?" she asked. "I think you can be cruel," I said and we laughed.

I remember the first time I saw that coffin back in 1977. I not only stepped back, I nearly ran out of the room! We had buried my father a few months before and at that point I wasn't quite ready to view my mother's final resting place. I just stared at it, horrified, while she quickly explained that Dad's funeral costs were so high and she didn't want to burden us when she died so she decided to take care of it herself. I've gotten used to it over the years, I guess. She keeps the stereo on top of it, and on the inside—in the space that will one day hold the husk that housed her open-handed and ever-curious spirit—she now stores clothes (and materials for future projects).

When she finally does die, my entry for most-often-used expression will be: "Ooooh! Isn't that interesting!" Although, I don't know why I bother with possible obituaries, when she told me that she's written her own. It was last Christmas and I was decorating her tree and minding my own business. She was rummaging through the file cabinet in her bedroom, looking for something. She called out, "Hey, wanta read my obituary?"

"Your WHAT?"

"My obituary. I wrote my own obituary. Wanna read it?"

"NO! Surprise me!" I heard belly-laughter from the bedroom.

A Last Few Words

. . . BEGINNING WITH A STORY about this family photo. I couldn't be there but Mother was determined that I be represented. "It'll look like she's dead" my siblings said. Mother gripped the frame. "I don't care. She's going to be in this picture."

Just before the photographer bent over the camera, Jimmy explained that I had died recently in a horrible accident whereupon everyone—except the photographer—burst out laughing. Some things just don't change . . .

*   *   *

So many people who have read this story have wanted to know what we are doing now (and more than a few have jokingly asked whether Walter has spent any time behind bars. The answer to that is "no.") Of the ten children Mother and Dad had in thirteen years:

Steve, the oldest, is now sixty-one and has three children. After graduating from Providence College, he went on to get a master's degree in social work and from 1973 to 2000 worked for the Diocese of Providence at Catholic Social Services and the Life and Family Ministry. (He still enjoys long driving trips...)

Marty is remarried, has five children and is a recent breast cancer survivor. She worked in real estate for years and is presently a receptionist at the Rhode Island State Lottery and living in Cranston, Rhode Island. (She still mothers and grandmothers her growing brood and is a warm and loving hostess.)

Florrie is a sculptor and a potter at Salmon Falls Stoneware. She has brought up three beautiful children and given them her gentle, loving spirit. She now enjoys throwing pots and living near her grandchildren in rural New Hampshire. (She can find her way out of the woods without a problem...)

Gem has been a music director since 1974 and has created shows in Italy, Hawaii and Okinawa, Japan. She is recently widowed, has four children and is a choir director in Havelock, North Carolina. (She still turns heads, adapts to new environments easily and has Mum's style and dramatic flair...)

John has two children and lives in Foster, Rhode Island. After serving in Vietnam, he joined the Providence Fire Department in 1970 and retired after fighting fires for twenty-six years. (He still does the funky chicken, spins and does the

James Brown slide at family parties, but slowly ... and he leaves the floor-splits to the younger set ...)

Since his return from Vietnam in 1973, Jimmy has worked for the U.S. Postal Service and is presently a supervisor at the Esmond office in Rhode Island. Of all of us, it seems he has passed on the "music genes" to at least two of his four children, who are attending the Berklee School of Music in Boston. One plays jazz piano, the other plays bass. Sounds like a new Burke Brothers orchestra in the making ... (Jimmy is still outrageously funny and I just found out that he actually has "crying loon" as part of his e-mail address ...)

Annie got married and had one son and then twin sons with a severe seizure disorder, an ongoing illness that has changed her life. A few years ago, she was drawn back to Wake-field, Rhode Island, to be near the ocean and her roots. She is presently single, has a housecleaning business and a sometimes cosmic spiritual life. The girl is tuned in. She's got a channel goin'. There's very little "snow" on her TV screen. (She still loves chocolate, dancing and calls herself The Scrabble Queen, even though I beat her that one time she won't admit to ...)

Walter has survived to his present age which, last time I checked, was one year older than me. He has four active sons (which, of course, is *just* what he deserves) and lives in Cumberland, Rhode Island. For twenty-two years he worked at the Rhode Island Catholic Orphan Asylum, better known as St. Aloysius Home and for the past seven years, he has been the parks and recreation for the Town of Bristol, Rhode Island. He has always worked and continues to work with children. (He has, however, given up the "slap game" ...)

I am next in line, the ninth of ten, the ten percent, and the only lefty. I added guitar and other instruments to my flute playing and for many years have performed either alone or as part of a musical duo. I graduated from Clarke College in Dubuque, Iowa (where we sang in 1963), and like my father, I play music in church—with the Lutherans as well as the Catholics. I wrote this book in beautiful Wisconsin and now live with my longtime partner in an old farmhouse in rural Connecticut. (For breakfast out, I still order "the usual"...)

Peter has one son and lives in Providence, Rhode Island. For fifteen years he worked for the Rhode Island Department of Administration delivering government food to prisons and schools and for the past seven years he has worked at the Rhode Island Department of Corrections. (Things have changed between Pete and me. Now he often takes *me* for a ride...)

Dear Mum passed over into eternal life on July 27th, 1999, and has left us broken-hearted with one foot in this world and the other in the next. Sometimes I feel glad for her. After all, her whole life was lived toward that moment, that reunion. And sometimes I know she is still with us, praying for us as she always did. Interceding. There wasn't another like her...and if you don't think that the same woman who had challenged God to send a rose years earlier had anything to do with the book you now hold in your hands, then you don't know Anne Devine Burke...

Photo Credits

All photographs are from the Burke Family Archives, with the exception of:

Providence Journal Photo: pp. 3, 54, 130, 150, 194 (top), 212, 286
CBS Photo Archive: pp. 2, 167
Mark McCann: pp. 7, 44, 55, 69, 232
Paul Ladd: pp. 32–33
Fr. Joseph Murphy: pp. 80, 81, 213, 324
Fay Foto/Boston: p. 96
Paul Darling:: pp. 159, 184, 194 (bottom), 203, 298 (bottom), 325
Album cover courtesty of EMI Records: pp. 224, 261
Narragansett Times Photo: p. 260 (top)
WBZ-TV, Viacom Boston: p. 332 (top)
L'Osservatore Romano Citta del Vaticano Servizio Fotografico—
    Arturo Man: p. 356
Olan Mills: p. 363

Every attempt was made to locate the holders of copyrighted photographs so that appropriate credit could be listed. If you have information about any of the photos, please contact us.